Marching Along

LIEUTENANT-COMMANDER JOHN PHILIP SOUSA, USNRF

Marching Along

John Philip Sousa

GIA Publications, Inc.

G-8620
Marching Along
John Philip Sousa

Copyright © 2015 GIA Publications, Inc.
7404 S. Mason Ave., Chicago, IL 60638
www.giamusic.com

ISBN: 978-1-62277-138-7

Contents

GRATEFUL *acknowledgment is made to the editors of the* Washington Post *for their kind permission to reprint excerpts from their Fiftieth Anniversary Number; to the editors of the Saturday Evening Post for excerpts from their serial "Keeping Time," by John Philip Sousa; and* The Bobbs-Merrill Co. *for "I've Bin Fightin'," and "The Feast of the Monkeys," from Mr. Sousa's novel* Pipetown Sandy, *Copyright 1905.*

Illustrations

Dedication

My Great Grandfather was taught music at a young age and thanks to his music teacher's persistence, John Philip Sousa became the most notable musician of his time. His knowledge of music helped to make him one of our countries most prolific composers and outstanding world ambassadors.

Because of this, I would like to dedicate this book to two groups of people:

The first is to every music educator in the United States. Thank you for all you do to make the lives of EVERY student who attend your classes become better people because of your efforts. Grades improve, social skills improve, grades in unrelated classes go up and the kids are happier human beings because of the success they have in your classrooms or band rooms. Your contribution to their future wellbeing is almost immeasurable.

The second is to each and every school board member in every school district in America. PLEASE make sure you allocate a reasonable percentage of the budget to music and the arts. For the sake of the kids and their future, you must stop cutting the arts budgets.

We are all painfully aware of the pressure you get to allocate more money to sports or to off the wall classes for purely politically correct reasons....Neither of these, at the end of the day, will improve a kids life like learning music and the arts...You and I and millions more know this to be a fact. Be strong and be forceful for the kids and their futures.

And the facts are clear...Teach a kid music and every aspect of his or her educational and personal life is going to be vastly improved. Teach a kid how to shoot hoops, and not so much. Math, languages, English all improve because a person learns music. Team spirit, cooperation, coordination are all results of music education...There is simply no down side.

I'm not saying that by increasing your music or arts budget will cause the next John Philip Sousa or Michael Jackson or Beethoven to emerge, but teach the kids music and you will produce less welfare recipients, more successful middle class productive Americans....and they will be forever grateful to you.

Talk to leaders of our military bands, or to directors of the few community bands left in America and they will all tell you the same thing...We can't find good musicians because the schools aren't teaching the kids music; how to read music or how to play an instrument.

There was a time in America when virtually every community, every town had its own band...many had multiple bands. They marched in local parades celebrating the 4th of July or Veterans Day. They played summer concerts in the park where families gathered and even in the frigid Northeast, they held Christmas concerts that people of all denominations enjoyed.

Music crosses the barriers or race, of religion, of borders. Music brings kids together to play together, to learn together, to celebrate accomplishments together.

So please, if you are a school board member, or know a school board member, stop cutting the music education of our kids. It's causing more harm than you can possibly know.

Thanks

John Philip Sousa IV

P.S. I very much hope you will enjoy my great grandfather's auto-biography. I also hope you will keep in mind that this was written in the 1920s and some of the language is not necessarily language we would use or even find acceptable today. It was acceptable 90 years ago which is why I have decided to ignore political correctness and republish the book just as John Philip Sousa wrote it. He was not a racist and he was not a bigot. He loved all mankind, worked and toiled with people from all walks of life, and spent his life promoting America and the American people...all of them.

Chapter I

FIDDLING VERSUS BAKING — SELF-INFLICTED ILLNESS AND ITS PENALTY — SCHOOL DAYS — THE AGONIES OF SOLFEGGIO — THE CONSERVATORY — A CONCERT TRAGEDY

WHETHER pastry and music can be prevailed upon to go hand in hand is a question. Of course there is one classic instance — M. Rageuneau in *Cyrano de Bergerac*, whose pastry-cooks delighted in presenting him with a lyre of pie crust! The fact remains, however, that I once came very near being a baker instead of a bandmaster.

A violinist begins a tone with a turn of the wrist which may best be described as the compelling impulse. A compelling impulse turned me baker's apprentice! My father had enrolled me in the conservatory of music of Professor John Esputa, Washington, D. C. and, at the end of my last year there, our pleasant relationship of master and pupil was marred by a personal combat.

The professor had been afflicted with boils, and was reclining in a hammock swung near the stove in the recitation room, when I came for my violin lesson. I observed that he was in a very bad humor but began my exercises, unheeding. Nothing I did met with his approval. Finally he told me to "draw a long bow."

"I am drawing the bow as long as I can," I said.

That seemed to incense him greatly and he shouted, "Don't you dare contradict me!"

"But I am drawing the bow as long as I can," I repeated. "My arm is up against the wall now."

He was holding in one hand a valuable violin bow, recently presented to him. Just what he intended to do, I do not know, but in his anger he jerked the bow back and struck the stove, breaking the bow in half. His rage knew no bounds!

"Get out of here," he yelled, "before I kill you!"

Taking my fiddle by the neck, I said clearly, "You attempt to kill me and I'll smash this fiddle over your head."

"Get out," he raged.

"I'll get out," I replied, "but don't you dare hit me, because if you do you'll get the worst of it."

I put my instrument in its green bag and walked home.

My father, sensing something wrong, said, "What's the trouble?"

"Oh, I have just had a fight with Esputa," I answered and, still shaking with wrath, explained the whole thing.

"Well," said my father, "I suppose you don't want to be a musician. Is there anything else you would prefer?"

With a heart full of bitterness I said, "Yes; I want to be a baker."

"A baker?"

"Yes; a baker."

"Well," he mused, "I'll see what I can do to get you a position in a bakery. I'll go and attend to it right away," and out he went.

In about half an hour he came back and said, "I saw Charlie (the baker just two blocks away) and he says he will be glad to take you in and teach you the gentle art of baking bread and pies; but," he added, "I have noticed that bakers as a rule are not very highly educated, and I believe if you would educate yourself beyond the average baker, it would tend to your financial improvement in this world at least; so I insist, as gently as a father can, that you keep on going to public school and pay no attention to your music. Give that up, and when you are through school the baker can start you."

Father then went on to say, "The baker has consented that you come to-night. You should be there by half-past eight."

That night I went to the bakery, and I am sure that no apprentice ever received such kindness as was shown me by Charlie and his wife and his journeyman bakers. I was there all night, and in the morning helped load the wagon and went out with the driver delivering bread to the various customers. I was particularly impressed by the intelligence of the horse, who knew every customer's front door along the route.

After I got back to the bakery about eight in the morning, I went down home, ate my breakfast and, since my father had said he wanted me to be a highly educated baker, I went to school. I had had probably half an hour's sleep that night. The bakers, after all the bread was in the ovens and the pies were ready to be baked, threw a blanket on the troughs and took forty winks of sleep, and so did I.

When I came home from school that afternoon I suddenly lost interest in playing baseball and hung around the house. After supper I went up to the bakery for my second night.

As I look back on it, I remember thinking that the baker and his assistants and his wife were slightly severe with me, for I was kept on the jump pretty constantly the whole night. When everything was in the ovens and we had had our usual half hour's sleep, we started loading the wagons. I went around delivering bread, returning home about eight o'clock, with an appetite, to be sure, but very drowsy. At school that day I learned nothing, and when night came I dragged myself to the shop. Alas, the baker was no longer the kindly employer, but a dictator of the worst description, and I was hounded at every step. About half past twelve the baby upstairs began to cry and the baker's wife snapped at me, "Here, you, go on up and rock the cradle."

I was only half awake, as I wearily mounted the stairs, and I must have fallen asleep before I had rocked the cradle three times, although Master Baby was yelling in my ears! I was awakened by a smart cuff and "You miserable lummox!" from the busy baker-lady.

When I reached home the next morning after delivering the bread again, I was absolutely tired out. My father said, "How do you feel this morning?" with a solicitude that did not ring true to me. Before I could answer, I had fallen asleep. He woke me up, called my mother and said,

"Give the boy some breakfast and put him to bed. Let him sleep all day. Of course you want to be a baker, don't you, Philip?"

"No," I moaned; "I'd rather die than be a baker!"

"Then" said he, "I think you had better make it up with Esputa and start in with your music again."

Thus it was that my father brought Professor Esputa and myself together again and we buried the hatchet for good. Ever after that (years later I orchestrated a mass for him) we were the best of friends. To prove my sincerity, I studied hard and made great progress in orchestration, harmony and sight-reading.

The incident of the bakery is ample proof of my father's kindly wisdom and common sense. We were, withal, an odd family. Father, being a Portuguese born in Spain, remained a votary of the daily siesta, Mother supplied the Nordic energy, and I, being the first boy, was inclined to despotism over my devoted parents. I was born in Washington, D. C., on the sixth day of November, 1854, and a tyrannical youngster I must have been. When I reached my fifth year Mother refused to allow me my full quota of doughnuts, and I informed her she would be "sorry later on," planning meanwhile what I intended to be a cruel revenge.

It was raining hard, and I moved out a plank in our front yard, placed it on two trestles, and then proceeded to make it my

BIRTHPLACE, WASHINGTON, D. C.

bed. In fifteen minutes I was soaked to the skin, and in half an hour my mother discovered me shivering and chattering with cold. I was carried into the house and put to bed. In a few days pneumonia developed and I was not able to leave my home for two years. My warning to my poor mother was correct — she was sorry later on!

Had I exterminated Sousa on that rebellious day, in my heartless attempt to punish Mother for having refused me the extra cruller, a kindly musical public would never have given me the title of "March King," King Edward VII would have presented his Victorian Order to some more deserving artist, the French Government would have bestowed the palm of the Academy on some other fortunate mortal, and five Presidents of the United States would have sought another bandmaster than myself.

During the two years of my illness my sister Tinnie and my father taught me to read and write and I became quite a student. It was a very common thing, however, for me to hear from some whispering neighbor, "I don't believe they will ever raise that boy!"

When I was at last able to be out again I was sent to a little private school opposite my father's house on 7th Street, from there to a larger one half way down the block, and, soon after, I applied for admission to the primary department of the public school in our district. I was there only a few hours when I was transferred to the secondary school; it seemed that the teacher thought I knew too much for a primary pupil! So I spent the rest of the term at the secondary and then was transferred to the intermediate, where I remained the following year; I was then about nine years old, and at ten I was in grammar school.

From childhood I was passionately fond of music and wanted to be a musician. I have no recollection of any real desire ever to be anything else. Washington was, in those Civil War days, an armed camp, and there were bands galore. Strange is the boy who doesn't love a band! I loved all of them, good and bad alike. So far as I know, there was no question of heredity in my love for music; I simply loved it because it was music.

The first to initiate me into the mysteries of the art was an old Spanish gentleman, a friend of my father's, who, with his wife, came to our home nearly every evening. One night when I had been particularly active in rolling a baseball around the room, to the evident discomfort of our visitors, the old gentleman suggested that a few lessons in solfeggio would do me no harm. My father thought I was too young to begin the study of music but finally consented.

The start was not particularly encouraging. The old Spaniard was a retired orchestra player and knew instrumental music, but he had an atrocious voice. All musical intervals were sounded alike by him. When he was calm he squawked; when excited, he squeaked. At the first lesson he bade me repeat the syllables of the scale after him.

"*Do*," he squawked.

"*Do*," I squawked in imitation.

"No, no," he cried, "sing *do*," and he squeaked the note.

"*Do*," I squeaked, in a vain effort to imitate his crow-like vocalization.

He grew very angry, stormed and abused me. His mental ear was alert and true enough, but the articulated sounds of his voice conveyed nothing but a grating noise to my child mind. For an hour he roared, and I floundered hopelessly after him. At last the lesson was over, and I almost a nervous wreck. During the entire time that I remained his pupil, the sound of his toneless voice hung over me like a pall.

One night after my highly irascible teacher had come to the house for my usual music lesson, he discovered the loss of his spectacles. He searched in his pockets and in his cloak which hung on the balustrade, but all in vain. His wife, who accompanied him, was positive that he had the glasses when they left home, which was but a few minutes' walk from our house; so it was proposed that the entire household should search the street.

The younger members of the Sousa family took lighted candles and the hunt began. Soon I was far ahead of the others. The street was deserted, and as I came near the old gentleman's house I saw the glasses on the lawn. Quickly I picked them up and put them in my pocket and then continued the search more assiduously than ever. When some one would point out the futility of our efforts, I would, by proposing new hunting-grounds, reawaken interest. Anything to prolong the search, so that I might escape the horror of at least one evening's lesson. My plan succeeded. We finally gave up and my teacher, with many imprecations on his ill luck, dismissed from his mind any idea of solfeggio.

Finally we returned to the house; I sat on the stair near the place where the old gentleman's cloak was hung, and when the family and their guests were engrossed in conversation, I slipped the spectacles into the inside pocket of the cloak. Then, with a cheery "buenas noches" I stole to my room, not to sleep, but to listen. On the stroke of nine, I heard my teacher walk into the hall, and when he wrapped his cloak about him, there came a loud cry as his hand struck the pocket containing the spectacles. "Caramba! Maldito! To think we have been hunting so long for that which I have just found. And I searched my pockets," — and with many angry mutterings he stamped out of the door. I crept back into bed, well satisfied with the evening's exploit, and closed my eyes for the first peaceful slumber since my introduction to solfeggio!

It was this eccentric old fellow's son, John Esputa, who started the conservatory of music in our neighborhood, and with whom I had the quarrel over the violin bow. Esputa's suggestion to my father was that "even if I didn't learn anything, it would keep me off the streets."

I was duly enrolled in 1861 as a student in Esputa's class of some sixty pupils. I am sure that during my first three years I was the silent boy of the class. I was noisy enough out of the classroom, but Iago himself couldn't have outdone me for silence when a class met. It was the result of Professor Esputa's remark to my father that if I didn't learn anything it would keep me off the street. I resented the imputation and so said little to the offending speaker but at the same time I drank in knowledge thirstily.

At the end of my third year at the academy, the first examinations were held. The Professor went to my father next morning and with the emphatic way peculiar to himself, said:

"That damned boy of yours has won all five medals, but I can't give them all to him — it would excite comment."

My father smiled as he replied, "Why, John, it isn't necessary to give him any, I'm happy to know that he has won all of them. The possession of the medals won't make him any smarter, and if you can make better use of them, by all means do so."

"Oh, no," said Esputa, "I'm going to give him three of them and I'll give the rest to other pupils." And he did. I have those three medals to-day — little gold lyres — a constant reminder, when I see them, that I had fooled everyone by silence — always golden.

When I had reached my eleventh year, I had made sufficient progress on the violin to be selected by Esputa as one of the soloists for his annual concert at St. Elizabeth's Asylum for the Insane, just outside of Washington. I was already playing as a professional. Unfortunately, on the day of the concert, I was scheduled to pitch a game of baseball. I returned home after the game hungry, tired and dirty, to find the house in a state of confusion; the usually faithful maid-of-all-work absent, my eldest sister away on a visit, and my mother so ill I was not allowed to see her. As it was near the hour for me to dress for the concert, I had but a few moments to eat a sandwich. Then, going to my room, I got out my Sunday clothes and my clean shoes and stockings, but for the life of me I could not find a shirt, the laundress having failed to return our linen. I hurried to the Conservatory to tell my teacher of the predicament.

"That's all right," he said, "run over to my wife and tell her to give you one of my shirts."

I went over, and the good-natured Mrs. Esputa put one of the professor's shirts on me. The bosom seemed to rest on my knees, and as the collar was many sizes too large, she pinned it together and I started with the party to the Asylum.

When it came my turn to play I tuned my violin and began the first movement. As the physical effort of playing became greater, the pins that held the shirt in place suddenly gave way and it fell from my neck. I forgot my notes, looked wildly at the dropping shirt and the laughing audience, and rushed off-stage in confusion, where I sought an obscure corner of the anteroom and wished that I were dead.

At the end of the concert, the superintendent invited the professor and the pupils into the dining-room to have some ice-cream and cake. I thought only of escape, but the professor intercepted me, and said:

"You made a nice mess of it. You should be ashamed of yourself and do not deserve any refreshments. You should not have spent the afternoon playing ball, but should have prepared yourself for the more important work of the evening." His lecture and punishment, for I had no ice-cream, had a salutary effect upon me, and from that day to this I have made it a rule never to swap horses in crossing a stream. I either play or work, but I never try to do both at the same time.

MR. SOUSA'S FATHER AND MOTHER

Chapter II

WASHINGTON IN THE SIXTIES — THE GRAND REVIEW — "I'VE BIN FIGHTIN' " — A BOY "ON THE NAVY YARD" — FATHER AND I — MUSICAL MUTINY — THE CIRCUS AND FATHER'S ANTIDOTE — IN THE MARINE CORPS AT THIRTEEN — STUDENT, TEACHER AND SOLOIST — FIDDLING IN FLOODTIME — TRIALS OF A YOUNG COMPOSER

IN MY boyhood Washington was just a sleepy Southern town. There were omnibuses but of course no trolley cars and the appearance of the first horse-car was a momentous event. The street railway company decided to equip its conductors with a sort of portable cash register worn around the neck like a yoke. One conductor refused to wear it — we learned later that he was "well-fixed" and lived in a fine residence on the outskirts of Washington. When cable-cars arrived, the drivers appeared in all the glory of great raccoon coats; I have no doubt that I regarded them with much the same admiration and awe with which the prep-school boy regards the 'coon coats of college undergraduates.

When I see the hectic hurry and the complexities of present-day life, I realize how simple was life in Washington in the sixties. Mother always went to market herself, though I went occasionally on errands. Once she entrusted me with money to buy some things for the household. On my way I was lured aside by an auction sale, where the eloquent barker enticed me, and before I knew it I had bid in several gross of knives and forks made of pseudo-silver. I found that I hadn't money enough to pay for my purchase, but when I tried to explain my plight to the auctioneer, he only shouted, "This damned boy hasn't enough money!" I gave him every cent I had and went home with an assortment of worthless knives and forks instead of bread and meat for the family.

I remember well the fright of Washingtonians at the time of Early's raid, when the Confederate cannon boomed only a few miles away. Every man capable of bearing arms went out to protect the city. As for the Grand Review, after the war was over, surely no normal boy of eleven would miss that spectacle. It is as vivid to-day as if it all happened only yesterday. I have described it in fiction form in my novel, "Pipetown Sandy," and I venture to quote here that account which is based on my own recollection of the impression the historic event made upon me.

"I'VE BIN FIGHTIN' "

'Twas jest a little while after Gen'ral Grant an' Gen'ral Lee had their great confab at Appermattox, an' settled things. I guess everybody wuz mighty glad they talked it over an' made up their minds to quit fightin' each other.

My father wuz readin' the Evening Star after supper, an' he ups an' sez, "Jennie, I sees by this 'ere paper that the army is comin' home." "The Lor' be praised fer that," sez mum, "an' I hopes an' prays they'll stay home, an' never go off fightin' ag'in," at which my dad sez, "Amen."

"Jennie," he sez, "I'm a-feelin' it's almost 'Lights out' with me, but if the Lor' wills to let me stay till the army comes back, I'm a-goin' to put on my uniform, an' jest go out an' see 'em marchin' up the street."

My old dad was ailin' a terrible lot jest then. Between three or four lead slugs that had never been dug out, an' his sawed-off leg, he was full of mis'ry but he never croaked. The only way we knowed he wuz sufferin' wuz when he'd holler in his sleep, an' then he wouldn't 'low he did, when we tol' him. He'd say he was jest dreamin' o' nothin' in partic'lar, but, in course, we know'd better.

Sure 'nuff, the corporation begins cleanin' the streets an' hangin' out buntin' an' flags an' evergreens, an' there wuz stuck up ev'rywheres signs what said: "Welcome to the Nation's Heroes," "Welcome to the Army of the Potomac," "Welcome to the Gallant Fifth and Sheridan's Invincibles," an' sich-like.

The old man gits his uniform out an' has mum to sew up the bullet holes, so people wouldn't think it was moth-eaten or wore out, an' when the day come, he spruces up, an' me an' him legs it up town to see the sojers come back.

When we gits up by the capitol, the school children wuz standin' aroun' on all sides a-waitin'. The gals wuz all dressed in white an' the boys had duck pants on an' blue jackets an' all of 'em had red, white an' blue rosettes pinned on their shirts. Some of them had bo'kets an' things like that to give to the sojers when they come along.

We stan's there a little while an' hears 'em sing *Rally Round the Flag*, an' *When Johnny Comes Marchin' Home*, then the old man sez, a-startin' off: "Let's mosey along to where Andy Johnson an' Grant's goin' to review the boys."

We kep' on a-walkin' until we got up by the President's house, an' we steps up, brash as yer please, on a stand, jest across from the place where Andy Johnson, Gen'ral Grant, and the other big guns wuz goin' to sit an' look. Nobody said nothin' to us, so we squats right down an' watches the people come a-pilin' in.

It wuz Guv'ner this, an' Guv'ner that an' Guv'ner t'other; it wuz jest a-rainin' Guv'ners. We warn't no guv'ners, an' we knowed we didn't b'long there, but we didn't holler it outo so folks could hear us, an' nobody noticed the diff'rence. Afore long ther' wuz some clappin' an' shoutin', an' Andy Johnson and the Gen'ral comes out on the stand opposite. Then a lot er high-up officers, an' sich folk, hustles on, lookin' mighty well-kept an' important. There wuz two boys 'mong that crowd, an' somebody sez they're the Gen'ral's children. I spec' they wuz orful proud o' their daddy, fer yer could hear the people hollerin': "Grant, Grant! Hurray fer Grant!" more'n anythin' else just then.

Well, sirs, we hears a rumblin' down the street an' we knowed the Army wuz comin'. There wuz a fine-lookin' gen'ral ridin' in front. One of the pack er guv'ners sez, "There's Meade!" I'd never seen him afore, but I took the guv'ner's word fer it. Then come a lot 'er officers, some clean an' new-lookin' an' t'others consid'rably s'iled, an' as they passed the President, they s'luted with their swords an' kep' right on.

I wuz wishin' it would get a little excitin' when, lickety-split, the devil's own horse comes tearin' up the street fer all he wuz worth. He cert'nly did look bad. The crowd stops cacklin' an' rose up like bees a-swarmin', an' strains their necks peekin'. There wuz 'n officer on the horse without no hat on. His long lightish hair wuz jest blowin' ev'ry-way; ther' wuz a great wreath swung on his left arm, an' that 'ere horse wuz runnin' as if Satan hisself wuz chasin' it. I wuz so scared I jest shet my mouth fer fear I'd spit out my heart! My father grabs my arm tight as a vise; yer could see the place a week afterwards.

"My God, he'll be dashed to pieces!" hollers a lady, holdin' on to the rail.

"Who is it?" shouts a guv'ner, shakin' like a aspen leaf.

"It's Custer!" bellers a officer, jumpin' on a chair, mos' dead from excitement.

"That's all right!" yells my daddy, as loud as he knows how. "Set down, an' enj'y yerself."

Jest then the horse rears up, an' when he come down I thought he wuz goin' heels over head.

"Oh!" cries all the people at onct, a-shudderin'.

"Set down!" yells my dad ag'in. "Set down; it's Custer, an' it's all right. He don't ride a horse 'cause he has to; he rides 'cause he kin."

Fer a minute yer could hear a pin drop. An' lo an' behold, we sees the Gen'ral comin' back, an' his horse was steppin' soft an' actin' as gentle as a parson's nag on Sunday. Custer was a-bowin' to Andy an' Grant an' the ladies as he passes, an' he wuz jest as c'am an' smilin' as if he wuz in a parlor.

Oh, my, how that crowd did clap an' hurray! Yer'd a-thought it wuz a house er-fire. My dad said he felt like he had hair clean down his back, an' ev'ryone a-standin' up, when he seen that horse runnin' away, but when he heard it was Custer he jest lay back, an' could er snoozed, he felt so peaceful like. Pop sed Custer wouldn't know how to start gittin' scared.

Pretty soon along comes his cav'lry, an' they cert'nly did look scrumptious with their carbines, an' sabers an' red scarfs a-danglin' sassy-like 'round their necks. They had a band, an' it was tootin' chunes that ev'rybody was keepin' time to, an' even Dad was a-pumpin' up an' down with his cork leg.

After a while the Zoo-Zoos comes by, all in red trimmin's an' red tassels on the caps, an' it wuz jest great, an' the *Tramp, Tramp, Tramp the Boys Are Marchin'* stayed with me till I got home. Lots of the flags had crape on 'em. One of the guv'ners sed it wuz 'cause Mr. Lincoln had died, an' that wuz mighty sorrowful to ev'rybody aroun' to say nuthin' of poor ol' dad.

When dad an' mum an' me was sittin' talkin' 'bout it that night, pop sez: "It wuz fine, an' no mistake." But after he had lit his pipe, he sez: "Jest wait till to-morrer, an' then yer'll see somethin'. My Army is comin'. The Bummers with Uncle Billy an' Black Jack'll be marchin' in, an' they'll make Rome howl!" Pop was powerful fond of Uncle Billy an' Black Jack, an' proud he'd been with The Bummers. When he wuz argufyin', he'd say it might be a matter o' dooty fer a sojer to lose his leg with any army, but with The Bummers it wuz a pleasure, an' I don't believe he'd a-taken it back if hell had froze over.

Well, sir, nex' mornin', bright an' early, me an' dad starts up, an' when we gits to the Botanical Gardens by the Tiber Creek bridge, we finds a pile o' bricks, an' they looks handy to set on, so we preempts 'em, an' we could see hunky-dory.

At nine o'clock, "Boom!" goes the signal gun, an' afore yer got tired waitin' along comes The Bummers. They looked like they had been mos' too busy to change their fightin' clo'es. Their broad-brimmed hats looked great, an' the crowd got stuck on 'em mighty soon.

Officers come 'long with wreaths on their horses' necks an' lots an' lots er the sojers had bo'kets stuck in their guns, an' Lor' alive, but they did hoof it. Yer could hear 'em plunk, plunk, plunk, the boys are marchin', till yer couldn't rest.

Well, sir, here comes a sojer marchin' 'long with his comp'ny, an' I-hope-I-may-die, if he didn't have a raccoon a-settin' on his shoulder. That raccoon jest put his face down by the side of the sojer's cheek an' looked out at the crowd, jest as sharp an' bright as yer please, an' it seemed to me he was sayin':

"I've bin there, I've bin there; I've bin fightin'."

The crowd clapped and laughed to split their sides. Then up comes a tall sojer carryin' a flag pole, an' the flag was faded an' shot to pieces. There wuz stains on it that looked like blood, an' all at once the breeze jest flung that flag out, proud an' defiant like, an' I thought it sed, plain as possible:

"I've bin there, I've bin there; I've bin fightin'."

The crowd clapped till the flag was out er sight, an' pretty soon along comes mules, an' donkeys, an' goats, an' dogs, an' cows, an'-I-hope-I-may-die if there wuzn't a rooster perched on a horse's back, an a-crowin':

"I've bin there, I've bin there; I've bin fightin'."

An' we jest went crazy, clappin'.

When the sappers an' miners comes, their blouses tucked in their pants, an' their belts tightened, an' shoulderin' their shovels, picks an' axes, we knowed they'd bin there. We knowed they had chopped, had dug, had shoveled their way to vict'ry an' to Glory Hallelujah. An' when they passed, the line comes to a halt fer a minute. My ol' dad wuz keepin' both eyes open, an' all of a sudden I seen a sojer lookin' at dad, an' he hollers out:

"Well, I'll be damned; there's Dan Coggles!" And afore yer could say Jack Robinson, he tosses his gun to another feller, an' rushed over to dad an' honest-to-goodness, if they didn't hug each other like they wuz two mothers.

"I thought yer wuz dead, Dan," said the sojer, as if he wuz goin' to cry.

"I heerd you wuz, Sam," said dad, an' he wuz a-blubberin'.

"No; I'm all right," said Sam, laughin' happy like an' pattin' my head.

"An' I'm all right, too," said dad. He wuzn't, but he didn't let on.

An' then I know'd the sojer was Sam Dickson who had gone to the war with dad, an' they had marched an' starved an' almost died together. I knowed it, fer one of the other sojers told me.

Well, sir, what must we do, but dad jest takes his place in that 'ere comp'ny right 'long side o' Sam, an' Sam handed his gun to me, an' I walked in front a-totin' it at right-shoulder-shift, jest like all the sojers in the regiment.

An' *Tramp, Tramp, Tramp the Boys Are Marchin'* we went up the Av'nue. Dad stepped out jest as if he hadn't enny cork leg, an' I stretched my shanks fer all I wuz worth.

The people clapped an' clapped, an' give me a bo'ket, an' dad got a lot of 'em, an' the officer who wuz marchin' right in front er the comp'ny kep' his eyes glued ahead, an' pretendin' he didn't see nothin' which cert'nly was mighty white er him.

We wheeled round the corner. Jest as we got to the gran' stan' the officers shouted out their orders. Me an' the Bummers presented arms, an' dad s'luted as we passed the

President. The crowd seemed jest crazy happy but I wuz orful lonesome, 'cause I wuz the only one in that 'ere hull review who couldn't say:

"I've bin there, I've bin there; I've bin fightin.'"

When I was a boy in Washington everybody who lived east of 6th Street, S. E. and south of Pennsylvania Avenue lived "on the Navy Yard." In fact, it was not a difficult matter to find out in just what section of town a boy lived by asking him what he was. The city was divided, in our boyish minds, into regions — the "Navy Yard," "Capitol Hill," "Swamp Poodle," (which is now in the vicinity of the Terminal Railway Station and the Post Office) and "the Island," which was south of Pennsylvania Avenue between Tiber Creek and the Potomac River. The nabobs who lived in the Northwest hadn't reached the dignity of a neighborhood nickname and the nearest approach to their vicinity was the "Northern Liberties," which was out 7th Street, N. W. While the "Navy Yard" section was probably ten squares from the United States Navy Yard near where I lived, I always said, "I live on the Navy Yard."

The boys who lived "on the Navy Yard," with scarcely an exception, toted a gun as soon as they were old enough to shoot and went out on the river — the Potomac or "Anacostia," as we called the eastern branch — and into Prince George County whenever game was in season. A boy who couldn't shoot a gun or sit out all day in the sun fishing had no standing "on the Navy Yard."

Thus very early in my life I was inoculated with the love of duck and quail shooting, my father being an inveterate hunter, and whenever he had the time, he was out hunting quail or decoying ducks during the season.

When I was still too young to carry a gun, but not too young to lug the provender, my father took me on hunting trips. We would usually be up at four o'clock in the morning, for a hearty breakfast, if it was to be a quail shoot over Bennings Bridge and into Prince George County.

I remember one occasion when I everlastingly disgraced myself. My mother always prepared a lunch for us of four boiled eggs, two rolls and a couple of apples, which was enough for anybody's luncheon. On this particular morning we started out happily, and, when we got over in the cultivated fields where there were quail, the dogs made a point, the birds were flushed and my father brought down one of them. He then started in a relentless pursuit of the squandered birds. About ten o'clock he was so far ahead of me that I could just hear the occasional sound of his gun, and suddenly I became very hungry. It was two hours before luncheon and in my boyish mind I felt I should probably starve to death if I hadn't something to eat before the lunch hour. So my hand stole into the haversack and I felt a hard-boiled egg in the corner. I took it out, looked at it admiringly, almost reverently, took off the shell and ate it. I next took one of the rolls and ate that. Instead of appeasing my appetite it seemed to give me more, and, to hasten matters, before twelve o'clock had come I had eaten four eggs, two rolls and one apple.

About twelve o'clock I caught up to my father and he, putting his gun against a tree, said cheerily, "Now we'll sit down and have luncheon."

Suddenly, at the word "luncheon," it dawned on me that I was probably the most abject scoundrel in the world, but I said nothing. My father lifted the haversack off my shoulders, put his hand in it, and then a puzzled look came over his face and he said, "Strange, strange; your mother never forgets," and drew forth one solitary apple left of the entire luncheon.

He raised his eyes and saw my guilty face and the telltale egg around my mouth. He looked at me for perhaps half a minute, then said, "You're not a hunter; you're a loafer."

He went down to the brook, took a drink, came back and offered me the other apple, saying, "Before eating it, I would wash my face if I were you." And that was the end to the incident!

This quiet father of mine was one of the best-informed men I have ever met. A most accomplished linguist and an inveterate reader, he had stored up wisdom from a multitude of sources. In the last days of his life, when he was an invalid, I have noticed on his table four or five books in different languages, each of which he delighted to read. I am happy now, to recall that I was not only his son but his companion, and whenever there was a hunting trip or a fishing expedition or any other pleasure, I was always with him. Many of his observations made an impression on my youthful mind and, with his wide knowledge, he had a story suitable for any incident in our daily life. One thing he fastened in my mind very strongly: never assume that you know all about a thing, or try to talk the other man down; instead, agree as nearly as possible with his opinions and so gradually force him to see yours. No better way can be found to get at the truth.

Father had his lovable and amusing little foibles. For one thing, he was not fond of work despite the fact that he was wonderfully handy at doing the things he liked. And like all Portuguese, he liked to take a siesta after his luncheon hour. I can recall Mother, who was charged with ambition and energy, saying despairingly, "O, Tony, Tony, don't go to sleep this afternoon!" But he would continue slowly upstairs, saying: "Elise, the night is for sleep, and the day is for rest."

Father was very reticent about his boyhood days, and almost never talked of Spain, or his days on the sea, but I did know that his parents were driven out of Portugal during the Revolution of 1822, and went over into Spain where he was born in Seville, on September 14, 1824. As a youth, he left Spain and went to England, and from England came to America some time early in the forties. In Brooklyn he met Elizabeth Trinkhaus, a young woman who was visiting the United States with some school friends (she was a native of Franconia, Bavaria) and after a short courtship they were married. Mother used to recount with much pride in Father's ingenuity (for if ever a wife worshipped her husband it was she!) how Father got out her German Bible and his English one, and how thus she learned English, and he conveyed his tender sentiments to her by that highly respectable medium! Father never let us know — and if he told Mother, she kept her own counsel — just what his standing was in the Old World, but I have read so much about the Sousas since I have grown to manhood that I have every reason to believe that he was a man exceptional in education and family. He was a gentleman in the liberal and the accurate significance of that much-abused word. He was always keenly interested in literature, language and current events, and although his technical knowledge of music was limited, he possessed an unusually acute ear.

While I was a pupil of Esputa, I began to attract kindly attention as a violinist, and began to do some solo work in amateur concerts, besides earning money with a little quadrille band which I had organized. This band had a second violin, viola and a bass, clarinet, cornet, trombone and drum. They were all grown men; in fact, the bass player was a very old man indeed. We became popular as a dance orchestra in Washington, and continued prosperously, until I listened to the anarchistic utterances of my associates and so talked myself out of a job.

We were playing for Professor Sheldon's dances. They came to me and said, "You're a great favorite here and you ought to make Sheldon pay you more money for the music."

Professor Sheldon was probably paying us the fair market price for a small orchestra and I couldn't understand why he should pay more, just because I happened to be popular. But my fellow musicians egged me on until I finally yielded and told Sheldon that he must advance our wages two dollars per man thereafter.

"And if I don't, what will happen?" he asked.

"I'll quit," I replied.

"Well, I am very sorry to lose you, but it's all I can pay, and all I propose to pay."

"Then," said I stoutly, "I quit."

At the next Saturday hop there was another man in my place, but the same seven anarchists were meekly playing there at their old wages! It was a lesson I have never forgotten and never shall forget!

One day while I was playing one of de Beriot's Concertos there came a rap at my door. I found a gentleman there who said, "I have been listening for five minutes to your playing. I was anxious to know just who you were so I rapped at the door."

"Won't you come in?" I asked.

He began, "You play very nicely. Have you ever thought about joining a circus?"

"No, indeed."

"I am the leader of the band in the circus that is showing near Pennsylvania Avenue," he said, "and if you would like to join I can get you a place."

Visions of beautiful ladies in spangled tights, of pink lemonade in buckets, flashed through my mind and I said, "I'd like to do it, but I don't think my father would let me go."

"There's no necessity of asking your father," he replied.

I told him I wouldn't think of it without asking him, since he was an awfully nice father.

"Yes, but fathers don't understand the future for a boy traveling with a circus; he might object."

"Yes, probably he would."

"I tell you what you do," he urged. "To-morrow night we are going to 'strike the tents.' You come over with your fiddle and go along with us, and then, after we've been away for a day or two, write your father and tell him what a good time you are having; perhaps he won't interfere then; but if you tell him now he might forbid you. And, by the way, do you play any brass instrument?"

I said, "Yes, I play baritone." And I got out the baritone and played him a few measures.

He enjoined secrecy, and I agreed to report the following night. The more I thought of it the more wonderful it seemed to follow the life of the circus, make money, and become the leader of a circus band myself. What a career that would be!

Inevitably, however, I had to let somebody into the secret. Next door to my house lived a good-looking boy and a great playmate of mine, Edward Accardi, so I must go and tell Ed my good fortune, pledging him to secrecy. Ed, I suppose, immediately told his mother, and she, with woman's wild desire to have everybody know everything, told my mother.

Next morning, while I lay a-bed, dreaming contentedly of circus triumphs — conducting a gigantic band beneath a monster tent that reached upwards to the stars — I was roused by the gentle voice of my father, "Good morning, Son."

"Good morning, Father."

"When you dress to-day," he said, emphasizing every word, "put on your Sunday clothes."

It was not Sunday and I didn't like at all the idea of making such a radical departure from custom, but I obeyed, put on my Sunday clothes and went downstairs where Father and I had breakfast together, and chatted casually. At the end of the meal he said, "We'll take a walk."

We took the walk in the direction of the Marine Barracks, — through the gate in silence and across the Parade Ground to the Commandant's office.

The record of the Marine Corps says that John Philip Sousa enlisted on the 9th day of June, 1868. Somewhat over thirteen years of age, and not fourteen until the following November!

This father of mine, bless his soul, had played trombone in the Marine Band since 1850, and was very much liked by everybody in the corps from the Commandant down. He had been to see General Zeilin, the Commandant, and they had discussed the matter as two fathers would, and concluded to enlist me in the corps as an apprentice boy to study music until I got over my infatuation for the circus, for my father knew that I was so much a law-abiding boy that I wouldn't desert.

Being a boy in the band was not a novel situation for me, for from my tenth year I had played triangle, cymbals and E♭ alto horn (God forgive me!) at various times with the band, and was a great friend of all the musicians in it.

The first time that I heard really fine music (apart from the ordinary orchestra or band programmes), was when the Franko family of five wonderfully talented children came to Washington for a concert. Professor Esputa announced to the school that they were exceptionally gifted and that he wanted every student to be sure to attend the concert; and most of us did so. It was the first time I had heard real violin playing, and the exquisite performance of little Nahan Franko, who was a wonder on the instrument, inspired me with zeal to do better. His sisters and his brother, too, added much to the pleasure of that excellent concert.

My youth up to this time had been spent largely "on the Navy Yard" but as I developed into a professional musician, I became acquainted with people who lived in the Northwest section of Washington, and, until I left the city, my companions were almost entirely from the Northwest. Some of those interesting young people had organized a club which they called the Vis-à-Vis, a literary society which issued a little magazine, containing their own articles. I do not remember what I wrote for them, but I am sure I was active in it.

While I played more and more in public, I became a member of the Orchestral Union, of which Mr. George Felix Benkert was the conductor. Mr. Benkert was a remarkably fine musician and one of the greatest pianists of that day. I played first violin in the Orchestral Union and evidently looked younger than I really was, for, on one occasion when they gave the oratorio, "The Creation," Clara Louise Kellogg, the famous American prima donna, who was singing the soprano role, came over and patted me on the head. I have no doubt she did it because she thought I was in the infant class. I was too shy to reciprocate, which shows I still had something to learn.

A great admirer of my ability as a musician, Dr. Swallow, introduced me to a Washington music lover, the Hon. William Hunter, who was Assistant Secretary of State. Every Tuesday evening during the concert season, Mr. Hunter had a string quartette party come to his house and play from eight until ten o'clock, after which he served a supper, and I was invited to come and take part in one of these musical evenings. I must have favorably attracted the attention of Mr. Hunter, for, until

I left Washington a couple of years later, I invariably spent my Tuesday evenings at his home, and my knowledge of some of the leading composers, such as Frescobaldi, Haydn, Tartini, etc., — what they did and what they wrote — was entirely due to him. He would place advertisements in the London, Berlin, Paris and Vienna musical papers for certain rare works that he could not obtain in the ordinary music store and, when they came, he would read me the biography of the composer out of a European encyclopedia, translating as he read, and in that way I grew to know much about the old-timers.

Knowing that I was earning my living as a musician Mr. Hunter took a very delicate way of paying me for my services. Every Tuesday evening after the quartette playing, when we were packed up and about to leave he would come over to me and say, "Young man, you did very finely to-night."

Of course I would utter a modest "Thank you."

He would then say, "What a splendid vest you have on to-night," and would slip five dollars into my vest pocket. Five dollars was a lot of money in those days.

Gradually I tired of my position in the Marine Band. At a change of leadership of the Band I had written a march, "Salutation," and when the new conductor came on the Parade we were playing it in his honor. When he reached the band he said, "What is that you're playing?"

The assistant leader answered, "That's a march by that boy there," pointing to me.

"Take it off the stands!" he ordered. Needless to say, he and I never became friendly.

I went to Mr. Hunter and told him I was unhappy in the band and asked him to see the Secretary of the Navy and secure my release, which he did.

The very moment I was released from the Marine Band, Mr. Hunter said, "You should go to Europe and complete your musical education."

I told him that was impossible; that my father had a number of children and could not afford to do it.

"I know a gentleman," he said, "who, I'm quite sure, would send you."

"But I wouldn't want anybody to support me."

"I wouldn't be so particular about that," he said. "If the man wants to spend money to educate talented young musicians, why not let him do it? I'll see the gentleman to-morrow and make an appointment."

It was Mr. W. W. Corcoran, the great philanthropist. Mr. Hunter made me promise a few days later, after he had seen Mr. Corcoran, that I would call on him. So I went to his house, pulled the bell rather timidly, and an overwhelming footman came to the door and asked me, in the splendid manner of footmen, what I wanted. I told him that I had called to see Mr. Corcoran, and also told him to tell his master that I had been sent by Mr. Hunter.

In a little while, Mr. Corcoran descended the stairs, came over to me, and asked me my name and ambitions. Finally, he said, kindly,

"Well, now, I'll think over your case and you call again in five or six days."

I never got out of a house quicker than I did out of that one, and I *didn't* call in five or six days; in fact, I haven't called up to date! The idea of being under obligations to anybody was very distasteful to me and though Mr. Corcoran might have sent me to Europe, I feel that I am better off as it is — even without the benefits of European education — for I may therefore consider myself a truly American musician.

Meanwhile, I was beginning to get pupils. I had three or four nice little Italian boys who played the violin in the streets, to a harp accompaniment. The little fellows had talent, even though they smelled of garlic.

I had a cornet pupil who wanted to learn only one tune, *The Last Rose of Summer*, and my efforts to teach him exercises went for naught — he wanted the fingering for the cornet part of *The Last Rose of Summer* and nothing else! That is all he studied with me for a period of three months. He had a yacht and his great delight was to take friends down the Potomac, get out his cornet and play this old melody. He was a fine swimmer, and when he had a party of men aboard, and *The Last Rose of Summer* had become a bit wilted with repetition, they would throw his cornet overboard, whereupon he would immediately dive after it and fish it up!

The variety theatre of those days corresponded to the vaudeville of to-day, except that the only ladies present were on the stage. The principal variety theatre in Washington was Kernan's Théâtre Comique. Mr. Kernan decided to open a summer garden on a lot adjoining this theatre. The lot was below street level, but seemed otherwise well adapted to such use. The stage was built, the singers and orchestra engaged, when suddenly they realized that there was no conductor, since the regular conductor of the Théâtre Comique had gone off for the summer with his orchestra to a watering-place in Virginia. Leaders of variety were scarce in Washington and Mr. Kernan was in a dilemma, until one of his musicians said, "I know a boy up on Capitol Hill who would, I think, suit you as an orchestra leader."

Kernan immediately sent a messenger to my house and asked me to call on him, which I did with a speed that would not have shamed Nurmi.

Kernan said, "What experience have you had in variety?"

"None."

"Do you read music?"

"Of course."

"Well, I'm willing to give you a chance."

"Thank you."

"Rehearsal will be on Saturday morning and we'll give a performance on Saturday night."

When I joined the orchestra to lead it for rehearsal it was a very easy matter to play songs and dances and so on, and I got through swimmingly, with everybody delighted.

I went home and in order that I might be on time for the performance at eight o'clock that night I returned to the Théâtre Comique at five! About half-past five one of those well-known Washington summer showers came down and flooded the Garden until everything was afloat except the piano, and the waves were lapping the black keys. As I stood there with Kernan looking out upon the deluge, he groaned,

"We can't give a show there to-night. We'll have to give it in the Théâtre Comique, indoors."

"All right," I answered, pulling on my rubber boots, "but if you're going to do that, we must have the piano moved up right now."

Three or four husky Africans were summoned, who exhibited such a fine carelessness in the process that the instrument finally reached the Théâtre Comique and was installed in the orchestra pit with every wire, from middle C down, torn from its moorings!

This was before the days of a steel E string for fiddles and when you sometimes got a lot of bad strings. Before we had finished what they were pleased to call on the program *The*

AT TWENTY-ONE

IN LONDON, FIRST BRITISH TOUR, 1900

Overture, I had snapped my E string and was giving an exhibition of jumping up to positions on the A which would have done credit to a half dozen Paganinis rolled into one.

One of the admirable qualities of a vaudeville entertainment is its incessant action; so we had no more than played the last note of the overture (I frantically trying to put on a new E string) when the bell rang for the beginning of the performance.

During the short dialogue that intervened, I managed to put the E string on; but I had played only fifteen measures of the next movement when the D string broke, and before the performance was over I think every string on the violin broke from one to five times, except the G, and that was a hardened old sinner and stayed by me the whole evening. The pianist couldn't hit a bass note because there was no note there to hit; the cornet player worked hard but was wheezy; the clarinet player was extremely nervous, and the drummer thumped irregularly. It was without any doubt the worst orchestral performance that was ever given in this imperfect world.

Kernan's reputation as a dangerous man in an argument was already known to me and, before the performance, I had been told that he didn't hesitate, in a fight, to bite off a man's ear or gouge out his eyes. He had been a sailorman.

When the performance finally came to a close, the stage manager apologized for its obvious faults and informed everybody that it would be improved the following day. I had one wild desire while he was talking — because it seemed as if everything he said must be directed at my miserable work — to have the floor open and swallow me up!

While I was putting away my violin the cornet player leaned over and said, "Here's Kernan coming down the aisle. I hope he doesn't kill you!"

I turned my head quickly and saw him striding towards me. Just as he got to the orchestra railing I wheeled around and shouted at him, "I never want to play in your theatre again!"

He looked at me, as if I had gone hopelessly insane.

"What's the matter with you?" he said.

"Matter with me? This is a great way to treat a man. You brought me up here in the hottest theatre the Lord ever allowed a man to work in, had a lot of darkies smash the piano so we couldn't play a note on it, and then you expect me to stand here and submit to it. I never want to play in your theatre again!"

"Now, son," he said, "listen."

"I don't want to listen!"

"Now you listen, or I'll get angry!"

"Well, go ahead; what do you want to say?"

"I know you're right. It was no place to put you. We should never have attempted to give a performance. But we'll have a rehearsal to-morrow morning, and everything will be all right." He was almost gentle — because he knew of no other leader for his orchestra. I shook my head dubiously at first but soon relented and agreed to try once more.

Next morning, when I arrived, the lady who sang, *We Used to be Friends, But We're Strangers Now*, or some such classical selection, descended on me with fire in her eyes: "You spoiled my song last night!"

Kernan, who was sitting in the first row, called out to her roughly,

"That's enough from you; sit down! We've heard all we want. Go ahead with the rehearsal."

We rehearsed, everything was all right and I stayed there until the winter season opened.

However, all was not so pacific where my studies were concerned. I was often disheartened. Professor Esputa was a kind man, but he believed that the way to manage boys was to "treat 'em rough." He was considerate and kind to his girl students but invariably severe with the boys. This was no way to treat me, for at home I was used to kindness and love. Moreover, since I was following a profession quite foreign to the atmosphere of my home life (since Mother was unmusical and Father was not an especially good technical musician) I felt that every other music student of my acquaintance knew more than I did, and so I required much encouragement to keep me from becoming depressed and unhappy.

On one occasion I brought my professor an arrangement of my very first musical composition. I had heard the *Träumerei* of Schumann played very beautifully, and thought it a perfect melody — to this day it still seems to me surpassingly beautiful — and I wondered if I could write something a thousandth part as lovely. So I evolved a little piece which I called *An Album Leaf* for piano and violin, which I played to my unmusical mother, who said it was beautiful, and to my father, who asked me to play it over again. Even the neighbors remarked that, while it wasn't as jolly as *Dixie* or as solemn as *Nearer My God to Thee*, still it was pretty! So when I went for my first lesson that week, I took it to the professor and placed the piano part before him and we played it through. As we completed the last chord, he took the piano part between his fingers, tossed it over the instrument, and said, "This thing is nothing but cheese and bread, and bread and cheese." Probably he intended only to stimulate me to greater efforts but, had he struck me, he could not have hurt me more than by that expression. I picked it up and, even though it is only "bread and cheese, and cheese and bread," I have kept that little piece among my treasures even unto to-day.

Another of my teachers was Mr. Benkert, with whom I studied harmony, violin and piano. Mr. Benkert took unusual interest in me and under his genial instruction I made rapid progress, especially in harmony, which would occupy most of the hour's lesson; although he would sometimes, when his engagements permitted, give me two- and three-hour lessons. My violin playing would begin after we had finished the harmony lessons. He would pick out a sonata of Beethoven or Mozart and I would play the violin part to his piano accompaniment; but he never gave me any instruction on the piano. Happening to mention that fact to my father, I was told, "Will you kindly say to Mr. Benkert I am anxious that you should know something about the piano?"

This I repeated to my teacher. He went to the piano and struck C on the ledger line below the staff of the right hand and asked what note it was. I said, "C."

Then he struck the same note again and said, "What note is that?"

"Why," I said, "That is C on the ledger line above the staff in the G clef.

"I think that's as much piano as I want you to know. You seem to have a gift of knowing a composition by looking at it, and you may develop into a very original composer if you follow that line of procedure; whereas, if you become a good pianist you would probably want to compose on the instrument and, if you are not careful, your fingers will fall into pleasant places where somebody else's have fallen before."

After I had been with Mr. Benkert I grew to love him. He seemed to me the perfect man. Brown beard, deep sunken eyes, and æsthetic features, he appeared to me a modern embodiment of the Saviour.

I was past nineteen by that time and playing first violin at Ford's Opera House, where the Alice Oates Opera Company was giving Offenbach's *Les Bavards*. I took the violin part with me to my lesson to have Mr. Benkert mark the fingering in one or two more or less intricate passages, and at the end, after going over it I said, with an outburst of boyish enthusiasm, "Mr. Benkert, do you think I will ever be able to write an opera?"

He put his hand on my head and said, "My son, you will write a better opera than this one you have just been playing." That was encouragement. The nearest he ever showed his displeasure at any of my exercises was slowly to raise his nose. He died in his forties, beloved by every one who knew him, one of the finest musicians to whom America has given birth.

I published a few compositions while he was still with us; and, although he did not approve of a young man rushing into print too rapidly, he was good enough to go over the proofs of one with me. Its publication came about in an amusing way: a man much older than myself was very much in love with a pretty girl and he thought that a piece of music, dedicated to her, would smooth the road to matrimony. So he offered to pay for the publication of the piece. That brought into existence (they long since dropped into oblivion) a set of waltzes entitled *Moonlight on the Potomac.*

My next compositions were a march called *The Review* and a galop, *The Cuckoo.* I took them to Philadelphia to the then well-known firm of Lee and Walker. Their editor was the late Thomas á Becket, a fine musician and a splendid man. When he played my compositions they sounded much better than when I played them myself. I sold them to him for a hundred copies of each piece. They did not electrify the public, but were played by a few bands here and there.

Chapter III

ONE evening at the Opera House in Washington the conductor of the orchestra was taken suddenly ill and I was called upon to assume his duties. The play of the week was *Bohemians and Detectives*, the work of Milton Nobles, who was also the star. I sat on the high chair of the conductor, and I think that no one ever took up the cues of that melodrama with greater alertness than I. Mr. Nobles left the Opera House at the end of the week, but before the following week was up, a telegram arrived from him, in Chicago, offering me the position of leader of the orchestra of his company. Evidently my eagerness had impressed him; I had a real offer.

Just at this time, I was head over heels infatuated with a clergyman's charming daughter. This young lady was a member of the Vis-à-Vis Club, wrote very good poetry, and painted with unusual skill. With that impetuosity characteristic of nineteen and twenty, I made my love known and we became engaged, but the girl insisted on secrecy, which I couldn't understand because I wanted to yell from the housetops that I had won this wondrous creature.

We wrote various songs together, one of which made what you might call a little hit. This song, the words of which are given below, was written after we had had a tiff — still, I believe, a common practice among all young lovers. I had kept away from her house for several days, and she sent me this lyric, which was an absolute peace offering:

AH ME
A KNIGHT there was of noble name,
Ah me!
A knight of wond'rous deeds and fame,
Ah me!
He wooed a lady, wooed and won,
No fairer lady 'neath the sun,
She lived and smiled for him alone,
Ah me!
A shadow crept into the light,
Ah me!
The lady's face grew strangely white,
Ah me!
The knight one morning rode away,
Nor came again, Ah well-aday,
The sunset's glory turned to gray,
Ah me!
And love is fleeting, love will go,
Ah me!
No hand can stay its ebb and flow,
Ah me!
And death is sweet when love has fled,
A rest of heart, a rest of head,
A fold of hands and we are dead,
Ah me!

Secrecy is hard to achieve in this world. How our romance was revealed, I do not know. I only know what happened!

Her father and mother had been extremely fond of me, I thought, but when I called one night, expecting the sunshine of her smile, the maid who opened the door said, "The Doctor told me to tell you, if you called, that he would like to see you in his study."

I was suspicious. Had my charming inamorata whispered something to some bosom companion? And had the whisper reached the family?

He was a very large man with an oratorical voice. Glaring at me with piercing eyes he said, "Young man, you have come into my house like a thief in the night and stolen my daughter!"

If he had said he was going to hang me just then it wouldn't have surprised me more; but I quietly said, "Will you kindly explain?"

"What right have you to become engaged to my daughter?" he asked.

Thinking that perhaps levity would be the strongest weapon, I replied, "Well, she had to become engaged to somebody."

He ignored my flippancy. "This engagement must end now."

"Let's argue the point," I replied.

"I have no desire to argue the point. I simply insist that it end now."

"Why? Do you object to me as a man?" — drawing myself up.

"No."

"Do you object to my family?" I inquired, a little louder, and more impressively (as I thought).

"Not in the least."

"Then just what is your objection?"

"I object to you because you are a musician."

"There is no nobler profession in the world," I stoutly declared.

"I am willing to grant that," he said, "but point out to me, if you can, one musician who ever had a dollar!"

"That is no reason why I shouldn't get one," I replied.

"Perhaps not, yet the history of your profession proves that musicians invariably live in poverty. My daughter has been brought up with every luxury and I shall never consent to her marrying a musician."

"Well," said I, "I have one proposition to make to you, and only one. I promise to abide by it, and you must, also."

He looked at me curiously, and I continued (thinking of Mr. Nobles' offer from Chicago), "I will leave Washington and stay away for two years, and if at the end of that time I have not made some progress in the world in a financial way, I will give up your daughter. But if I have made progress, I shall come back here and marry her, whether you agree to it or not — providing she still cares for me.

"I'll not consent to that," said the clergyman.

"And I don't care whether you consent or not. That is my proposal. I shall get out of Washington just as fast as I can. I will not write to your daughter or have any communication with her whatsoever, for two years, and if at the end of that time, she still loves me, we will marry, whether you are at the wedding or not. Good day!" And I walked out of the room proudly, my head in the air.

I went back to the Opera House, handed in my resignation, and said to the man who had received the telegram from Mr. Nobles, "Telegraph Mr. Nobles I accept."

The next day I left for Streator, Illinois, reaching there at about the same time that his company did. I reported to him and the first question he asked was, "Have you had any experience in engaging musicians?"

"No," I said, "except with a little dance orchestra in Washington."

"You go down to the theatre," he said, "and find out who the leader of the orchestra is, then go out and engage not over ten men at the best price you can, have a thorough rehearsal, for they'll need it, and then report conditions to me."

I found the local leader in a paint shop, weighing out white lead and putty, his arms and face smeared with many-colored daubs. He assured me that he was ready to talk "art" and that he was the man with whom to do business. I told him that I was the leader of the traveling company which was to perform that night and asked if he could supply ten men for the orchestra. He took his cigar from his mouth, and said, "Can supply you as many as you want."

"How much do you charge per man?" I asked.

"Two dollars a skull," was his reply.

"Well," I said, falling into his mode of expression, "I want ten skulls — one first skull, one second skull, viola, 'cello, and bass skulls for the strings, and flute, clarinet, cornet and trombone skulls for the wind, and a drum skull besides."

"Anything else you want?" he asked.

"Yes, I would like them at the theatre for rehearsal at two o'clock sharp," I said.

He looked at me with a pitying expression and said,

"Stranger, there are just two things that you don't want here. One is that you don't want any first fid, and you don't want any viola or 'celly and you don't want no flute, 'cause we aint got 'em. The second thing you don't want is a rehearsal at two o'clock or any other time."

"But," I said, "we must have a rehearsal."

"Rehearsal be blowed," he said, "we never rehearse here."

"But," I persisted, "my music is difficult and a rehearsal is absolutely necessary. Several numbers must be transposed. Can your orchestra transpose?"

With a wave of his hand he disdainfully said: "Transpose? Don't worry. We transpose anything."

No argument could budge him; and he finally stopped any further discussion by saying that I could take his orchestra or leave it, just as I liked. It was Hobson's choice with me, so I said, "Well, I'll take your orchestra and I do hope everything will go all right to-night."

"Don't you lose any sleep over us. We're all right," he called to me, as I was leaving his store.

Shortly after seven I went to the theatre and found the orchestra in the music room under the stage. The leader said, "You might as well know the boys and I'll just introduce you. What is your name?"

"My name," I answered, "is Sousa."

"Well, Sousa," this with an awkward bow, "allow me to introduce Professor Smith, our second fid; and, Sousa, this is Professor Brown, our clarinet player; and, Sousa, this is Professor Perkins, our bull fid, and this," pointing to a cadaverous-looking fellow, "is Professor Jones, who agitates the ivories on our pipe organ. Sousa, these are Professors Jim and Bill Simpson, solo and first cornet; this is Professor Reed, who whacks the bull drum, and yours truly, solo trombone. Now that all of us know each other, what is your overture?"

I explained that the overture we used I had written myself and it had met with some favor.

"I ain't sayin' that's so or not, but it won't go here. Will it, boys?"

A unanimous "*No*" from the orchestra dispelled any doubt as to their feelings. I expostulated with warmth and injured pride:

"But you have never heard my overture, you know nothing about it, and I can assure you it is all right."

"It may be all right in Chicago or Bosting, but I tell you it won't go here. I got the overture that our people want and that's the one we are going to play to-night."

"But I think —"

"Don't think," said the leader, putting his hand on my shoulder; "just make up your mind that you are going to play our overture. Do you read first fid at sight?"

I mildly admitted that I could.

"Well, just take a look at this thing," and he held up the first violin part of his "overture." "Now, I want to explain this piece to you. When we open up on her we go along quietly, not making any fuss, almost sneakin'-like," and he pantomimed the tempo. "When you are playin' that first strain you do it just as if you didn't have no train to ketch, but when we get here," he pointed at the next strain marked Allegro, "just go as fast as hell! You'll have to chase your fingers all over the fiddle."

I sighed and answered, "All right, I think I understand."

After we were seated in the orchestra box I rapped for attention and we began the overture. I noticed immediately that all of them were wretched players and, when I started into the movement which the local men told me was to be taken "fast as hell," I began playing the strain with a rapidity evidently unknown to the orchestra, and pandemonium reigned. But curiously enough each man felt that it was his duty to play the notes to the end regardless of what the rest did, and they finished one after the other, stretched out like a bunch of horses in a race. I had no time to express my disgust, for the curtain was raised immediately and the first number was to be sung. It was Come Back to Erin in E flat. When we began the introduction of the song every member of the orchestra was blowing a note either in a different time or different key.

I shouted, "It's in E flat."

The louder I shouted, the louder they played. The singer sang on, trying to appear oblivious to the cacophony that reigned. As soon as the song was finished I turned to the leader and said, "This is the rottenest orchestra I have ever heard, you do not know one note from another.

He looked at me calmly and said, "You're too particular. If you don't like our style of playin', pay us and we'll go."

"Pay you?" I cried. "You have not earned a cent."

"Well, if you don't like us, give us our money and we will go."

I was much excited, and I shouted, "Give you your money? Not under any circumstances. Pack up your instruments and get out of this theatre."

"We'll go when we are paid, and not before," said the leader.

"I'll see about that," I said, jumping up and walking through the centre aisle of the theatre. Going to the box office I explained the situation to my manager. He called the manager of the theatre over and the latter said, "All right, just call in the constable and put them out as usual."

As the constable walked in to drive out the orchestra, I said to the local manager, "Just think, these men told me they could read anything and when I wanted them to come to rehearsal they said they never rehearsed in this town."

"Yes," said the local manager, "that is true; they never have a rehearsal because if they did they would be discharged before the performance."

I was very happy in Mr. Nobles' company. He was a fine man and a scholar, and we got along splendidly the entire season. After we had been out six or eight weeks, through some disagreement, the actor who played the part of *Dionysius O'Gall*, the Irish lawyer, in *The Phœnix*, suddenly resigned his part and left the company. Mr. Nobles was in a dilemma, until a little Englishman, valet to one of the actors, volunteered to do the part. He had heard the play so often that he was letter perfect and went on immediately.

Those familiar with the play will recall that the first act ends with a great fire scene. Mr. Nobles played the part of *Carroll Graves*, and while he is sitting at a table writing the famous story, *The Villain Still Pursued Her*, the Irish lawyer makes his entrance. On the night of the valet's debut, the exigencies of the stage required that one of the fire traps would be immediately in front of the door marked for the entrance of the Irish lawyer. Through some inadvertence, the young valet actor had not been informed of the situation of the fire trap and the necessity of stepping over it. When the cue came, the door was swung quickly open and with a hearty, "Good morning, Carroll, I have brought you some oysters," the valet rushed forward and stepped into the open trap.

The audience, who thought it was part of the play, gave the most spontaneous laugh I have ever heard, while I, sitting in the orchestra, felt my hair stand on end. Believing the valet must be maimed or killed, I rushed through the orchestra door to the stage, while Mr. Nobles, with a look of great anxiety, motioned to the stage manager to ring down the curtain. When I reached the stage, I found that a ladder had been lowered into the trap to the caverns beneath and a group of actors and "grips" were peering into the abyss, all fearing that the poor fellow was dead; but at that moment the valet poked his head above the trap.

Mr. Nobles grabbed him by the arm, and said, "Are you hurt?"

The little Englishman looked at him much perplexed and replied very slowly, "No, I am not hurt, but greatly surprised."

We were gradually working into the extreme Middle West, and when we were to give a performance in a town in Kansas, the manager of the theatre said to Nobles and myself, "If you want to pack this house to-night, just get the city band to play out in front of the theatre from half past seven to eight o'clock. By that time you will have the whole town out." "And," he added, "they won't cost you a cent; all they ask is that you let them in to see the performance."

MRS. JOHN PHILIP SOUSA

I hunted up the leader of that band and he was sure that his boys would be delighted to play. All they wanted was to see the show afterward, and they would use their instruments as a passport into the theatre. At half past seven the band, resplendent in their uniforms, struck up a march and for half an hour entertained the audience that gathered in the street; but no one seemed to be enthusiastic about entering the house. Finally the leader of the band said, "Guess we'll go in now."

The theatre was a ground-floor one, barn-like, and had a number of windows on one side, not far above the ground. The band passed in. I went to the music room to tune up my fiddle and had been there perhaps ten minutes, when the call-boy came running back and said, "How many men are there in that band?"

"Oh," I said, "perhaps twenty."

"Well," said he, "about a hundred men have already gone in with their instruments!"

"That's impossible," I replied, "I'll go and investigate."

As I entered the theatre, I noticed a man come in with an instrument, immediately go to an open window and hand it to a fellow outside, who went round to the front door and came in with it; he in turn handed it to someone else outside. If I hadn't closed the window the entire town would doubtless have viewed the performance, and all for the half hour's work of the band!

Most of the towns we played were small, and I very soon got used to the depth of musical degradation a country orchestra could reach. Their so-called musicians were men employed in other walks of life; and, without an opportunity to practice their instruments daily, they made a sorry mess of the melodramatic music which was used in the performance.

The original name of the play was *Bohemians and Detectives.* The hero is rescued from fire in the tenement house where he lives and is lying in a hospital reading John Hay's poem Jim Bludso. An officer of the hospital asks his name, and it occurs to him to rename himself Jim Bludso. Dramatically he says, in an undertone, "From the ashes of Carroll Graves will arise Jim Bludso."

I suggested to Mr. Nobles that, since here was the rebirth of Carroll Graves, *The Phœnix* would be a good title for the play. Nobles immediately adopted it and the play for the greater part of the season (and even to-day) is known as *The Phœnix*. One of its lines, "The villain still pursued her," is still quoted.

This journey through the Middle West was replete with amusing experiences. As we travelled from Council Bluffs (our next stand after Omaha) to Lincoln, we learned from the morning paper that the Opera House, where we were scheduled to play, had burned down the night before, just after the theatre had been emptied of its audience. I was met at the station by the leader of the orchestra, who gave me a detailed account of the fire, and at the end of it, said very dramatically,

"The Opera House is burnt and I have lost my violin. But, thank God, I saved the *Poet and Peasant* overture!"

When, in our journeyings, we reached Mobile, I found a fairly capable orchestra, with an old German leader. In those days it was customary, at the end of a rehearsal, to invite the orchestra out to have a drink — which, of course, it never refused — and the old leader attached himself to me, staying till lunch time. I invited him to lunch, and he remained for the afternoon. I invited him to dinner, then we went to the performance, and at its close, out we went to sup together! And then he conveyed to me his great respect for my musical ability, adding that he wished to honor me with the dedication of a new composition of his. If I would call the orchestra for Thursday morning, he would play it.

Accordingly, the orchestra met Thursday morning at ten o'clock. I rehearsed one or two numbers and then he played his composition — a very pretty concert polka which the orchestra played with an ease and smartness that struck me as most uncommon. Then he lunched with me (he had lunched, dined and supped with me on the Tuesday and Wednesday preceding; this was Thursday, and Friday still to follow!) They changed the bill on Saturday night for a number without music, so I was sent to New Orleans to rehearse the orchestra; it was the first time in my life that I had led a Sunday dramatic performance.

I found in New Orleans the leader of the orchestra a Mr. Maddern, to be a very interesting gentleman and a good musician — who for a long time when I recalled the incident in later years, I assumed was the father of Minnie Maddern Fiske. At the end of the rehearsal, I happened to say something about Mobile. Mr. Maddern smiled. "Did they dedicate a piece to you?"

"Yes," I replied, "the leader is going to send a copy over here to me."

"That piece has been dedicated to every leader that has gone to Mobile," said Mr. Maddern, "since that old fellow has been leader of the orchestra there, which is a great number of years. In fact, it will continue to be dedicated until he passes in his checks, for it has paid his board for half a lifetime. I don't believe he can write a note, but he plays the trick on every leader who comes. He is a regular Old Man of the Mountain until the leader departs, and then he prepares for a new victim." Maddern must have been right, for I never received that piece!

On my return to Washington, they immediately made a position for me in my old theatre. After playing there a short time, there came to the theatre a very sensational series of tableaux known as *Matt Morgan's Living Pictures*. I believe it was the first time that America had seen the undraped female on the stage, in any numbers, and America gasped at the spectacle. From an artistic standpoint the tableaux were certainly very beautiful. Matt Morgan, who had been the artist for *Frank Leslie's Weekly*, had painted some very effective scenery and there were seven statue girls and one statue man to depict such paintings as *Phryne Before the Tribunal, Cleopatra Before Casar, The Christian Martyr, The Destruction of Pompeii, The Shower of Gold,* and others equally famous.

The audiences were almost entirely men and the performance, though a harmless one, was generally considered as risqué. During the week, the management, dissatisfied with their conductor, approached me and I was engaged to join the company as leader of the orchestra.

When we reached Pittsburgh, the morals of that city were so affronted that the statue girls, all seven of them, were arrested and locked up in the police station. Why they arrested neither the manager nor myself, who shared an equal prominence on the bill, is a mystery.

The manager engaged one of the best lawyers in the city and the trial proceeded the next morning. Charges were made by a police officer, who, after he had given his opinion of the depravity of the exhibition, was cross-examined by our lawyer. The latter began to discourse learnedly of art, especially in the nude. Finally, taking a photograph of Minerva from his case, the lawyer said, "Did you ever arrest this party?"

The patrolman looked at it long and intently; then slowly mopping his perspiring brow, he said,

"I arrest so many people — I can't remember all of them!"

There was loud laughter in the court-room. The judge dismissed the case. We turned people away that night!

Our arrival in St. Louis coincided exactly with the delivery of a message to the manager offering him an engagement in San Francisco for a protracted period. I, however, had no wish to spend the entire summer of 1876 in California, and had set my heart on going to Philadelphia to the Centennial. So I left my orchestra and proceeded to Philadelphia, where I first heard the famous Gilmore band and where I was told that I should starve to death since the city had no work for even local musicians! Far from starving, I was given most agreeable fare—the opportunity to play first fiddle under Offenbach, who had come over from Paris to show at the Centennial.

This engagement was a pleasant and profitable one. I vividly recall an incident while we were rehearsing. The orchestral platform was in the centre of the building, which was called the Offenbach Garden, on the corner of Broad and Cherry streets. One morning, a most effete composer came in with a big bundle under his arm and approached the kindhearted Mr. Simon Hassler, who was directing at that time. After some conversation, Mr. Hassler turned to the orchestra and said, "Gentlemen, this is Mr. So and So, a composer whom I have known, and who has just finished a new composition which he wishes you to play over.

Anybody who knows orchestras, knows just how they feel about playing a thing over just after a long rehearsal; but when Mr. Hassler said he would be glad if they would do it, they acquiesced and the parts were handed out. Mr. Hassler handed this society composer the baton, which he eagerly grasped. He mounted the platform and began the number. As I remember, it didn't amount to a great deal; besides, the copyists had not been over-scrupulous in keeping it free from wrong notes. At the close his head was buried in the score, and while he was so engrossed, evidently looking over pages where things hadn't sounded just right to him, each member of the orchestra of at least eighty men — with the exception of the young fellow who sat next to me, and myself — silently walked, or I might say slid, off the platform, "Now, gentlemen, that we understand each other, we will go through the composition again."

He raised his head and his baton at the same time, and there, in front of him, sat two boys! The rest of the orchestra was on its way home, and I don't think he could have brought them back even at union rates!

Offenbach was a small man with mutton-chop whiskers or "sideburns." He had in America an unusually large orchestra, but conducted his own works. The arrangements of his works were poorly copied and had many mistakes. The *Trip to the Moon* ballet was printed and correct. His attention was called by Max Maretzek, the assistant conductor, to an arrangement of his most famous melodies by Conrad called *Offenbachiana*; this he played at every concert. We also played very often a polka — I think it was called *La Belle Americaine*. Offenbach was a kindly man and got on splendidly with the orchestra. He spoke in French only.

I played in the Offenbach orchestra during his entire season, which ended some time in July. I wrote one piece for the orchestra, *The International Congress*, since published for wind band. It started with a short fugue on *Yankee Doodle*, then ran a gamut of the principal national songs of the world, winding up with *The Star Spangled Banner* treated in imitation of the last part of the *Tannhäuser* overture.

At the end of the season I was in doubt whether to remain in Philadelphia, return to Washington, or seek my fortune in New York; but dear old Simon Hassler settled the question for me by giving me a position in his orchestra at the Chestnut Street Theatre.

This was probably the best equipped and largest of the theatrical orchestras of that day. The theatre was run as a stock company under the management of Gemmill, Scott and Mackey, and had in its company Minnie Conway, McKee Rankin, W. J. Ferguson, Lizzie Harold, and many others who became famous as great actors. The star of the company was one of the finest actors it has been my pleasure to see, W. E. Sheridan. I thought his Louis XI was far superior to any other I had seen, including Irving's.

In 1876 Byron's play, *Our Boys*, ran nearly two hundred nights. It always interests me to meet somebody who corresponds to a character I have met in print. We had a viola player in the orchestra who always recalled to me that well-known story of a certain society lady calling her footman and saying, "James, I want to rest to-day and don't want to see anyone; so, if anybody calls, I don't want you to indulge in an untruth, but give them some evasive answer." James, with that deference characteristic of footmen, said, "I understand, Madam." So when Mrs. Nouveau Riche called in the afternoon, the footman went to the door. She asked, "Is Mrs. Brown in?" The footman said, chattily, "Is your grandmother a monkey?"

Well, our viola player always reminded me of this footman, because if you asked him if it was going to snow, he'd probably tell you his baby had the croup. Mr. Hassler tried on several occasions to pin him down to an answer, but without success. One night as we sat in the music room smoking and playing cards, awaiting the end of the act, the viola player got up quickly, and said, "I guess I have time to run to the drug store before the act's over." The acts were being timed to the minute. He pulled out his watch and noticed the time. Mr. Hassler believed he saw his opportunity and called to him, "What time is it, Joe?"

Joe took out his timepiece for a second look, put it back in his pocket slowly, and, starting for the door, turned and said, "I'll tell you when I get back!"

As I said before, *Our Boys* ran nearly two hundred nights. There was an old German in the band who had the reputation of being a great grouch. We very seldom heard his voice, and he used to reach the theatre at least fifteen minutes before the overture was played, tune his instrument, and sit down waiting for the rest of the orchestra to come in. He did that every night during the run of *Our Boys*!

Mr. Hassler, who always had some funny idea in his head, said, "Sousa, I'll bet you a supper that old Diffendorfer, although he has heard *Our Boys* for at least a hundred and fifty nights, can't tell us what the first line in the play is."

I accepted the bet. Mr. Hassler sent for Diffendorfer at the end of the act and said, "Mr. Diffendorfer, I have just made a bet with Sousa here as to what the first line in *Our Boys* is. You've heard it for a hundred and fifty nights. Will you kindly tell us what it is?"

Diffendorfer stood on one foot, shifted to the other, thought a long while and finally said, "Vell, it vas somedings."

The following season found me back with Mr. Hassler in the Chestnut Street Theatre and part of the time playing with the Permanent Exhibition Orchestra that was giving concerts at the Finance Building of the Centennial. I was also making money at teaching, and was assistant to Thomas à Becket, correcting music proofs for the W. F. Shaw Company. Also, I occasionally sold a composition; it was during those days that I wrote a Te Deum and began to look about for an opera libretto. Two libretto prospects failed to materialize. Charles Heber Clark, the funny man of the *Philadelphia Bulletin*, was suggested as my librettist by Mr. Hassler, who had unbounded confidence in me, after my dramatic music for the plays at the Chestnut Street Theatre, but Mr. Clark's price was too high. Mary Dennison, the other prospect, a charming and gifted author, had finished only a portion of a projected first act, when she gave up the work at the death of her husband. Thus was success spiced with disappointments.

I was greatly surprised, walking down Chestnut Street, to come face to face with the girl I had left in Washington two years before! Her father was with her, and they were planning to return to Washington the next day. I invited them to dine with me, and then we went to their hotel for a chat. Of course she wanted to know all about my activities, and I gave her a rosy account of the number of pupils I had, the pages of proof which I had corrected (at 12 cents a page!), the two orchestras of which I was a member, and of my compositions which were beginning to attract favorable attention.

They left next morning, but two days later I received a letter from my fiancé, telling me that her father was much pleased at my progress and would be glad to see me whenever I could call. I left Saturday night for Washington, attended church with her family Sunday morning, and had a long and highly satisfactory interview with the doctor. All was merry as a marriage bell — *until* — the girl's mother appeared on the scene. She had no sons of her own and, from our first meeting, was wonderfully kind to me and interested in everything I did. While my beloved was changing her dress after luncheon, to take a stroll with me, her mother entered the room, placed her hand on my shoulder maternally, and said,

"Philip, dear boy, I am worried."

"What is it?" I asked, perturbed.

"Em may love you, but I am not at all certain. There is a man who has been paying her attention for more than a year. He is much older than she, but he is a splendid man. He was an officer in the Confederate Army, and is fine and admirable in every way. I am sure he loves her dearly. And she — well, of course, she will marry you if you insist; but are you sure you will be happy?"

This was indeed a thunderbolt from a clear sky!

I took her hand and said, simply, "I understand."

Not long after she had left the room, Em came in, smiling and ready. But I took my hat and overcoat and said, "I'm going."

"Where?" she inquired.

"To Philadelphia."

"But you said you weren't leaving until midnight!"

"I am going at four o'clock." (It was then three.)

"What made you change your mind?"

I looked at her intently, then said, "Ask your mother." Then I left the house and returned to Philadelphia.

Monday morning I received a letter from her telling me not to be a "foolish boy." I tore the letter up without replying. Wednesday I received a warning that if I didn't answer that letter she would marry the other man. I did not answer it, and the following Wednesday I received a marked copy of the *Evening Star* of Washington, containing the announcement of her marriage. Thus ended my first romance!

Life, however, was very full for me. J. M. Stoddart engaged me to write a series of fantasies from such operas as *Carmen*, *The Sea Cadet* and others, which gave me a new interest and kept me busy. When the fortunes of the Chestnut Street Theatre began to wane, I accepted an invitation to fiddle at Mrs. John Drew's Theatre on Arch Street. Mrs. Drew was a gifted actress and a splendid stage manager whose only business mistake, during my acquaintance with her, was the production of the *The Sorcerer*, a play singled out for failure because of inadequate rehearsal, over-exploitation, and actors unused to musical pieces. With Zimmerman, the leader of the orchestra, I was guilty of the orchestration!

Just then, *Pinafore* was winning its way into the hearts of the public, and one day when I went to W. F. Shaw's to correct proofs, I had a conversation with Tom á Becket, in which he said, "A bunch of society amateurs want to give *Pinafore* and they want me to drill them. I have neither the time nor the inclination, so I have recommended you. They start rehearsing to-morrow night at 7:30. They pay ten dollars for each rehearsal, and if you please them you may get the engagement to conduct all the performances!"

Accordingly, I went there the next night and found the finest assembly of voices and beauties I had ever met! Being young, I was extremely stern at rehearsals. It is wonderful the amount of drilling competent people will take. Only the stupid, vain ones, who are ill-equipped for the work anyway, get "hot under the collar" at correction or reproof. When we finally gave our first performance it created a sensation. I believe ours was the best singing cast of Pinafore among the innumerable companies then interpreting the piece.

The operetta took America by storm. However, in Gilbert's life, he complained always that he "had consistently received unfair treatment from the professional critic," and it is amusing nowadays to read the many futile criticisms written of *H. M. S. Pinafore* fifty years ago, in the light of its acceptance now as a charming bit of musical frivolity. It was claimed then that the story itself did not contain sufficient genuine humor to balance the studied absurdity of many passages; it was described, too, as a "frothy production destined soon to subside into nothingness."

As a famous gentleman once remarked, "If this be oblivion, 'tis surely very pleasant!"

The immediate success of *Pinafore* was, to some extent, due to an admirable topical joke. Just before it was produced, Disraeli had appointed as First Lord of the Admiralty, W. H. Smith, head of a firm of publishers! Mr. Smith was a keen business man, a clean politician, and an excellent administrator but the connection between books and battleships was not apparent to the sea-dogs of the British Navy. Gilbert worked the joke for all it was worth in Sir Joseph Porter's song, *And Now I'm Ruler of the Queen's Navee.*

Pinafore was first produced at the Théâtre Comique, London, Saturday, May 28, 1878, and had a non-stop run of more than 700 nights. *What, Never? Well, Hardly Ever*, was heard numberless times each day, and everybody sang, whistled, or went to see *Pinafore*. It was a poor town that didn't have at least two companies. The original American company held forth in Philadelphia, at the South Broad. At the North Broad, Fatty Steward had another permanent company, and at the other theatres there were always travelling companies to regale audiences with the melodies and satires of the piece.

Its popularity in America was enhanced, not so much by the British joke, above referred to, as by an editorial in the *Public Ledger* — the very standard of Philadelphian respectability — known most descriptively as the "Philadelphia Bible." Mr. Childs, its editor (a highly respected gentleman who presented all his callers with a cup and saucer as souvenirs of the happy occasion!), enthusiastically brought forth an editorial, pointing out the innocence, the cleanliness and purity of *Pinafore*, in contrast to the tights and coarseness of the French pieces so often produced. The effect was electrical! People who had never been in a theatre in their lives came to see *Pinafore*. Here was emancipation for pent-up youth; all the myriads of Puritanical parents suddenly discovered that the theatre really gave innocent enjoyment, and was not such a den of the devil as they had been taught to believe.

We called our *Pinafore* company the Philadelphia Church Choir Company, and gave performances in Philadelphia and neighboring towns like Wilmington, Trenton, and Pottsville, always with the greatest success. This company finally went into the hands of professional managers, John Gorman and William Mead; most of the amateurs faded out of the picture and were replaced by professionals, and then we invaded New York. Opening at the Broadway Theatre, afterwards Daly's, under the management of Edgar and Fulton, we achieved an unusual success, and remained there the entire season.

On the 22d of February, 1879, was introduced by the *Hebe* of the company to her understudy who proved to be quite the loveliest little girl I had ever seen—Jennie Bellis of Philadelphia. She had a cloud of chestnut hair, and a perfect complexion. She was wearing a little gray poke bonnet and was charmingly dressed. I liked everything about her, her manner, her speech, her face, her voice. After I had shaken hands with her, she said, laughingly, "There are two birthdays to-day. I am celebrating Washington's and —"

"And," I broke in, "whose?"

"Mine," she said; "I'm sixteen."

We were married before a seventeenth birthday rolled around, I can assure you! It is no wonder that *Pinafore* has a special place in my heart, since it brought me Mrs. John Philip Sousa and our three splendid children, Philip, Priscilla, and Helen. Like all good love stories, the last sentence of ours is, "And so they lived happily ever after."

Chapter IV

IN NOVEMBER, 1879, there came to one of our performances, Gilbert and Sullivan and Blanche Roosevelt, who had journeyed from London to give *Pinafore* and *The Pirates of Penzance* over here. Although they were unheralded and sincerely trying to attend incog., our very alert stage manager, Peaks, recognized them and sent a young woman of the staff to sit by them and catch whatever comments they might make upon the presentation of the piece. This was the burden of her report:

"Piece finely sung," said Sullivan enthusiastically; "couldn't be better."

Blanche Roosevelt declared that she could not vocalize, as well as our American soprano, the passage which begins:

This very night, with bated breath …

Gilbert was indignant because Dick Deadeye had the presumption to interpolate a song by Malloy.

Sullivan thought the orchestration excellent. (This of course, delighted me, since it was mine!)

Gilbert, however, said the acting was below par. (In this respect, I agreed with him, for we had organized the company with an eye to singing talents, and had thus paid little attention to the dramatic side of the cast.)

A TROPICAL SONG OF YOUNGER DAYS
The Free Lunch Cadets, 1877

A few weeks after this "review by the generals" we were off on a tour of New England, and as the season advanced, it was seen that *Pinafore* was becoming a little threadbare, and a new opera seemed advisable, so it was suggested that we take Sullivan and Burmand's opera, *The Contrabandista*, re-write the libretto, and make it more of a chorus piece. (Ensemble numbers were our strong point.) It fell to my lot to prepare the music. Charles Gaylord, author of the successful play, *Our Fritz*, was to write the libretto. The opera was finished in an incredibly short time, rehearsed as each new number was written, and finally produced in Jersey City for the first time. It met with only moderate favor, not enough to fire us with enthusiasm. We took it through New England and closed it in Holyoke, Massachusetts. I hurried to Philadelphia for a new adventure, — to be married!

Now it was that I picked up my fiddle and played substitute in various theatres; and presently Mr. F. F. Mackey wrote that he would like to meet me. We met, he showed me the libretto of a musical comedy, *Our Flirtation*, by James Bird Wilson of Cleveland, and asked me to write the music. I made a contract with him, took my bride, a couple of quires of music paper and a large capacity for work, to Cape May and straightway wrote the piece. It went into rehearsal late in July and was first produced at Abbey's Theatre on Arch Street, Philadelphia.

The flutist of our orchestra was a Scotchman, John S. Cox, probably the finest artist on that instrument in America. He was quick-tempered, with a chronic grouch against all composers for the reason that they never succeeded in writing anything he couldn't play. He delighted in the most difficult music; so, knowing his weakness, I inserted in the overture to *Our Flirtation* an extremely difficult cadenza for the flute. The copyist, in writing out the parts, placed that cadenza on a turn-over page. The first thing Cox met when he turned the page was a display of notes that ran the gamut of the instrument. Cox, like most old time players, proud of sight-reading ability, never turned a page until he reached the bottom. How his eyes opened in surprise when he saw that cadenza. He looked up at me, and said, "Just a minute." Bending over, he softly played the passage through and then said, "All right, I'm ready," whereupon he phrased and played it beautifully. The entire orchestra applauded him. Indeed, so long as we were at the Philadelphia theatre, there was always generous applause for him.

After closing in Philadelphia, we went on to Reading and when the orchestra was assembled I noticed the flute player was a very rotund and very short German, bespectacled and taciturn. The rehearsal began. When the flutist turned the page and his eye fell on the notes, which seemed as numerous as the sands of the sea, his eyes opened wider, and a puzzled look came into his face. "Go ahead and play it," I urged. He looked daggers at me, slowly took his flute apart, placed in it the case, and said, "I vill not blay vot I cannot May," and walked out. The inhabitants of Reading never heard the cadenza!

We travelled West, and when we reached St. Louis, I received a letter from my father telling me that he had had an interview with the Colonel Commandant of the Marine Corps and I was wanted in Washington as quickly as possible to lead the Marine Band. Mr. Mackey, however, was unwilling to let me go. After much wiring, however, between Father and myself, Mr. Mackey finally agreed to let me go, and I secured Charles Zimmerman to take my place as leader of the orchestra.

I reached Washington on the last day of September, 1880. For the first time in my life I was conducting a military band. And how rich with incidents was that existence!

One of those memories never fails to bring a smile to my lips. There was a little old man who had been a member of the band for years and years who always started out by making a great to-do over each new leader, but, alas, ended by hating him. In all other respects he was a most commonplace musician with an exalted idea of his own importance. When I arrived, with my wife, at the station, father was waiting for me, and so, too, was this little old fellow, who, stepping out of the crowd, shook hands very cordially and said, "Mr. Philip, we will bring you a serenade to-morrow night."

I tried to explain to him that we had no need of a serenade, but could not move him from his purpose. At last I said, "Mr. Demona, I will not allow you to serenade me to-morrow night; but if you are equally fond of me one year from to-morrow, I shall consider it a great honor if you will serenade me then." Forty-five years have passed and I am still waiting for my serenade! I suppose he has passed on to the land of eternal serenades.

The band work provided a fascinating occupation; moreover, I had a decided advantage in my new position since my father had been a former member of the band, a trombonist, though long on the retired list — and I had been in the band for a short time in my boyhood. The Commandant had impressed upon me the necessity of a complete reorganization of the band. The men were dissatisfied with the present state of affairs, and to use the Commandant's words, "The band gives me more trouble than all the rest of the corps put together."

I found its music-library limited, antiquated, and a good deal of it poorly arranged and badly copied. There was not a sheet of Wagner, Berlioz, Grieg, Tschaikowsky, or any other of the modern composers who were attracting attention throughout the musical world. I immediately selected some first-class compositions from the leading catalogues of Europe and proceeded with the most rigid rehearsals, in order to bring that band up to modern requirements.

The small pay received by the musicians and the impossibility of getting a discharge from the service, except through disability or bad conduct, developed in the band a perpetual grouch. It bothered me so much that I went to the Commandant and explained to him the condition of affairs, and my diagnosis of the case; I suggested that he grant a discharge to any member of the band who applied for a release with my approval. With great reluctance, he finally consented. At the next rehearsal, one of the best players in the band put down his instrument and said the rehearsals were beyond his endurance.

"Well," said I, "what do you propose to do about it?"

"I want my discharge," was the sullen reply.

I knew he didn't really want anything of the sort, but I said, "Make out your application and I will get it for you."

Much to that musician's surprise, he received his discharge in twenty-four hours.

By the end of the first year the band was reduced to thirty-three men and even the Commandant was a little alarmed; but I gradually gathered about me an ambitious and healthy lot of young players, and the public performances of the band were such that it began to attract very favorable attention from Washingtonians and visitors to the National Capital.

From a motley mob of nurses and baby carriages and some hangers-on, the audiences at the White House Grounds concerts grew into the thousands, and the Saturday afternoon concerts at the White House became a social event. Thursday concerts at the Barracks were splendidly attended and Wednesday concerts at the Capitol drew large audiences, although we suffered from the noise of street cars and carriages passing near the bandstand. The harmony and good behaviour of the men became proverbial; for be it said to their everlasting credit that, during the last eight years I was in the band, not a man was reported for dereliction of duty or unsoldierly conduct.

When the men found that I played fair with them and that my approval for discharge brought immediate action, they never asked for it unless they really wanted to go, in which respect they were very much like the rest of the human family.

The many and various parades we had took on the character of events and we would be followed from assembly point to the end of the march, not only by small boys but by many of the business men of Washington — and, perhaps, some unsophisticated Congressmen. I believe there was no better marching band in existence during the last ten years of my leadership. The front file consisted of trombones and basses, finely built young fellows who could step out and keep up a cadence of one hundred and twenty a minute from start to finish.

But during my first days with the Band, and the preceding years, it was a hot-bed of feud and dissension. The members were mostly Italians and Germans, with a few Americans and English. The main cause of the trouble was "outside business" — the engagements the men made apart from their Governmental duties which was their principal means of existence. The Government pay ran $38 a month for a first-class musician, $24 for a second, $21 for the third, and the grandly remunerative sum of $13 for the fourth, or private class. Of course there was thirteen cents per day for rations, besides some fuel and clothing money, but it was all so pitifully small that it was hard to recruit men and equally hard to keep them satisfied after you got them. "Soft words butter no parsnips," I knew, but if I could build up the private practice of the band something would be gained, I thought. The repertoire of the organization was very limited: some selections of old Italian operas, a few of the standard overtures, and a great number of ordinary marches, polkas, etc. I knew from former experience that the music played at the White House receptions, state dinners, and Saturday afternoons in the winter was too robust for the limits of the White House, and I began almost immediately to soften the burst of sound for the guests who came to meet the President.

The first appearance of the band under my direction was at a New Year's reception. The first to enter are the ambassadors, then the cabinet, then the supreme court, then the officers of the army, navy and marine corps stationed in Washington, the bureau chiefs of the departments, winding up with the general public. As the first-named arrived we played music of a subdued character, eliminating the percussion instruments, so that the drums, tympani and cymbals were largely squelched, all of which did not please the drummers, who had from long usage believed that they came not only to be seen, but to be heard. Then as the guests came in greater numbers, light operas were played, and when the general public arrived, I ran into marches, polkas, hornpipes and music of the liveliest character. I think my method gave the President a chance to shake hands with double the number of people he could have met had I played slow pieces. President Hayes' secretary told me it was a splendid idea, that the President was less fatigued than he had been after previous receptions. The President evidently appreciated the work I was doing.

As a band, we played in the ante-room which was an entrance to the Portico; as an orchestra, beside the staircase between the East Room and the reception rooms. When we had orders to play for the President we assembled at the Marine Barracks and went to the White House in a street car.

General Hayes was an American of Americans, distinguished by a rare devotion to his duties. He was a gallant soldier and a gifted statesman whom the Electoral Commission had placed in the White House by the close vote of 8 to 7. The dispute over his election no doubt made him more serious than was necessary, even for a President, yet everybody who knew him loved and respected him. Hayes calmed the after-war hysteria, and won over the country to tranquillity. He withdrew the Federal troops from the South, the very troops who were supposed to have been the cause of his election, and diligently served his country, many times in direct opposition to the dictates of his party. Mrs. Hayes was a beautiful woman and looked a very queen in the White House; in my opinion, she was the most charming First Lady of the Land we ever had. She dressed always in exquisite style and possessed personal beauty in full fruition. Moreover, no more gracious hostess could be found in Washington.

On the occasion of my second appearance at the White House, at a dinner given to the ambassadors and to members of the Supreme Court, I had a set-to with a man of African descent, which brought about an immediate reform in the matter of refreshments for my band. The members of the band had complained to me from time to time that when they were called to get something to eat, after playing several hours, they found, on reaching the dining-room in the basement of the White House, that a motley crowd of waiters, garden helpers and policemen had devoured nearly everything on the table. One bandsman told me that the last time he attempted to answer the supper call, he received only a plate of oyster soup — without the oyster.

On the second night we had been playing almost incessantly from 7:30 until 10 when a burly, dictatorial colored man — a left-over from General Grant's administration — came over to my stand and grumbled, "You an' yo' musicianers can go downstairs now and get something to eat."

CONDUCTOR OF THE UNITED STATES MARINE CORPS
BAND, 1885

I looked at him a moment and then, a faraway look in my
eyes, replied,

"It has been my privilege to see the Jungfrau in all her snowy
grandeur; I have seen the lazy Tyrrhenian lap the Neapolitan

pebbled shore; I have heard the melodic words of the silver-voiced orator expound the beauties of America. I have heard much, and seen more, but I never expected to hear a menial of the President of these United States use a word not in the dictionary and never used in polite society in any part of this mundane sphere. What, precisely, do you mean by 'Musicianers'? Explain yourself."

"Explain? Hell!" said he. "If yo' don' go downstairs to the dinin' room, you won't get nothin' to eat."

I turned to the band and said, "This colored man, evidently deputized by someone higher in authority, says if you don't hurry, you will get nothing to eat. Those who wish to go are excused."

Eight or ten went. They returned shortly, however, reporting an entire absence of food. The next time we played, the same colored man came to me and said, a trifle less aggressively than before, "There's some grub downstairs for the band if dey wants it." I said, "Just a moment, please, and I will give your order." Turning to the bandsmen, I said, "This dusky factotum reports that there is grub downstairs for you. Whoever wants it may be excused."

Not a man left his place. The old darky went off, shaking his head and muttering, "I'll be damned!"

Next morning there was a message at the barracks asking me to call at the White House as soon as possible. I went immediately. Colonel McCook, the officer in charge, informed me that the summons was from Mrs. Hayes, who entered very soon and said in her kindly fashion,

"Mr. Sousa, the President is anxious at all times to contribute to the welfare of those who entertain his guests. It was reported to him that neither you nor your band accepted his invitation to have some refreshments last night. There must be some mistake; possibly it is on our part. Won't you talk it over with Colonel McCook, who, I am sure, will set everything right?"

Consequently, I told the Colonel just what had happened, giving him an account of the colored man's attitude and the disappearance of the food before my men could get there. "Mrs. Hayes was very particular about ordering luncheon for your men," he said, "and, hereafter, we will see that they, and they only, get it." At the next White House affair, when lunch-time arrived, a young man came up to me and said respectfully, "Mr. Sousa, there is a luncheon for your men down in the dining room. Please tell each of them to rap twice on the door and they will be admitted. The President has arranged for your luncheon in the State Dining Room and will be pleased to have you accept his invitation." Such thoughtfulness was characteristic of General Hayes.

The next President was General Garfield, whose tenure of office was so short that I had little opportunity to form any estimate of him as president or man. We played only once at the White House during his administration, — that is, we should have played there, but by a curious circumstance, we failed to connect, much to Mrs. Garfield's disappointment, and to our own. We were ordered with the Marine Battalion to take part in the dedication of the Farragut statue. Leaving the barracks about 8 A.M., we marched to the northwest of the city, waited until the ceremonies commenced, took part in them, and reached the barracks again about 6:30 that evening. The tired band was dismissed. All the men who lived out of barracks left immediately. I went home, changed to "civies" and sat down to dinner. Presently the doorbell rang and a maid brought me this message from an orderly, "The Commanding Officer wants you as quickly as possible."

I jumped up, re-assumed my uniform and hurried to the barracks three blocks away. "Sousa," said the Commanding Officer, "a message has just been received for the band to report at the White House in full dress at eight o'clock."

"But," said I, "it's after seven now, the band has been dismissed for the day, and the men are probably scattered all over the town, and no doubt many of them are playing at private engagements and I know it will be hopeless to try to find them in time."

"Well," he replied tersely, "those were my instructions and those are your orders."

We sent our messengers and they found just one man, the bass-drummer. So at eight o'clock, I, in my gorgeous red uniform, sat at one end of the platform, and the bass-drummer at the other. There was a dazzling array of music stands and empty chairs, but no men. The President, evidently, saw the humorous side of it, for when I explained it to him, he said it couldn't be helped. All evening long we sat there, the drummer and I. When the reception was over, I dismissed the drummer with proper military ceremony and we filed out. We had reported for duty, were present and accounted for, though the President and his guests heard never a note.

That was the only time I met Mr. and Mrs. Garfield, for an assassin's bullet ended the life of the President. I was so confident that the President would recover that Wilson J. Vance, at that time the Appointment Clerk of the Treasury Department, and myself, were planning a hymn of thanksgiving for his recovery. We had several interviews and were about to begin work when the terrible message came that the President had died at Elberon. I had retired when I heard the newsboys shouting the sad tidings.

I got up, dressed, and told my wife I wanted to get out in the air, and I walked all night, in fact, until ten o'clock next morning. I came home, took music paper and wrote the dirge *In Memoriam*, which we played when the President's body was received at Washington and when he was put to rest in the cemetery in Cleveland.

When Mr. Arthur became President we were still idle because of the period of mourning over the death of General Garfield, and we did not appear at the White House for several months. One day in the late Spring I met the President's private secretary on Pennsylvania Avenue. He stopped me, and said, "The President wants the band next Thursday evening."

Next morning I told the Commandant that the band would be required at the White House on the following Thursday, to which he replied, "Of course they'll send their orders through the proper military channels."

When Thursday arrived and no order had been received at the barracks I went to the Commandant and asked him to telephone the Navy Department because I felt sure there must be some mistake. He reluctantly telephoned, for he was a military man and did not approve of slipshod methods. The message was returned that the band was not required. I was anxious to go, as it would have been our first appearance during the Arthur administration; but the answer from the Department led me to believe that the period of mourning was not over, and that Mr. Arthur had decided not to have music at his party.

Next morning, while I was at breakfast, a messenger came from the barracks saying the Commandant wished to see me immediately. Straight to the Commandant's office I went. "Did you go to the White House last night?" he asked.

"No, sir," I replied, "I was told by you that I was not needed."

"Well," he said, "the Secretary wants to see you to find out why you were not there." And off I went, puzzled but determined to defend my band.

Mr. Hunt, the Secretary of the Navy, very evidently expected me.

"Sousa," he said, "the President is much displeased at your failure to be at the White House with the band last night. You go over to the White House and make your peace with the President. Explain your absence, then come back to me." I could see that he was very much worried.

At the White House I was escorted to the office of the private secretary. When I entered I said, "I am more than sorry the band was not here last night, but I desire to make an explanation."

"We don't want to hear any explanation. The President will get a leader who will obey his orders."

"I wish to explain," I reiterated.

"We don't want your explanations," he replied, angrily, waving his hand towards the door.

Without another word I returned to the Navy Department — to the Secretary's room.

"I hope you fixed things up," he said.

"No, Mr. Secretary," I replied, "it's worse than ever."

I then recounted my interview at the White House, and Mr. Hunt asked, "What will you do?"

"Do?" I repeated. "Mr. Secretary, did you order me to appear at the White House? No, you didn't. I get my orders from the Commandant, who gets them from you — not from a private secretary, and I did not receive any orders from you to appear at the White House. Had I, I would have been there. I would have been pleased to go, but I received no orders," and I bowed myself out.

Although I knew I was right, I immediately went to see Senator John F. Miller of California in his Committee Room at the Capitol. He was a friend of mine and a great friend of the President. He laughed heartily.

"That's a great joke on Arthur," he said. "Don't you worry; he'll appreciate it. He was in the sutler's department during the war and probably didn't understand military etiquette or he wouldn't have allowed you to be ordered out at the command of a private secretary. Don't worry."

I didn't, and the matter ended. I never knew whether Senator Miller talked with Mr. Arthur or not, but I know there was no further trouble during his administration. While the President was much more reserved when he talked to me than was President Hayes before him, he never showed any indication of resentment.

The coming of Chester A. Arthur had placed the office of President poles away from the American atmosphere of the Hayes era. One snobbish official said to me in high glee, "At last we have a gentleman for a President!" If he meant a President who differed from Grant, and from Hayes, as I knew him, then he was right. But if being a gentleman involves following lines of pure Americanism, he was wrong. Mr. Arthur would have done admirably in an absolute monarchy, but that he carried out the American tradition of cordiality, I do not believe. The austerity of President Arthur was reminiscent of the effete aristocracy of the Old World; the genial activity of Hayes, Cleveland and Harrison suggested the pioneer stock of America.

I can hardly credit the oft-repeated story that General Grant knew only two tunes, one of which was *Yankee Doodle* and the other wasn't. I have known more than one President, relieved from the onerous duties of a great reception, to find rest by sitting quietly in the corner of a convenient room, and listening to the music.

At one of Arthur's state dinners, the President came to the door of the main lobby of the White House, and beckoning me to his side, asked me to play the *Cachuca*. A young lady wanted to do a Spanish dance to that tune. When I explained that we had not the music with us, but would be glad to include it on our next program, the President looked surprised, and said: "Why, Sousa, I thought you could play anything. I'm sure you can. Now give us the *Cachuca*."

This placed me in a predicament, as I did not wish the President to believe that the band was not at all times able to respond to his wishes. Fortunately one of the bandsmen remembered the melody and played it over softly to me on his cornet. I hastily wrote out several parts for the leading instruments and told the rest of the band to "vamp."

We played the *Cachuca* to the satisfaction of Mr. Arthur, who came to the door and said, "I knew you could play it."

Chapter V

MY MARCHES BEGIN TO APPEAR — THE MANSFIELDS EXCHANGE
COMPLIMENTS — "DÉSIRÉE" AND DE WOLF HOPPER — "THE
PRESIDENTIAL POLONAISE" AND "SEMPER FIDELIS" OUST "HAIL TO THE
CHIEF" — CLEVELAND — WHITNEY — MR. CLEVELAND'S WEDDING —
GENERAL HARRISON AT HOME — MAJOR HOUSTON DISCIPLINES THE
MARINES — THE FIRST TOUR OF THE BAND

B Y THIS time I was beginning to make real progress with
my marches. Bandmasters were now playing *Across the
Danube*, written in commemoration of the victory of the
Russians over the Turks; *The Resumption March*, written after our
return to specie payment, and *Our Flirtation*, which still enjoyed
a considerable popularity.

Once more I turned to light opera, and Colonel Wilson Vance
offered to write a libretto, using the music of *The Smugglers* as
much as possible. We retained that name and gave an amateur
performance in Washington. With our more than friendly audience, together with volunteers from the National Rifles (one
of the crack military companies of the city) who appeared in a
chorus of soldiers, the piece seemed to make a good impression
and Vance insisted we should form a company and send it on the
road. We engaged a very clever English girl, Fannie Wentworth,
for the principal part; James Rennie, a good comedian, and Henry
Mansfield (a brother of the famous Richard) for the principal
baritone. When I was in New York and engaged Mansfield, his
brother was playing in *The Black Cloaks* at the Standard Theatre.
I went to see the performance with Henry, and after the performance he introduced me to his brother. "So you have engaged

my brother to take a part in your opera?" Richard asked me, after shaking hands.

I nodded in acquiescence.

He looked at me, then at his brother, and said, "Well, he'll make a hell of a mess of it!"

Richard was correct, for that's exactly what his brother did. We kept the piece on the road about three weeks, closing in Philadelphia at the Chestnut Street Opera House. All our money was spent and we had to borrow to bring our company back to Washington. Thus *The Smugglers* was buried in the vast dramatic cemetery of musical failures.

After the company had departed on the midnight train I went to my hotel disillusioned and disconsolate. I examined myself and could only see that I was a colossal failure as a composer, as a dramatist, and as a man. I buried my head in the pillow. If ever a man berated himself as the smallest and most insignificant specimen of the human race, I did that night. If only I could crawl into a hole and pull the hole in after me! Finally I fell asleep and when I awoke it was nearly midday and the sun was shining through my window. My wife was sitting nearby, demurely hemming a handkerchief and waiting for me to dress. I got up. She came over, put her arms around my neck and said, "Don't grieve. It's going to be all right some time."

"You bet it will be all right," I said. "I'm going to start on a new opera to-morrow and it will be a 'knockout.' "

The next day I began on the score of *Désirée*, collaborating with Edward Taber and, though not exactly a "knockout," it was more or less kindly received as one of the pioneers in American comic operas. On May 1, 1884, it opened in Washington and the following autumn transferred to the Broad Street Theatre in Philadelphia for several weeks. One feature, at least, made it

memorable, for it introduced to the public that perennial comedian, DeWolf Hopper, who made his debut as a comic opera star.
The plot was taken from an old English comedy called *Our Wife*,
the subject of quite a number of pieces before that time and since,
and Hopper played the part of an old haberdasher whose beautiful daughter is loved by the Count de Courville. She loves the
Marquis Delavare and finally marries him; this marriage is the
subject of a topical song which was presented with great success
by Hopper and was also used in many musical pieces, after the
opera had ceased to run. The verse was:

> GENEROSITY'S a virtue that evinces
> The noble family from which I spring;
> When our daughters marry marquises or princes,
> We never fail to do the proper thing.
> Now if I find it possible to do so,
> Within so small a fraction of a day,
> I'll get the most expensive sort of trousseau,
> For all of which my son-in-law shall pay.
> This excessive liberality,
> Approaches prodigality,
> For all of which my son-in-law will pay.

Taber wrote a multitude of verses for this song, and Hopper
rarely sang less than nineteen or twenty of them at a performance.

Speaking of *Désirée* never fails to bring to mind an experience
I had with John McCaull, the producer, an experience which has
convinced me that the very worst medium for interpreting my
music is, beyond a doubt, my own voice. Cottrelly and I were
showing the score to McCaull. I proceeded to "sing" the second
number, in what seemed to me my very best manner. McCaull
listened, with a pained expression.

"It won't do," he said, "that thing is unworthy of the rest of the opera."

Accordingly I promised to write something else in its place. The second attempt was a pretty little polka movement, in the manner of a French chansonette, with which I was much pleased. I took McCaull into the Casino in New York, sat down at the piano and once more tried to sing. "Damn sight worse than the first one," was his terse comment. I was in despair; but Rose Leighton, one of the principals in *Désirée*, was charmed with the composition and insisted upon singing it herself. It is not strange that McCaull swiftly changed his mind, for the singer this time was a lovely young woman with the voice of a thrush, instead of the mere composer with the voice of a crow. "That," he said meaningly, "is different!" The song was a great success. Composers are the only people who can hear good music above bad sounds. The average music-lover hears only the production under prevailing conditions. Which, as McCaull remarked, is different!

And now the Arthur administration was drawing to a close. From time immemorial at White House receptions when cabinet members, ambassadors, generals and admirals were assembled in the East Room to greet the President, they were informed of the approach of the executive by the pompous strains of an old Scotch boating song, *Hail to the Chief*. This smacked more of royalty than of the proverbial Jeffersonian simplicity, but neither I nor any bandmaster before me had dared to break the precedent.

President Arthur, however, left his guests in the East Room one evening, and, coming out into the corridor, beckoned to me.

"What piece did you play when we went in to dinner?" he asked.

"*Hail to the Chief*, Mr President."

"Do you consider it a suitable air?"

"No, sir," I answered. "It was selected long ago on account of its name, and not on account of its character. It is a boat song, and lacks modern military character either for reception or a parade."

"Then change it!" said he, and walked away.

I wrote the *Presidential Polonaise* for White House indoor affairs, and the *Semper Fidelis* March for review purposes outdoors. The latter became one of my most popular marches, and is played, I think, more often than any other march ever written, by bands possessing a trumpet and drum corps. It is the official march adopted by the Marine Corps, by order of the general commanding, and I am very proud of the fact that it is the only composition which can claim official recognition by our government.

With the coming of Grover Cleveland, his sister, Miss Rose Elizabeth Cleveland, assumed the duties of White House hostess. If there ever lived a kindlier or more charming woman than Miss Cleveland, it has not been my lot to meet her; and if ever there lived a finer man than Colonel Dan Lamont, the President's private secretary, I have never met him. Mrs. Lamont, too, was a lovely, gracious and considerate woman. Add to this company the name of the great Secretary of the Navy, W. C. Whitney, and one can readily see what an admirable administration began with President Cleveland's entrance into office. Cleveland was a very great man, despite the fact that his enemies have accused him of being "successful in his failures."

If I had seemed to lose the beat at the beginning of the Arthur administration, I was in perfect tempo with the Cleveland régime. I wrote a set of waltzes called *Sandalphon*, dedicated to Miss Cleveland, and not long after, a set for Mrs. Whitney called, *La Reine de la Mer*, which still enjoys some favor.

TWO SOUSA OPERAS (with page 87)

On the occasion of the first New Year's reception of President Cleveland, Secretary Whitney came over to me and said,

"Sousa, when you get through here I want you to bring the boys of the band to my house. I want them to have lunch as my guests."

So at the end of the White House reception the band marched over to Mr. Whitney's house. He had instructed his butler to find a place for the men to put their instruments, and left the message that the men were his guests and were not to play any music, but simply eat, drink and enjoy themselves. The band, therefore, had an hour of good cheer and good wine. One of the newspaper correspondents, who was present, made a special story out of the occasion, and, among other things, said that when the Italians in the band were asked what they wanted, with one voice they answered "spaghetti and Chianti"; that the Germans shouted for sauerkraut, speck and Munich beer; while the Americans demanded hog, hominy and hard cider. Of course it was pure hokum, but it was copied widely.

Mr. Whitney always showed great consideration for his "boys." From days of old it had been the custom for the band to wear red coats and full dress uniform at White House and Capitol concerts. One very hot summer day in Washington, directly after a rendezvous of the Band at the White House, along came a carriage whose sole occupant was a man wearing a thin alpaca suit and fanning himself vigorously. It was Secretary Whitney of the Navy, and he beckoned to me, saying graciously, "Whew! Mighty hot, isn't it?"

"Yes, sir," I agreed with fervor.

"Those uniforms must bother you, don't they? Why not change 'em?"

"The order must come from your department, Mr. Secretary," I replied.

"Well, haven't you got an undress uniform, light and cool?"

"Yes, sir."

"Then I must see what I can do," he declared.

Next morning the Commandant informed me that the band would thereafter wear undress uniform at all White House and Capitol concerts during the summer — with "no brasses on your helmets!"

Finally the news was given out that Mr. Cleveland was to be married. When the time for the wedding was drawing near,

Colonel Lamont and I carefully measured the number of steps from the place where they were to stand, and I measured off *Mendelssohn's Wedding March* to correspond to the exact number of steps.

A week or so before the wedding I was notified that the President desired me to submit to him the program of music for the wedding, if I had made it out. I had not only done this, but had thoroughly rehearsed it, and went to the White House at once. Mr. Cleveland read the program carefully. He noticed a number by Arditi called *I Am The Rose*. "Of course, that is a compliment to the bride," he said.

"Yes, Mr. President."

Another number was from my opera *Désirée*. On the program it appeared as "A Quartette, *The Student of Love*." He read it very slowly, then said, "I think I'd play that number just as 'A Quartette,' leaving out *The Student of Love*."

"It's quite an effective number, Mr. President," I rejoined.

"Yes," he said, "doubtless an effective number, but I think it will sound just as well as 'A Quartette,' without *The Student of Love*."

At the wedding each member of the band received a bouquet of flowers with the compliments of the bride, who was a very beautiful young woman and was able in every way to assume, with distinction, the position of First Lady of the Land. Her youth and beauty and the romance of a White House wedding surrounded her with such a glamour that she was at once permanently enthroned in the hearts of the populace. The only time I ever had any direct communication with Mrs. Cleveland was a request she once sent me that I play the *Tannhäuser* overture; I was pleased with her excellent taste in music.

Although the President was congenial and fairly approachable before his marriage, he afterwards became more serious and decidedly distant. Perhaps the affairs of state weighed heavily upon him, or he took too keenly the new responsibilities of husband. Whatever the cause, he was a changed man. But even then he never lost the American traits which endeared him to me. At the very beginning of his succession to office it was plain to be seen that there would be a return to American ideals. He was always most democratic in his manner toward me.

He was once escaping from a Saturday afternoon reception held by his sister, Miss Rose Cleveland, and found it necessary to open a door near where the band was stationed, and thread his way through their numbers. In squeezing past them he probably disturbed twenty men, and with a warm smile and apologetic word or two, won the hearts of his musicians. When he finally reached my stand, he said, simply, "I'm a terrible lot of trouble, Mr. Sousa, but I'll be out of the way in a minute."

I scarcely ever met the President or his wife after their marriage, but saw the delightful Lamonts more than ever. When we were playing at a state dinner, they often came in and sat for hours listening to the music.

Finally the administration came to an end and General Harrison moved in. His inauguration certainly stressed the return to the simplicity of American family life as I had known it. American traditions and customs were steadily coming into their own at the White House. Few intellectual giants have graced the presidency, but General Harrison was one of them. He was a great wit. His sense of humor was ever alert, and his conversation consistently scintillating and satirical; the most brilliant speech I have ever heard was one he delivered at a Gridiron Club dinner.

Mrs. Harrison impressed me with her kindhearted, considerate attitude toward those about her. She was, in every way, a splendid type of American womanhood, a personality never to be forgotten by the many who were privileged to know her.

Certain it is, however, that there are men ready to depreciate the most admirable president. During one of my transatlantic voyages, I spent many hours on deck with a United States senator who was particularly severe in his comments on Mr. Harrison, whom I defended as best I could. I believe the man's bitterness arose from an interview which he described to me. He had called on the President a month after his inauguration and had requested him to withdraw his objections against a man whom the Senator desired to have appointed to a certain office. The President replied that he would not change his decision, and the Senator angrily retorted:

"You seem to forget, Mr. President, that, during your campaign, when the Republican party needed money badly, I went out and got it and thereby assured your election."

The President's answer was, "I appreciate your efforts, Senator, but you forget I am not President of the Republican party, but President of the United States. I must represent the people at large, and the people at large are not in favor of the appointment of the man you mention."

"Darn the little runt!" the Senator added to me. "His posterior is too near the ground to make him great, in my estimation."

"Remember," I said quietly, "size is no gauge of bravery or brains!"

And Mr. Harrison continued to prove in his administration that he was the President of the United States, and not the President of a party.

Courteous and kindhearted, he was a gracious man to meet — if your presence was desired. He very quickly became a national hero to those who had no axes to grind. Mrs. Harrison and Mrs. McKee, his wife and daughter, followed out the custom of giving Saturday afternoon receptions during the social season — that is, from January 1 to the beginning of Lent —, and, in addition, an occasional children's party for "Baby" McKee, the much-talked-of despot of the White House. At one of these children's parties, the grown-ups at the mansion had evidently planned how the children were to go into the refreshment room and] how they were to be seated. The President was there looking on, but when he attempted to place "Baby" McKee next to a shy little girl, the ungallant baby screamed "I won't!" and broke away.

After him went Mr. Harrison and pulled him back forcibly, but he decamped again. The President turned to me, "Don't play the march until I get him."

"Mr. President," I replied, "it's easier to control eighty million people than that little fellow."

"Watch me!" the President rejoined, very decidedly. He caught the refractory youngster, held him tight, plumped him down on his feet at the head of the line, and, making him shake hands with his selected partner, started the march into the refreshment room. "Baby" McKee's sulkiness vanished at the sight of the ice cream, candies and cake.

One drizzly day I was driving to the White House, when through my cab window I saw a short man with a big umbrella almost run down by a street-car. As I looked, I noticed that it was President Harrison. I entered the White House, and so was awaiting him when he came in from his walk. I remarked,

"Mr. President, I saw you a while ago picking your way across the street in the rain entirely unattended, and quite like the humblest citizen."

How different from a Presidential promenade that I had seen in Paris not long before! First there had appeared a platoon of hussars with drawn revolvers, clearing the streets. Following these at a short distance another platoon with sabres flashing. Then a hollow square of cavalry, in the centre of which was a barouche bearing President Carnot of the French Republic.

We were occasionally complimented by members of the Diplomatic Corps attending White House receptions. I suppose it was tactful for them to praise the President's Band. We were also very popular at the British Embassy where we played every year on the Queen's birthday. After each of these annual appearances Sir Julian Pauncefote gave the band a handsome honorarium.

There had been for some time a new commanding officer of the post at the Marine Barracks. The Barracks were divided into Headquarters and Post — that part of the barracks on the G Street side, with offices of the various members of the staff of the Marine Corps.

The officer in command of the post on the west side of the Barracks was Major George Porter Houston, who, though soldierly in his bearing, walked lame from the effects of Chagres fever, contracted while he was in command of the Marines in Panama; one of the finest men in the Marine Corps, he was as brave as Napoleon and possessed a steely blue eye that looked clean through you. My first introduction to Major Houston was a rather trying one. I have always tried to be diplomatic, but I sometimes speak more warmly than I should; and one morning, after the Major had been in command of the post for nearly three weeks, I was summoned to see the Commanding Officer. On my entrance into his office, he looked up and said sternly,

"You are the bandmaster?"

"Yes, sir," I replied.

"Well, I want you to distinctly understand that these German dukes and Italian counts that constitute your band can't run the barracks!"

"I do not understand you, sir."

"Then I shall make myself understood. Three of them were late at guard mount this morning, and they can't run me or the barracks, I want you to understand that!"

I looked at him steadily and replied, "If I am not greatly mistaken, there are certain rules and regulations governing a marine be he bandsman or soldier, who fails to arrive punctually at guard mount."

He returned my gaze for fully a minute, then said,

"Sit down; we'll talk this matter over."

We talked it over. His apparent anger was all assumed, and in twenty minutes Major Houston and I were the closest of friends, and remained so until his death. He had many admirable qualities. No troops were ever better fed than his. He often took some of the money intended for the purchase of beef and diverted it to oysters! He was determined that the Marines should have a varied bill of fare.

The major was extremely just in all his dealings with his men; he would not tolerate deceit, but he was not over-severe in punishing dereliction of duty if it was accompanied by a truthful attitude. I remember an occasion when the first sergeant reported a man for jumping the wall, getting full of whiskey and returning to have an altercation with the guard.

Houston said, "Show him in."

The door opened, and Private Smith entered, limping painfully, his head bandaged, and looking as if he had been through a threshing machine. Houston turned to me seriously and said,

"Sousa, what do you think of a man who enlists in this glorious service, the Marine Corps, receives three good meals a day, a good bed to sleep in, medical attendance when needed, and who cannot be arrested for bastardy, and yet jumps the wall, gets full of bad whiskey, comes back and assaults the sacred person of the corporal of the guard?"

Of course it was my cue to look very grave, but keep silent. Turning to the culprit, Houston said, "Well, what have you to say for yourself?"

The marine straightened up slowly.

"I'll thank the Commanding Officer to hear my story."

Houston gave him permission to grow eloquent.

"Well, sir," began the battered private, "I was sitting in quarters at eight last night, and I got thirsty for a drink so I went up to the gate and said to the sergeant of the guard, 'I'd like to see the officer of the day.' He ordered me back to my quarters. I went back, but I was trying to figure out why I couldn't see the officer of the day, and I was getting thirstier and thirstier; so I tried again. I said, 'I'd like to see the officer of the day. I want permission to leave the barracks for fifteen minutes.' 'You can't see him,' said the sergeant. 'You go back to your quarters, and the next time you come up here to see the officer of the day, I'll chuck you in the brig.' I went back to quarters, but darned if I could see why I should be chucked into the brig; so I jumped the wall, got one drink, and then I was so mad to think the sergeant had threatened to chuck me in the brig, that I took a couple more. I wasn't drunk, though. I walked up to the gate to go in and the corporal said, 'How did you get outside?' 'Jumped the wall,' I told him. He came up and said something to me that I wouldn't allow any man to say, and I struck him. He struck back, and before I realized it, there was a general rumpus, and I got the worst of it. They chucked me in the brig, and then they had to take me to the dispensary to bandage me up. But I wouldn't allow any man to say to me what he did, without fighting him back — not if it killed me!"

Houston said quietly, "It's a serious case, Smith, and requires some thought on my part. Go back to your quarters, and I will consider the affair."

The woe-begone marine limped out dejectedly. Houston turned to the first sergeant.

"Release that man from custody immediately, and see that he is sent to the hospital and properly cared for." Then, to me, "Sousa, it's pretty damn hard to get all the cardinal virtues for thirteen dollars a month!"

Major Houston, strange to say, was very fond of my music. One day an advertisement appeared in the Washington papers, stating that a concert would be given at Lincoln Hall by a Symphony orchestra from New York, and that the programme would consist entirely of music by American composers. When Houston looked it over, and found nothing of mine upon it, he dismissed it by saying that he knew it would be "rotten." I defended the programme however, for there were some fine composers represented upon it, and I added, "They are from New York, and probably I am little-known there."

The concert was given. Next morning, when I arrived at the barracks, the Major sent for me, and asked,

"Did you play last night at the Willard?"

"No, sir, I did not."

Whereupon he showed me a criticism of the concert, which stated that a reception had followed, at the Willard Hotel, and announced that the Marine Band was present at the reception.

"You answer that," said my superior. "Let the public know it is not so." So I wrote this to the Washington Post.

TO THE EDITOR:

In your account of the concert of American compositions given two evenings ago at Lincoln Hall, you state, "The Marine Band, stationed behind tall palms, played music in violent contrast to that heard earlier in the evening, at the American Composers' concert." I desire to offer a few corrections:

First: The Marine Band was not placed behind tall palms at the Willard Hotel.

Second: The Marine Band did not play music in violent contrast to that heard earlier in the evening at the American Composers' concert.

Third: The Marine Band was not present.

Except for these errors, the article is substantially correct.

JOHN PHILIP SOUSA

The Commandant of the Marine Corps, Colonel McCawley, suddenly went away on sick leave. I had been on the best of terms with him, although he had opposed any request I made to take the band on concert tour. The most he would allow was twenty-four hours' furlough which could carry us only as far as Richmond, Baltimore, or Philadelphia. I had applied many times for leave, but he had always refused to endorse an application to the Department for it. Since I was a member of the Marine Corps, I had no intention, even if the opportunity should present itself, of doing anything against his wishes. But as soon as he left Washington, I called on the Acting Commandant and obtained his permission to make the tour; he suggested that I call on the Secretary of the Navy.

General Tracy was the Secretary, a true friend of the Band. He approved of the plan but added that I "had better see the

President." My years in Washington had taught me that if you wish to see the President, see his wife first. So I asked for Mrs. Harrison. She liked the idea of the tour, and promised to speak to the President about it.

Next morning I was summoned to see the President. As I entered the room, he rose, shook hands cordially, and leading me to one of the windows which faced the Potomac River, he said,

"Mrs. Harrison tells me that you are anxious to make a tour with the band. I was thinking myself of going out of town, and," —with a smile, — "it would be tough on Washington if both of us were away at the same time. I have thought it over, and I believe the country would rather hear you, than see me; so you have my permission to go."

I immediately arranged a five weeks' tour which was a success both artistically and financially. The tour was directed by David Blakely, manager of Gilmore's Band. After we had completed our tour, Colonel McCawley, our Commandant, died. His son told me that his father had said to him, about two months before, "I see by the paper that Sousa is going on tour with his Band. He has got his own way at last!"

A newspaper notice of the period gives one of our early typical programmes:

The Marine Band, John Philip Sousa, Conductor, appeared at the Auditorium Theatre, Chicago, for the first of a series of three concerts, April 17, 1891. Marie Decca, Soprano, was the soloist. The band was made up of 14 B clarinets; two flutes; two oboes; two bassoons; four saxophones; two alto clarinets; four French horns; four cornets; two trumpets; two fluegel horns; three trombones; two euphoniums; three basses and drums, triangles, tympani, etc., a rather larger proportion of wood to brass than the strictly military band calls for, made necessary, however, by the greater variety of music which Director Sousa essays.

PROGRAM

RIENZI	*Wagner*
Invitation to the Dance	*Weber*
MOSAIC, *The Pearl Fishers*	*Bizet*
GRAND ARIA, *Perle du Brazil*	*David*
MARIE DECCA	
OVERTURE, *William Tell*	*Rossini*
Toreador et Andalouse Bal Costume	*Rubenstein*
Funeral March of a Marionette	*Gounod*
SYMPHONIC POEM, *Ben Hur's Chariot Race*	*Sousa*
HUMORESQUE, *The Contest*	*Godfrey*
STACCATO POLKA	*Mulder*
MARIE DECCA	
The Star Spangled Banner	*Arnold*

When the curtain rose a half hundred men were seen on stage in dress uniform of dark blue trousers, scarlet coats, liberal embellishment of silk cord, epaulets and gilt buckles. When conductor Sousa — a stalwart and pleasant-looking gentleman, with a large sword hitched in true military fashion to his belt, came in, there was more applause.

The tour was a very trying one, with two concerts a day, luncheons, banquets, civic demonstrations and incessant travel. The drain on my energy and the lack of sufficient sleep finally caused me to break down on my return, and the Post surgeon sent me to Europe to recuperate.

Chapter VI

MRS. SOUSA and I sailed on the City of Richmond of the Inman Line, in 1891.

Every phase of my life seems to have been packed full of adventures. Amazing experiences began immediately, on the European trip. The first day out, those passengers who craved excitement (or thought they did) complained that the Atlantic was about as rough as a duck-pond. By Tuesday, however, a terrible storm had arisen, and I have never seen such stupendous waves as washed the decks in that storm, although I have crossed the ocean many times.

The third night, shortly after midnight, we were summoned on deck by the terrible cry that the ship was on fire! It was raining, and the sailors were getting ready the life-boats. I doubt if the life-boats would have lasted five minutes in that storm. We waited patiently for day to break and before four o'clock the dawn crept slowly over those tempestuous waters. As soon as it was light, the captain asked for a volunteer to go down into the hold and locate the trouble. A brave Scotch engineer named Grant was lowered down into the hatch, supported by ropes. He put tackle on a burning bale of cotton which was hauled up onto the deck and thrown overboard to the accompaniment of our cheers. Another bale appeared, and then up came the Scotsman himself, overcome by smoke. When he regained consciousness he said something to the Captain, who immediately gave orders to batten down everything and to cover the ventilators with tarpaulin; this was speedily done. That day my cabin burned out. The weather continued rainy and dismal, and added to this was the horror of that fire eating at the vitals of the ship.

Finally we saw a vessel ahead, and made for it, throwing out our signals. She signalled back that she was the *Chancellor* of the Harrison Line, and when we told her we were on fire, her captain, in the excitement, dropped dead. The flags on both ships were placed at half mast and we travelled on together, not knowing at what moment the fire would burst out, uncontrolled.

That night we sighted a light to the northward. "It's a Cunarder," said the captain, and bidding farewell to the faithful boat that had stood by us all day, we cut after the Cunarder, sending up signal rockets. She could not understand our predicament, because we were making such speed. Signals were exchanged and she agreed to stand by us until we reached Queenstown. She was the *Servia*. Our crew, meanwhile, was steadily fighting the fire. On Thursday the prospect was not a hopeful one, for the linen room caught fire; by pouring tons of water into the hold of the boat and dampening the cargo of cotton at the top, with the aid of steam gauges, we finally put into Queenstown. The sensible ones disembarked, but some of the passengers (including the Sousas) decided to stand by the captain, who had, according to one gushing damsel, stood by us. The run from Queenstown to Liverpool, though short, was an exciting one, for the fire was making great headway.

Next morning we called a meeting to take up a purse of money for the crew. There were three old fellows aboard, who were going home to the old country, probably having made millions in America, and who had remained in the saloons during the crisis, drinking highballs. These sanctimonious rascals rose at the beginning of the meeting and said, "We'll open the meeting with prayer."

"No, you won't," I cried. "This is no prayer meeting, it's a business meeting." My sentiment was applauded, and we collected a handsome sum of money for the crew.

The ship was not allowed to dock when we reached Liverpool, but we were taken off on a lighter. The vessel was towed down to the mouth of the Mersey and some of the cargo salvaged. Then they opened everything and let her burn herself out. I believe that that accident caused the passage of the law which forbids a cotton cargo on a passenger ship.

In London, a couple who were very old friends of Mrs. Sousa and myself suggested that we go to their boarding-house in Woburn Square, for we were considerably upset after our terrible trip across the Atlantic. One day, just as I reached the house, some fire engines went roaring by. With the American's irresistible impulse to follow fire engines, I ran along after them. I found the fire, saw the engines put it out, and slowly started back. But in the meantime I had forgotten where I lived. I didn't know the name of the proprietor of my stopping place, nor that of the boarding-house itself. Not even the name of the street! Here was a pretty howdy-do; lost in London!

I stood on a corner fully twenty minutes, deciding whether I should go to a police station and have all London thoroughly gone over, or whether I should put an advertisement in the morning paper, when a pleasant-looking man came up to me and said,

THREE GENERATIONS OF SOUSA
John Philip Sousa, Jr.   John Philip Sousa   John Philip Sousa, 3d

"Can you direct me to Number Nine, Wo burn Square? I am a stranger in the city.

Fate was kind — it flashed across my mind, even as he spoke, that that was the number of my boarding-house, and I answered, "So am I, and I'm going to that very place; I'll take you along."

I called a cab, we drove for perhaps five minutes, reached the number, and, the Lord be praised, it was indeed the house where I lived!

It was in Europe that I learned how valueless are letters of introduction. We left London and went to Paris where we met at our hotel a very charming young lady from the Middle West, named Lattimer Gerard, who was travelling with her mother. James G. Blaine, Secretary of State, had given me a letter of introduction commending me to the mercies of the various American ambassadors and consuls in Europe. I took a fancy to see the great review at Longchamps on the Fourteenth of July, Bastille Day. Miss Gerard suggested that I see our Ambassador, Whitelaw Reid. I called at the Embassy, but Mr. Reid was out of town, and the very diplomatic chief clerk did not know when he would return, if ever. I was ready to give up the quest, but Miss Gerard was determined. "See the American consul," she urged me.

When I was ushered into the consul's office, the next day, he had half a dozen cronies sitting round the room, swapping stories of rather questionable genre, and as the point of each story was reached, the company indulged in hearty and prolonged laughter. I waited at the door several minutes, then stepped forward, and said, "May I present my credentials between some of these extremely funny stories?"

They looked at me in obvious surprise. I believe they thought me a Frenchman, because of my black beard and black hair. The Consul looked up. "What do you want?" I took out Mr. Blaine's letter and handed it to him. He read it carelessly. "What can I do for you?" he asked. I told him that I was anxious to get seats on the reviewing stand for the Fourteenth of July ceremonies. He threw the letter impatiently on his desk, and said, "Impossible! I haven't enough for my own friends; I can do nothing for you."

When I reported my interview to Mrs. Sousa and our Western friends that night, Miss Gerard exclaimed, "What a shame! I'm sure if the proper French official knew you wanted tickets, you would get them. You must go to-morrow to see the Minister of Beaux Arts, and I shall go with you!"

She was not to be dissuaded, so the next morning we called on that gentleman. She told him I was the conductor of the Marine Band, the official band of the President of the United States, and that I was a composer of considerable popularity in America. He touched a button, had a moment's whispered conference with a clerk and presently showed me a volume, *The National, Patriotic and Typical Airs of All Lands, By John Philip Sousa.* He then praised the work for its completeness and said, "What can I do for you, Mr. Sousa?"

He gladly wrote an order for the coveted box and said that he was happy to be able to serve me so easily. I thanked him cordially, concluding that personality was of more value than a thousand letters of introduction. I have never used one since that day.

After spending some time in Berlin, we went to Bayreuth for the famous Bayreuth Festival. I had written ahead for tickets, but for once, German efficiency was lacking, and I found it impossible to buy a ticket. Finally one farsighted millionaire-to-be offered to sell me his ticket at full price (twenty marks), provided I would come out immediately at the end of the first act. I accepted and witnessed the first act of *Tannhäuser.* Then I started to walk down to the Wagner villa, intending to stroll over the grounds and see the grave of Wagner, but the composer's widow, whom I suspect of having a temper of her own, had gone to the theater, leaving orders that no visitors should be admitted to that part of the estate. I tried all my powers of persuasion on the housekeeper, but in vain, so I went around to the back of the grounds, through a little park,

where the musician and the "Crazy King Ludwig" of Bavaria used
to walk together. I met a German student in the road, and told
him of my disappointment, as we went along. A little girl, with a
basket of bread, was walking directly behind us, and seemed much
interested in our conversation. Presently she spoke to me and said
she was sorry I could not get in, and that she would speak to the
housekeeper, whom she knew well. We all approached the front
door once more and the little girl called the housekeeper out and
said she thought it was a shame to send away a musician who had
come all the way from America to see Herr Wagner's grave!

A consultation was held among the servants, and the little
girl's eloquence prevailed, where mine had failed. They agreed
to admit me for five minutes. There was no name on the stone
which marked the great man's grave and I asked the housekeeper
the reason.

"He does not need it," she said proudly. "He is the first man!"

The collection of the national airs of all lands, which the
French Minister of Beaux Arts had praised, came about in an
interesting way. Secretary of the Navy Tracy was largely responsible for it. Tracy was an unusually efficient cabinet officer. He
had been a general in the Civil War, and was oftener addressed
as General, than as Secretary. He was a gifted lawyer, and had a
keen sense of humor. Both he and Secretary Whitney have been
called "The Father of the Navy." Modesty and the great qualities
of both men would have made it difficult to get their personal
views on that subject, but certainly from the time of Secretary
Tracy's appointment, the progress and development of the Navy
were phenomenal.

The band was frequently ordered aboard the *Despatch*,
known as "the President's boat," when foreign personages of
importance were to take a trip to Mount Vernon to see the home

of Washington and incidentally the key to the Bastille. Luncheon was served, and there was music by the Marine Band. On a very special occasion when the ambassadors of nearly every embassy in Washington were aboard, together with many men prominent in the official life of the Capital, the Secretary sent his naval attaché to me, with the request that I see him immediately.

"Sousa," he said, "if you have the music here, I should like you to play the national air of every embassy represented here to-day." His attaché reported seventeen embassies! I always carried the national songs of a great number of countries in a folio, so I promised to play all of them. I distributed what music I had and began with *God Save the Queen* at which the English Ambassador immediately rose, followed by the rest of the guests. I continued with the airs of France, Germany, Spain, Italy, Russia, Sweden, Denmark, etc., ending with *The Star Spangled Banner*.

A few days later, I encountered the Secretary and he congratulated me on my industry in collecting the anthems. I remarked that I had spent much time in getting them for the folio, and he said that they should be arranged and made into an official volume.

"I should like to publish them under your authority," I replied. He accordingly wrote the following:

NAVY DEPARTMENT

Washington, Oct. 18, 1889

SPECIAL ORDER:

John Philip Sousa, the Bandmaster of the band of the United States Marine Corps, is hereby directed to compile, for the use of the Department, the National and Patriotic Airs of all Nations.

B. F. TRACY, Secretary of the Navy

The work was issued in 1890, and is a standard all over the world. It remains the most exhaustive volume of its kind. In my collection I included many songs of the American Indians with representative melodies of the following tribes: Apache, Cherokee, Chippewa, Dakota, Eskimo, Iowa, Iroquois, Ponca, Vancouver. The titles were usually descriptive: *Apache Scalp Song and Dance*; *The Returning Hunter*, etc. Many of these songs were sung to me by ethnologists and others who had travelled and lived among the Indians. I sat at my desk and applied harmonic treatment to the tunes, without in any case changing a note of the melodies. Not only did the book cover all the principal countries of the world, but I assembled the airs of such faraway places as: Abyssinia, Boa Vista, Celebes, Dalecarlia, East Indies, Fiji Isles, Lapland, Moldavia, Nukahivah, Pfalz, and Samoa.

After we had discussed the compilation, he said,

"Sousa, I want to compliment you on the excellence of your band. I was very much impressed with the solo playing of your cornetist at your last concert."

Here was my opportunity to eulogize the band.

"Yes, Mr. Secretary, that young cornet soloist is a fine Western boy. He comes from Schoolcraft, Michigan; his name is Walter F. Smith; he doesn't drink, he doesn't smoke, his general habits and conduct are excellent, and all the Government pays him is thirty-eight dollars a month."

"You say he doesn't drink?"

"Not a drop," I firmly replied.

"And he doesn't smoke?"

"Not a puff."

"And you say, too, that his general habits and conduct are excellent?"

"He leads absolutely the simple life," I said, enthusiastically, warming to my subject.

"Well, Sousa," and the Secretary leaned back in his chair, "for Heaven's sake, what good will money do him?"

The band was not always greeted with open arms. At one time, the West Penn Hospital at Pittsburgh had secured permission from President Harrison for the band to go to Pittsburgh and give a concert for the benefit of the hospital. No sooner was the concert announced than some musicians in Cincinnati telegraphed the Secretary protesting against the band's accepting the engagement. The telegram ran:

> *To the* SECRETARY OF THE NAVY, *Washington*, D. C.
>
> We musicians of Cincinnati hereby protest against the Marine Band giving a concert in Pittsburgh, thereby taking the bread out of the mouths of American musicians.
>
> (Signed)
> WASSERMAN
> HESSLEIN
> HEYMEYER
> KRANTZ

I read the thing, and then said indignantly, "Why, Mr. Secretary, there isn't an American name signed to this telegram!"

He took the blank, re-read it slowly, and then remarked, "They're damn good American names for Cincinnati, Sousa!"

We proceeded to Pittsburgh and gave the concert. One of the Washington correspondents had amused himself by informing me that there was no city in the world which demanded such highbrow music as did Pittsburgh, and he added, "If you play anything of a so-called popular nature, they will hiss you off the stage just as sure as shooting!" He carried such an air of conviction that I believed him. I built my program of very solid material; something by Brahms, another selection Bach, some Wagner, and a bit of Strauss. The house was crowded, and when I finished the first number I turned to the audience, expecting salvos of applause. Absolute silence!

I thought, "Perhaps this piece was too trivial for them — they are certainly highbrows," and I started the next number. That too, was received in frigid silence.

"If the next is too light for them, I shall play something popular, and let them hiss me off the stage!" I said to myself, now genuinely worried. I began the Parsifal *Procession of the Grail*. When I finished it off, with a last slow flourish, half the audience was asleep, the other half yawning.

"Boys," I muttered desperately, "Get ready to be hissed off the stage. We are going to play *Annie Rooney*, and if any of you gets maimed or killed, I'll tell the Government that you died in line of duty, and your widow will receive a pension. All together!" and we sounded off for all we were worth.

Strong men wept with delight, husbands threw their arms about their astonished wives, and the rest of the evening was, without question, Annie Rooney's! As the band embarked for home, above the chug of the engine, there rang triumphantly in our ears the dulcet melody which accompanied the words:

SHE'S my sweetheart, I'm her beau,
She's my Annie, I'm her Joe,
Soon we'll marry, never to part,
Little Annie Rooney is my sweetheart!

And on we sped to Washington, our faith restored in Pittsburgh.

Meanwhile, my marches were gaining every day in popularity. The Yorktown Centennial did well, and *The Gladiator* became familiar in the musical arena. At a parade in Philadelphia, a friend of mine counted no fewer than seventeen bands playing it.

Some obscure brass-band journal, published in England, declared that America was entitled to the palm for the best military marches, and cited among the composers in America, who were doing good work in that line, Graffula, Downing, Reeves, Messud, Brooks, and Sousa. The article continued: "The last named, who, we understand, is conductor of the Government band at Washington, is entitled to the name of 'March King' quite as much as Strauss is to that of 'Waltz King.'"

My publisher showed me the article and an advertisement which he was issuing: "You can hear his music from the Atlantic to the Pacific, from the St. Lawrence to the Gulf Stream. The March King reigns supreme!" The title has remained with me ever since.

At this time plans were being made for commemorating the Mecklenburg Declaration of Independence. This declaration antedated the Philadelphia document by more than a year. Senator Ransom of North Carolina called on President Harrison, asking him to attend the celebration and deliver a speech, but the President's engagements were such that he could not accept. So the Marine Band was sent to take part in the ceremonies, which were to be held for a week or more in Fayetteville, North Carolina.

A committee of prominent citizens met us at the station and showed us to our quarters — a large hall well equipped as a barracks. The chairman of the committee said that he would call and discuss the programmes with me after we had eaten. This was only twenty-five years after the War of the Rebellion, and just what a Government band sent by a Republican president would play was a problem. I felt that this thought was uppermost in the chairman's mind when he requested such an interview.

When he arrived, he asked what I had intended for music at the ceremonies next day.

"Well," I began, "we will open with *The Star Spangled, Banner.*"

"O.K.," he agreed.

"Then we will play the *Coronation March* from the opera of *The Prophet,* by Giacomo Meyerbeer. We will follow with the *Overture* from *William Tell, On the Blue Danube,* excerpts from *Aida* and then, *My Country 'tis of Thee.*"

"That is all very fine," he said soberly, "but I should like to remind you that there's a tune down here that we love like mother's milk. I don't know whether your band plays it, but we surely would like to hear it."

"What is it?" I asked, in a most unconcerned and discouraging manner.

"It is called *Dixie,*" he said.

"I know the tune. I'll think it over whether we can make use of it or not. You know we are a very artistic organization and must always consider our programmes very seriously."

"Yes, yes," said my disturbed committeeman, "but if you can tuck it in, I know the people would love it. Some of them haven't heard it since the Surrender."

Of course I was only teasing the poor old fellow. A musician who went South in those days without *Dixie* in his repertoire was mentally, morally and physically damned by everybody—and doubtless should have been.

Next morning the ceremonies began. The town overflowed. People had come in from the mountains and the plains, from the forests and the fields. They bunked in covered wagons, and I saw boys asleep in drygoods boxes, under stoops and on benches.

Governor Fowle made the first speech. As he finished his address, I summoned my men to their feet and we played the national anthem, which was very quietly received. The next speaker was the Chairman, who made a short speech introducing Senator Vance, the idol of the State. As the Chairman sat down, just before Senator Vance rose to deliver his speech, I signalled to the band, and we launched into *Dixie*.

It was like an electric shock! A rebel yell, starting on the grandstand, went booming down the street, through the surging crowds. Never was there so tremendous and thrilling a shout! The very air seemed to quiver with excitement. A myriad of hats went rocketing upwards. Grim old warriors cried aloud, the women turned and hugged each other, and for fifteen minutes pandemonium reigned. After that, in fact during the entire time we were in Fayetteville, our programmes ran something like this:

OVERTURE, *William Tell*
SONG, *Dixie*
WALTZ, *Blue Danube*
SONG, *Dixie*
AIRS FROM *Faust*
SONG, *Dixie*
MEDLEY, *Favorite Tunes*
SONG, *Dixie*

And the encore to every one of those numbers was — *Dixie*.

How strange the ancestry of that tune, and of another Civil War favorite! *Dixie*, written by Dan Emmet, a Northerner, and first sung in New York at a minstrel show in 1859, and *The Battle Hymn of the Republic*, by Julia Ward Howe, set to a Southern hymn tune composed by Steffe, of Charleston, South Carolina! *Dixie* was originally written as a minstrel "walk-around," *The Battle Hymn of the Republic* as a sacred song, but when the populace wants a thing they take it wherever they find it. Albert Pike gave *Dixie* new words during the struggle, which awakened the Southerner to enthusiasm and defiance:

SOUTHRONS, hear your country call you!
Up, lest worse than death befall you!
To arms, to arms! To arms, in Dixie!
Lo, all the beacon fires are lighted,
Let all hearts be now united,
To arms, to arms! To arms, in Dixie!
Advance the flag of Dixie!
Hurrah! Hurrah!
For Dixie-land we'll take our stand
And live and die for Dixie.
To arms! To arms! To arms, for Dixie!

We gave a concert in the lobby of the hotel the next night. The crowd was so great that the musicians scarcely had room to move, much less play their instruments. I called the chairman to my side, and told him that unless he could prevent the crowd from pressing so close, I should be obliged to abandon the concert. He mounted a chair, and rapping for attention, began:

"The professor informs me that the professor's professors are unable to play, owing to the great crowd and their interference. And the professor says that unless you keep back from his stand, the professor and the professor's professors will be compelled to withdraw, thus making it impossible for the professor and the professor's professors to continue the concert."

Whereupon the "professor and the professor's professors" were given ample room to pursue the programme to its conclusion.

We returned to Washington with the pleasantest recollections of our week in the South and the delights of Southern hospitality. When I began concerts in the Capital that season, I discovered that my public had taken a tremendous fancy to the *Washington Post* march. Perhaps I can best describe the writing of this march by quoting portions of an article published December 6, 1927 in the fiftieth anniversary number of *The Washington Post*:

ON April 7, 1889, *The Washington Post*, in order to encourage learning and literary expression in the public schools, organized as a "permanent institution" The Washington Post Amateur Authors' Association and offered prizes and medals for the best essays written by pupils in the various grades in the public schools. It created the greatest interest in the schools, and many a literary ambition was fanned to flames in the juvenile breasts of the scholars of Washington. The undertaking had the cordial support of Prof. W. B. Powell, then the superintendent of schools, and the judges were prominent men and women.

It was planned to make the awards of prizes on the Smithsonian grounds on Saturday, June 15, 1889, when a part of the exercises was to be a musical program by the Marine Band. Of this famous band John Philip Sousa was the leader, having been appointed to that position October 1, 1880. One day shortly before the award of prizes in the authors' contest, Mr. Frank Hatton, one of the proprietors of the *Post*, chanced to meet Professor Sousa on the street and had a happy inspiration. He asked Mr. Sousa to write a march for the contest and to play it for the first time on the occasion of the award of prizes. Mr. Sousa was delighted with the idea and produced a stirring piece of music which he called *The Washington Post March*. It was dedicated to Frank Hatton and Beriah Wilkins and the first copies of the original edition bore on the cover a reproduction of the first page of the paper for which it was named. How many millions of copies have since been struck off nobody knows. Track of them has been lost. They have been printed in every civilized country on the globe ...

The great day to which the children of Washington had been looking forward came at last, and an enormous crowd assembled on the Smithsonian grounds for the exercises. By this time the association had 22,000 members, all of whom were there, and the other students and the mothers and fathers swelled the throngs to 25,000. Never before were so many children seen together in one gathering. Not even on "egg-rolling day" when the hillsides of the White Lot are covered with young-ones, was there ever such a swarm of boys and girls, almost full grown, half grown, and just begun to grow as congregated in the Smithsonian grounds to see the distribution of the gold medals to the winners in The Washington Post's Amateur Authors' Association …

The committee of judges who examined the compositions and made the awards was composed as follows:

Prof. W. B. Powell	Gen. A. W. Greely
Hon. A. A. Freeman	George F. Dawson
E. Francis Riggs	H. S. Bundy
Walker Blaine	R. Stuart Coleman
Mrs. A. G. Wilkinson	Mrs. Blanche M. Swope
Miss Sue Britton	Rev. W. A. Bartlett
Simon Wolf	Rev. Byron Sunderland
Frederick Douglas	Campbell Carrington
Thomas Wilson	R. D. Mussey
Gen. W. W. Belknap	Henry T. Stanton
Mrs. Chas. P. Lincoln	Mrs. Weston Flint
Mrs. Virginia Moore	

President Harrison was represented by Mr. Halford, his private secretary, and Colonel John M. Nelson, Superintendent of Public Buildings and Grounds. On the platform also were

Mr. Wilkins and Mr. Hatton, a delegation of prominent news-paper correspondents, Justice Miller of the Supreme Court, who delivered the prizes, and Mr. Willis B. Hawkins of the Post staff who at that time wrote a column on the editorial page known as *Postscripts*. The time-stained pages of the Post tell the story of the birth of *The Washington Post March*: "The day was beau-tiful, with a fresh breeze and occasional light clouds to temper the sun's heat. In the trees that surround the stand were birds and boys, and until the boys obtained too large a majority, the birds filled in the intervals of the band concert with their singing.

"Promptly at four o'clock John Philip Sousa took his place in front of his men and raised his baton and the instruments of the famous Marine Band poured forth the strains of the over-ture. Full as the space was all about the stands, people were still coming from every direction and the long lines looked like rays converging to the grand stand as a center. Hundreds arrived while the band was playing. Mr. Wilkins said: 'The Marine Band will now play a march composed by Professor Sousa and dedi-cated to the *Washington Post*.' This announcement was greeted with applause and the march was generously applauded; before that died away the High School Cadets came marching up from the east, and their appearance was greeted with a mighty cheer from the children.

The march was an instantaneous hit, and soon all the bands in town were playing it. It is probable there has never been a big parade in Washington from that day to this in which at least one band has not played the famous marching tune.

It was chosen almost immediately by the dancing masters at their yearly convention to introduce their new dance, "the two-step." I sold this famous tune to a Philadelphia publisher for thirty-five dollars!

I have smiled almost incredulously many a time at proofs of the world popularity of that march. It seems there is no getting away from it — even in the fastnesses of a Borneo jungle! Major Coffin of the Army, told me that one day as he was walking through a forest in Borneo he heard the familiar sound of a violin and suddenly came upon a little Filipino boy, with his sheet of music pinned to a tree, diligently working away on *The Washington Post*. As for more conventional places, the wildfire spread with even greater vigor. When I went to Europe I found that the two-step itself was called a "Washington Post" in England and Germany, and no concert I gave in Europe was complete without the performance of that march. It was the rage, too, in staid New England, for an orchestra leader in a New England town declared that, at one ball, the only obstacle to his playing the thing twenty-three times was the fact that there were only twenty-two dances on the programme. Even during the recent World War its cadences clung. One of our soldiers told me that he had stopped for a drink of water at a little house in a French village and the old peasant who came to the door invited him in and, learning that he was an American, immediately commanded his little girl to play some American music for the guest. The child obliged — with *The Washington Post*.

When I reached Washington after our stay in Fayetteville, David Blakely wrote me, asking if I could get permission to make a tour to the Pacific Coast. I obtained permission of General Haywood, the Commandant, that of the Secretary, and finally that of the President, for a seven weeks' tour from ocean to ocean. We left Washington in March, and arrived in San Francisco April 9, 1892, after playing in the leading cities all the way across the continent. I quote an article from the *San Francisco Argonaut* of those days, which was doubtless the work of an English writer:

THE United States Marine Band closed, on last Saturday, a season in this city which must have been profitable, if the proportion of paper in the Grand Opera audiences was not excessive. The management was distinctly bad; but the music was so good that people overlooked inconveniences arising from carelessness or inexperience, for the sake of artistic merit. As a rule, military bands have not been successful here, and if, as Mr. Haweis says, the connection between morals and orchestral music can be detected at a glance, we must be in pretty bad case. The Hungarian Band, Cappa's Seventh Regiment Band, the Mexican Military Band, all discoursed most excellent music, but they are none of them believed to have carried away many bushels of shekels.

It seems that the taste for orchestral music is a tardy plant, and flourishes chiefly in communities which have reached a high stage of development. Forty-four years ago, one of the most perfect bands that ever played in this country — the Germania band under Carl Bergman, which had been recruited in Berlin — made a tour through New York, Boston, Philadelphia, Washington, and other eastern cities. They played to empty houses. In Philadelphia, they played to nine dollars and a half, the rent of the hall being ten dollars; in the middle of the performance, the proprietor appeared on the stage, and threatened to turn off the gas if the other half dollar was not forthcoming; whereupon the bandsmen, with one voice bade him "turn her off." They kept on playing, at intervals, for six years; but when they finally disbanded, there was no money in the treasury. The members found work separately; Bergman became conductor of the New York Philharmonic — a post which he retained to his death.

Jullien, who came to New York in 1853, may be said to have created the taste for orchestral music in the United States. He was a man of genius, and knew a little of everything except the science of music. But he was an admirable conductor, and possessed the gift of imbuing his players with the feeling that they must deny themselves the luxury of expressing their own feelings, in order to render the conductor's conception of the composer's ideas. He was, also, an absolutely perfect judge of public taste. He used to say of himself that his vocation in life was to popularize music. He was a Frenchman, and like many Frenchmen, was nothing if not theatrical. Those whose memories go back forty years will remember him as he used to appear, graciously smiling, in an enormous white waistcoat, with huge wrist-bands folded back over his coat-sleeves, bowing his thanks for plaudits. As he stood before the footlights, a valet in full dress brought him a pair of white gloves on a silver salver. Having donned these and seized his jewelled baton, he gave the signal, and very capital music, indeed, ensued.

Gilmore, Cappa, Godfrey, and Sousa — who has just left us — conducted their bands less turbulently; Mr. Sousa's legs were as motionless as if he were a sentinel on duty; Jullien writhed and flung himself from side to side as if the violence of his emotions electrified his muscles. When the piece ended, he flung himself, breathless and panting, into a velvet armchair, and fanned himself with a lace handkerchief.

As he still figures as the prince of bandmasters, it is sad to recall the harshness with which he was treated by fortune throughout his life. He made money by his concerts, but invested it in a lease of Drury Lane, which landed him in bankruptcy. He wrote an opera and brought it out at his own expense at Covent Garden; it was a total failure. His entire stock in trade was destroyed by a fire. He started a company to give garden concerts; it went to smash, taking Jullien with it. Driven out of England, by poverty, he went to Paris, ran into debt, and was imprisoned at Clichy. His friends in London were raising money to clear him, when the news reached them that he had died in a madhouse.

It was he who introduced to the American public the most wonderful cornetist of modern times. This was Levy, a London Jew, who had sworn, in his youth, that he would either blow his soul out of the mouth of his cornet or surpass all previous performers on that instrument. He never performed the former feat, but lived to delight many audiences and to marry many wives.

There were many claimants for Jullien's mantle, some of whom are conducting orchestras today. Perhaps the most famous among them was Johann Strauss, the younger, who brought an orchestra to New York fifteen years ago, but did not come so far as this coast. He was a real musician, and genuinely felt what Jullien affected to feel. It is curious to contrast his style with the grave immobility of Sousa as a conductor. A critic wrote of him:

"His appearance was the signal for frantic applause, to which, fiddle and bow in hand, he bowed good-humoredly; then turning sharp around, he would seem to catch the eye of every one in the band, and raising his violin bow, would plunge into one of those rapturous dance tunes which, once heard, could never be forgotten. Now shaking his bow at the distant drummer, egging on the wind, picking up the basses, turning fiercely on the other stringed instruments; then stamping, turning a pirouette, and dashing his bow on his own fiddle-strings, the clear twanging of the Strauss violin would be heard for some moments above all the rest. Presently the orchestra sways as one man into the measure, which flows capriciously … now tearing along, then suddenly languishing at the will of the magical and electric violin. Johann Strauss danced, pit and boxes danced, the very lights winked in time; everybody and everything seemed turned into a waltz or galop by yonder inexorable pied piper, until some abrupt clang brought all to a close, and the little man was left bowing and smiling, to an audience beside themselves with delight."

It is, of course, unfair to institute comparisons between a military band, consisting of wind and reed instruments, with a complete orchestra with the usual proportion of stringed instruments. Much can be done with trumpets and cornets, trombones, flutes, oboes, and clarinets, and their various modifications; still, the highest form of orchestration cannot be attained without violins, viole, violoncelli, and contra-bassi. At any rate, that is the opinion of musicians whose opinion is law. To the common man, whose musical education has been neglected, a military band, well-drilled, is a monstrous good thing to hear.

When Godfrey, of the English Grenadier Guards — one of that famous trinity of brothers, who are the great bandmasters of England — came to this country a few years ago, his concerts were very popular indeed, and he must have made quite a sum of money. The Englishmen had learned a lot of American popular airs, and gave them in return to calls for encores, with good taste and feeling. His band, take it all in all, was no better than our Marine Band. Mr. Sousa's troupe is one of which any conductor might be proud. It might be called a band of soloists. He is himself a musician of no mean merit. His *Sheridan's Ride* and his *Race from Ben Hur* are stirring compositions, and he has drilled his men till they have sunk their individuality in the work of playing parts of one great machine.

His band is quite large enough for any ordinary hall and it is not too large to be handled. The monstrous bands which are occasionally gathered together at great celebrations often discourse discord from the impossibility of controlling them. There was one occasion when several hundred musicians played together with fine effect. That was in the old, old days when Louis Philippe was king of the French. An army corps was embarking at Marseilles for Algeria. The men were reluctant to go. They had heard weird tales of blighting heat and parched deserts in Africa. It was not deemed wise to employ force. General Bugeaud, who was in command, had the bright idea of ordering the military bands to play the *Marseillaise* — which was then a forbidden air in France. At the firing of a gun, twenty military bands struck up simultaneously the well-known air. The thrill which shot through their audience was indescribable. Everybody joined in; the stirring melody rose from the quays to the mountain tops which overlook the seaport of Provence, and filled the air with a joyful sound; and, without further ado, thirty thousand red-legged Frenchmen took up their knapsacks and marched, singing, on board the transports.

The notices in all the papers were most gratifying, and on our way back we gave concerts again in Chicago. Mr. Blakely came to me and said, "How much does the Government pay you a year?"

"Oh, about fifteen hundred."

"Well," he answered, "I have been talking the matter over with a party of business men. They are willing to organize a syndicate, pay you six thousand a year, and twenty per cent of the profits, if you will resign from the Marine Band and organize a private concert band."

"I'll think it over," I replied.

The next morning, before any reply had been given to the offer, the Associated Press carried a story that I was going to leave Washington and organize a concert band in Chicago. Within the week I received hundreds of letters, some congratulating me, others hoping that I would not leave Washington. *The Washington Post* of April 19, 1892, published the following:

WANT TO KEEP SOUSA

WASHINGTONIANS AMAZED AT THE PRESUMPTION OF CHICAGO

FEAR HE WILL ACCEPT THE BID

Washington, April 18:

"Chicago will want the White House next." The remark was made this noon in the Senate restaurant by one of a group of senators and newspaper correspondents who were discussing pie, milk and Chicago's attempt to capture Sousa, the leader of the Marine Band. The news that Chicago was negotiating with the leader caused not so much surprise as regret. The people of Washington would receive with equanimity the news that Chicago had determined to introduce a bill to remove the Capitol of the nation to her capacious limits or to annex the present capital. But they are not prepared to witness the attempt to deprive them of the able and popular leader of the Marine Band and are very much exercised over the prospect of losing him. They don't blame Chicago, nor in fact do they blame Sousa for considering the offer, and they would not blame him if he accepted it. But they do blame the Government, and, moreover, they are bringing to bear upon the devoted heads of the congressmen a great deal of pressure to induce them to vote for a bill that shall give to the leader of the Marine Band a salary commensurate with his worth.

Even Frank Hatton, who is used, from long practice, to view with unperturbed soul, the march of Empire toward the West, has devoted considerable time and space in his newspaper this week to sounding the alarm by declaring that the loss of Sousa means the loss of the Marine Band, it being naturally expected that if Sousa leaves, he will take with him such of the players whose terms of enlistment have expired, and others will follow in due course.

By the time I had reached Washington on May 6, I had fully made up my mind to request my release from the Government. The release was granted late in July, and with a number of gracious letters of appreciation from those in authority, I left Washington on the first of August for New York, to begin the organization of a concert band.

Twelve years of service under five Presidents of the United States had enabled me to draw some conclusions about the highest office within the gift of the nation and also about those men who occupied it. Moreover, the Marines, the White House, the routine of official life, had all grown inevitably dear and familiar to me. It was, in a sense, like leaving home, to leave the protection of the Government. Every year of the twelve had been packed with color and interest and excitement. I had been in close contact with the outstanding personalities of the time — men who possessed nobilities of character which gave them heroic qualities in the eyes of their musical director. I was not soon to forget the sane, impartial Hayes, with his clear vision and his valor, the integrity of Arthur, the democracy of Cleveland, the brilliancy and idealism of Harrison. The office of President is a great one; to every true American it seems the greatest on earth. And to me, as I was engaged in weaving a background of music for the pageantry of it, there came a deeper realization of the effect of that office on the man. Whatever acrimonious discussion might accompany a political campaign, the moment a man became President, the office glorified him. He would be ordinary clay indeed, if he did not respond to that stimulus, and live up to the grandeur of his position. I never knew a President who did not regard with reverence his duty of controlling the destinies of the nation.

Chapter VII

IT WAS a new sensation to be under private management after twelve years of official life in Washington. During the two tours I had made with the Marine Band, under the management of David Blakely, I had met him only a few times — when we started both tours and when we "settled up."

Blakely had been manager of Theodore Thomas' orchestra for several years and had also managed Gilmore's Band for a number of years. He told me that he had gone to Europe after his split with Gilmore, to find a conductor of equal popularity. He had come back from his quest empty-handed, and by chance happened to be in Chicago when we played our second engagement there. He was very flattering and, being an impressive sort of person, commanded my respect instantly. He said that he had been Secretary of the State of Wisconsin, Editor of the *Chicago Post*, and had entered the managerial world by organizing and bringing to a successful conclusion a huge musical festival in Minneapolis. Blakely had a nose for news, and wrote well, but he left the route-making and date-making of his attractions very largely in the hands of two assistants, Howard Pew and Frank Christianer.

Blakely asked if I had confidence in the success of our enterprise, and I assured him that I had. At that, he suggested that I buy some stock in the concern, and set the sum at a thousand dollars. I bought it then and there. We opened our season on the twenty-sixth day of September, 1892, at Plainfield, New Jersey, and continued on the road for eight weeks. On the day of our first concert, Patrick Gilmore lay dead in St. Louis. In respect to that fellow musician I arranged and played as the first number ever played publicly by my band, a composition of Gilmore's, *The Voice of a Departed Soul.*

We continued on the road with varying success. Sometimes business was wretched, again we would strike a town where I had previously showed, with the Marines, and then business was good. When we reached Boston, Blakely joined us. He called me into his room at the hotel, and said, "I'm going to close down this tour to-night." I was frantic!

"You'll do nothing of the kind," I cried. "The route laid out for the band has been hopeless, but that is not my fault. You booked me in a territory where Gabriel with a horn of gold wouldn't draw. And now you have the effrontery to propose ruining my career. You would disgrace me as a musician; the authorities at Washington would laugh at my humiliation, after I left them in such high feather. I won't permit you to close! We have two weeks more, and I insist that you carry out your contract!"

He finally consented to resume the tour.

We went from Boston to Portland, Maine, and had a very large house. From there we went to Lewiston, Bangor, Rockland, Manchester, Burlington, and other towns in New Hampshire and Vermont, all of which gave us excellent houses.

But Blakely and I never really were in harmony from the date of that tense interview in Boston. Although I realized his ability as a manager, I could not place my entire confidence in so poor a loser. As the band grew in popularity, he no doubt saw his mistake and became almost fatherly in his affectionate attitude toward me. I quote a letter which demonstrates his subsequent friendliness:

New York, October 30, 1896

MY OWN BONNIE BOY: —

Your note, received yesterday, from Vienna, was a delight for two reasons: One: because I found that you were receiving my letters through Brown, Shipley and Company, and the other because it contained the fine notice from the *Nachtrichen*, of your concert in Berlin. Be assured that the letter shall have the attention and wide circulation it deserves. We are receiving dozens of notices every day from the newspapers, containing the cables of the United and Associated Presses regarding the concert, and the written notice sent out by me. So that the country is familiar with the fact, and the country is happy because of the honors done its favorite and distinguished leader.

It happens every day just as it has happened today, that fully half of my time is taken up by callers — some wanting the Band, some wanting engagements, some wanting this and some wanting that, and sometimes I feel as if my time had actually been frittered away for a whole day with scarcely any compensation; but you will be pleased to know that the book is almost completed, and that it contains between its covers an amount of testimony in the way of unbought, unprejudiced, unselfish eulogy never before equalled in the history of music in this or any other country; and that I am classifying it under all its different heads, each department by itself, each section of the country by itself, each city which has given us more than one notice, each Fair, each Exposition, each class of matter by itself, and several magnificent pages concerning the new opera — the whole forming a bouquet of newspaper exotics such, I repeat, as were never before bound within covers since the birth of man.

MR. SOUSA IN VARYING MOODS

While going through the proof of some of these notices yesterday, I turned to Miss Allen, and said, "Could mortal man of whom such and so many of these things are said, escape from being vain or be blamed for being vain?" No, my bonnie boy, you have a title to self-appreciation beyond that of most men living. And if you succeed in keeping this fact under, or from seeming to be too frequently and continuously manifested, you must certainly be entitled to the credit of something more than human. In many respects, you are certainly an extraordinarily modest man. Your conduct on the stage in this respect is beyond reproach, and your general conduct in public is entitled to the same commendation: and they who find fault with you for sometimes dwelling too long upon matters connected with your career as a leader and composer, do not know you as I do, and do not know how few men there are living, or who ever lived, who do not show the effect of their honors more conspicuously than you do.

I am hurrying this letter for the morning's mail. I shall now write you more frequently because you are getting my letters. Dismiss from your mind any concern regarding my accident. It is not only behind me, but its damaging effects are there also. I am putting in my full number of hours in the office — everything is promising — Sousa continues to occupy the columns of the papers and the hearts and minds of his scores of thousands of his friends — the prospect of the election is good — our own tour promises well because of this fact — and you, I trust, are enjoying and being benefitted by your vacation and the appreciation which accompanies you on foreign shores, and hence all is well, and is going to be well with us in the future more abundantly than it has been in the past.

The last return from the opera — to wit, the second week in Brooklyn, has just come in, and amounts to $194. For a second week in Brooklyn, that was immense. Hopper never did so well there in his life.

Always affectionately and devotedly,

Your DAVID BLAKELY

In October, 1892, I had the honor to play in conjunction with Theodore Thomas' Orchestra at the dedication of the World's Fair Buildings in Chicago. The programme consisted, among other numbers, of *Columbus*, a march and hymn for orchestra, military band and chorus, written by John Knowles Paine of the Faculty of Harvard University. I had very thoroughly rehearsed the music we were to play in combination with the orchestra, and a general rehearsal was held in the Auditorium. Mr. Thomas stopped the orchestra in the middle of the number and turning to my band, said, "Sousa Band, start it from the beginning." He went through it, without once stopping them. Then he turned to me — I was sitting with Mr. Blakely in the front seat of the Auditorium — and smilingly said, "I thank you for the pains you have taken." After the rehearsal he came over to me and said, "Let's get some lunch." We sat in the Auditorium Hotel restaurant until after six. It was one of the happiest afternoons of my life. Thomas was one of the greatest conductors that ever lived.

It pleased my fancy to compare Thomas' career with my own, for they were much alike. He had played second horn in a United States Navy Band stationed at Portsmouth, Virginia, when he was but thirteen; I had played second trombone in the Marine Band at Washington when I was thirteen. He had played the violin for dancing; so had I. He had become an orchestral violinist, and so had I. He was an American by adoption, coming from Essen, East Friesland, at the age of ten. I was an American by birth, but my parents were Portuguese and German. He had conducted an opera at sight without ever having seen performance or score before: I had done the same thing for a German opera company in Washington. (The conductor missed the train, and I conducted *A Night in Granada* by Kreutzer, without ever having seen anything but the overture.)

I have heard it said of Thomas that a great violinist was side-tracked to become the greatest conductor in the world. No wonder I was thrilled to be with him! He ordered luncheon and then became reminiscent, and told me a number of interesting stories about his early career. He laughed especially over the memory of a concert in Terrace Garden, in New York. He had placed on the programme a piece entitled, *The Linnet Polka* for two piccolos, and he prevailed upon the piccolo players to get up into the trees. When the audience heard the sounds coming through the foliage above, they applauded so heartily that it was obvious that the performance was a real "hit."

I told Thomas that my early dream of heaven was his rendering of Schumann's *Träumerei* in Washington when I was a little fellow.

"That was some pianissimo," he commented. "But, speaking of concerts, you must be very careful about management. Managers will stick close when you are making money, but they'll desert you without a qualm when the first squall blows up. Beware of speculators, if only for art's sake. Barnum offered to undertake the management of my concerts years ago, but I declined because I had no faith in his artistic integrity, and felt that he would exploit me in much the same manner as he did the Siamese twins, the fat lady, or the skeleton."

We discussed many compositions I had heard him give, and when I became enthusiastic over some especially brilliant effect he had produced, he would inquire happily, "Do you really remember that?" adding, "I worked over that effect for hours but

I finally got it." The afternoon sped by, and I only left when I had to get ready for my concert that evening.

Late that night, as I sat in my hotel room, musing over our conversation, I continued the parallel between Thomas and myself. Like him, I was tenacious of my rights, but more diplomatic and less given to irrevocable dicta. I would listen to advice, and if I knew it was no good, would quietly say, "I'll think that over," leaving the other fellow with no ammunition to discuss the matter further. If I thought the advice good, I'd make the other fellow advance more arguments in favor of it and thereby convince me of its practical worth. Thomas had a highly organized symphony orchestra with a traditional instrumentation; I a highly organized wind band with an instrumentation without precedent. Each of us was reaching an end, but through different methods. He gave Wagner, Liszt, and Tchaikowsky, in the belief that he was educating his public; I gave Wagner, Liszt and Tchaikowsky with the hope that I was entertaining my public.

I do not believe there ever lived a conductor who interpreted Beethoven so perfectly as Thomas did, and he was the only one of the symphony leaders who idealized Wagner. Wagner to him was not a blare of brass or scraping of strings, but harmonies often ethereal in beauty. Thomas was primarily an educator, and nothing turned him aside from his purpose. It made him lose his sense of proportion, and at times brought him into sharp conflict with his public and his critics, yet I feel sure that nearly all the captious sayings reflecting on Thomas were directed against the man rather than the musician.

Thomas became the Director of Music for the World's Fair, and engaged our band to play at the Exposition during the spring and early summer of 1893. Our concerts were a tremendous attraction and drew thousands at every performance. Mr. Tomlins, the vocal director of the Exposition, came up to the bandstand one night, after I had played a selection of old-time songs, and said, "Sousa, while you were playing that last piece, thousands of these people were just crazy to join in with the band. Let me announce that you want the audience to sing when you play *Old Folks at Home*. So that night, we broke into *Way Down Upon the Suwanee River*. Before we finished, we had played half a dozen songs and hymn tunes near to the heart of America. We repeated the experiment several times during the season, with many encores.

The passing of Patrick Sarsfield Gilmore in the autumn of the previous year had saddened the musical world. Mr. Gilmore had organized and gathered together the very best wood-wind and brass players of both Europe and America. He had gone into the highways and byways of the land, playing Wagner and Liszt, and other great composers, in places where their music was absolutely unknown, and their names scarcely more than a twice-repeated sound. His concerts were extremely popular; indeed there is no doubt that Mr. Thomas had intended Gilmore to be the band attraction at the opening of the Fair.

On April 16, 1893, we gave a joint concert with Mr. Walter Damrosch's Symphony Orchestra which was billed as "the only permanent orchestra in New York." A notice from the *New York Press* records:

> The experiment of uniting the efforts of two of the chief musical organizations of the country resulted in a novel and enjoyable concert at Carnegie Hall last night. The Sousa Band joined the Symphony Orchestra and filled the stage with 150 performers.
>
> The volume of sound produced by so large a body of players was unprecedented in the annals of the house. This

effect was especially noticed in the concerted numbers that brought both bands under one baton, in which instances the gossamerlike delicacy of the Damrosch strings were quite lost in the richness and fullness of tone from the Sousa brass and percussion.

The rival organizations were best heard apart. It was a contest of skill between the two leaders and their superlatively trained musicians. The audience bestowed especially enthusiastic approval on both conductors. In his charming delivery of Grieg's *Solvejg's Song* from the Peer Gynt suite and Czebulka's dainty *Love's Dream after the Ball*, Walter Damrosch won as much applause as was given Mr. Sousa for his spirited rendering of Titl's *Military Overture*, Barnard's *Serenade Enfantine*, and three numbers from *The Damnation of Faust*. The competition between these talented conductors for the favor of the audience induced an unusually animated spirit in the musicians, and the concert was, in all matters, one of the most intensely interesting and enjoyable of the Music Hall series.

On May 5, 1893, we gave a Columbian Festival in Boston at Mechanics Hall. Besides the band, we had a large orchestra of women and a group of vocalists which included Madame Fursch-Madi, the Misses Behnke, and Van Cauteren and Messieurs Campanini, Guille, Merton and Vivian. Miss Leonora Von Stosch was the violinist and it was all backed by a large chorus. Most of the vocal artists were from the Metropolitan Opera. We gave five performances in Boston and although artistically it was highly praised, financially we just about "broke even." Presently we moved on to Buffalo.

M. Guille, who had been Patti's tenor on her tour through America, evidently doubted the momentary resources of our organization, for he refused to appear in Buffalo, unless he got his pay check three days in advance. The treasurer came to me with fight in his eye. He begged me to allow M. Guille to leave us. I said, "You can't do that. We have advertised the man, and the public expects to hear him, so pay him his salary, even though it isn't due." The treasurer obeyed me, and the concert was given. That night we left for Detroit, but to our astonishment, when we started the Detroit concert, M. Guille was not there. He had missed the train and came in just before he was scheduled to appear on the stage. The singer was profuse in his apologies; the train had been late, etc., etc. He ran the gamut of excuses, neglecting entirely to give the real one, which was that he had stayed up all night with a company of friends, and had forgotten all about his concert engagement.

But always the show must go on. I began the prelude to Guille's number. When the music reached the point where he was to begin, not a sound came from his throat — his voice had completely failed him! There was never a more agonized expression on a man's face. He left the stage, and I substituted one of the other soloists. Guille came to me at the end of the concert and, poor fellow, he was frantic. He could speak only in a whisper. I suggested he go at once to a hospital and let me know when he was well again, but asked him not to bother me until he was able to sing again and was fully recovered. He left and I have never seen or heard of him from that day to this.

The only other unpleasantness I had on that tour was with Madame Fursch-Madi. She was a consummate artist, one of the best of the Metropolitan opera singers, but she was temperamental. I had arranged a programme that included the finale of *Lohengrin*, in which the whole solo force of the organization, together with a chorus and band, was used. It was the grand climax to the concert. The number before the last one was by the band.

One night in St. Louis, Madame Fursch-Madi came to me and said, "Monsieur Sousa, I cannot understand the manner in which you make up our programmes. Nobody in the world makes up a programme like you."

Laughingly I replied, "Well, then, you should give me credit for originality, Madame."

"No, no," she continued. "You have arranged the last number for the vocalists. Why not have a piece for the band alone?

"Well, Madame, we have a number of excellent vocal artists with us, and I believe we should climax our concerts by bringing them all together at the end."

She answered, "Will you not change for me? It makes me so late for the supper which I always have after the concert."

"Anything to oblige a lady *once*," I answered. "I will reverse the last two numbers to-night, but never again."

I kept my word. The next concert was in Omaha, where the Apollo Society assisted us. I invited the Society's conductor to lead the closing number. As I left the stage, the local conductor, much excited, said to me, "Madame Fursch-Madi has left the hall. She says you insulted her."

"In what manner?" I asked.

"You promised to change the programme and failed to do so."

"I didn't do it because I distinctly told her that I would change it only for last night; but come on, we can't keep the audience waiting. I will have Miss Van Cauteren take the part."

Our next stand was Minneapolis. At my hotel I found this note:

M. Sousa: I would like to see you at once in my room.

FURSCH-MADI

WITH THE NORTHWEST MOUNTED POLICE

OFFICE OF THE MAYOR
OTTAWA CANADA

1st August, 1925.

Lt.-Commander John Philip Sousa.

Sir:

For a third of a century actually millions of persons in the United States, Canada and England have been thrilled by the music of the march king and his organisation. Surely in this commercial age a man who has given to multitudes music which they can admire is just a little higher than the ordinary in the plane of famous men.

Mr. Sousa's greatness is not national but is world wide. He has been honoured by many countries and by our late King Edward.

With more than ordinary pleasure, therefore, I welcome to Canada's Capital, Lieut.-Commander John Philip Sousa.

I should like also to include in this welcome, Miss Winnifred Bambrick, a daughter of a prominent citizen of Ottawa, who is rising to fame under the direction of Mr. Sousa.

John Bachum

Mayor.

IN CANADA

I went to the lady's room, rapped, and elicited a gloomy,

"Come in." I went in. The lady was in high dudgeon. I greeted her with great respect.

"You insulted me last night," she exclaimed, angrily.

"In what way?"

"You promised me to change the programme and you failed to do it."

"You are mistaken. I thought I made it very clear that I changed the programme for one night only. But do not worry. I have arranged everything."

She evidently did not like my tone, and asked impatiently, "What do you mean?"

"I mean, Madame Fursch-Madi," said I very slowly, "that I have instructed the treasurer of this band to fine you two hundred dollars for your nonappearance at the finale last night."

She glared at me like a tigress!

"If you do that, I'll not sing!"

"Very well, Madame, if you are not on the stage to-night when your turn comes, I shall go down to the footlights, and say, 'Ladies and Gentlemen: Madame Fursch-Madi, the great artiste from the Metropolitan Opera House, refuses to appear because she prefers to have her supper before she serves her public. To replace Madame Fursch-Madi, who has gone to her supper, the band will play *The Washington Post*.

Madame was on the stage at the crucial moment that night and sang like an angel!

Mr. Austin Corbin, President of the Long Island Railroad and owner of Manhattan Beach, had endeavored many times to engage me, when I was directing the Marine Band, to substitute for Gilmore, while he was in camp with his regiment. It was, therefore, quite natural that Blakely should sign a contract for me

to play at Manhattan Beach for the season of '93. This engagement brought me to the attention of the Director of the yearly
St. Louis Exposition and I suppose the additional élan of having
played at the World's Fair decided him in engaging me for the
entire season at the Exposition. Undoubtedly this led to my later
giving a series of concerts at the Trocadero in Chicago, for Mr.
Florenz Ziegfeld, Sr., the President of the Trocadero Company.

These engagements covered nearly the entire year of '93, and
every day was guaranteed almost from the start of the season to its
close. It was a signal achievement for an organization only in its
second year, and I could not help but remember with a smile that,
six months before, my management had sought to close me out.

During the Trocadero engagement I brought out *The Liberty
Bell.* I had finished the march, but had not determined what its title
should be, when, on entering the Auditorium one day, I chanced
to see a spectacle there, called *America.* I was impressed by the
very artistic scenic drop which depicted the Liberty Bell. At the
end of the performance I went into the lobby of the Auditorium
Hotel to inquire for my mail. A letter from my wife informed me
that our little boy, Philip, had paraded that day in Philadelphia
with his kindergarten class in honor of the Liberty Bell. The two
incidents decided me. I called my new march *The Liberty Bell*
and it was highly successful from its first performance.

At the Trocadero, Mr. Blakely had several interviews with Mr.
Michael de Young, a leading spirit in the forthcoming midwinter
fair to be held in San Francisco, beginning in January, 1894, but
Mr. de Young balked at the figure Blakely demanded and the
negotiations ceased. Early in December we returned to New
York, to plan the '94 tour. Scarcely a month passed before Blakely
received a telegram from Mr. de Young: "How soon can you reach
San Francisco?" Blakely replied that he could do so in three weeks

— at the terms previously laid down. We crossed the continent, giving concerts on the way, and on reaching San Francisco were amused to learn that the band which had been playing there before our advent had not succeeded in satisfying musical San Francisco; to placate the populace they had engaged us.

Of course we were in the pink of playing condition. When Gilmore died, we took into our organization about nineteen of his best men — such musicians as Herbert Clarke, the well-known cornetist, Gustave Stengler, Herman Conrad, Joseph Raffyola, William Wadsworth, and Albert Bode. These, together with our own Arthur Pry or (who had been a member of my band since its inception) Henry Koch, and many other talented men, gave us a host of brilliant players. The musicians of San Francisco were delighted with our work and at the end of the first week tendered us a magnificent banquet. One of their number, called upon to make a speech, said that he had been deputized by the Musicians' Union to attend the first concert of the band and report on "value received."

"Well," he smiled, "when you fellows played your first piece, I knew it was *Tannhäuser*, because the programme said so; but I soon found out something I never knew before — that the clarinet and the flute and the oboe can be played just as softly as a muted violin, and the rest of the band can play an accompaniment to them even softer. I never knew that clarinets and flutes had soft pedal keys on them, until I heard you fellows play."

This was received with great applause by everybody, and from that day to this there has always been a warm friendship between the musical fraternity of California and my band.

While we were at the Fair, Fritz Scheel, an excellent musician, who in after years became conductor of the Philadelphia Symphony, was giving concerts in a large auditorium in the Fair grounds, which I think they called "the Vienna Prater." The public attendance was very ordinary; while ours could be counted by thousands. Someone in authority suggested to Mr. de Young the advantage of boosting the enterprise by giving a double concert with Scheel's Imperial Orchestra and our band. I was consulted and told them I was engaged by the Exposition, and if they saw fit to have me play in conjunction with the Imperial Orchestra I would not object. They needed money and I would be extremely happy if I could assist in bringing money to the Vienna Prater people and the Exposition. So the concert was announced.

Scheel, a very nice fellow, had evidently been told that I was very dictatorial and would override him if he didn't watch out, which, of course, was all bosh, but he believed it. When we met to arrange the joint programme, he asked me how many soloists I intended to introduce.

"Only one," I said, "Mr. Arthur Pryor."

Then, said he, he would put on only one, Mr. Franz Hell (who afterwards became a member of my band). It was agreed that we should have two numbers by the entire aggregation, two numbers by the separate organizations, and the two solos.

"What is your piece for the combined orchestra and band?" asked Mr. Scheel.

"I'll take *Tannhäuser*," I replied.

"Nein, nein!" cried Scheel, "I must have it."

We argued, both getting pretty angry, when Frank Truesdale, the publicity man of the Exposition, whispered to me, "Let the Dutchman have it. Don't wrangle any more." I quieted down, and Scheel went on, "What is your next piece?"

"*The Second Rhapsody* of Liszt," I said.

"Nein, nein! I must have that!"

"Very well."

"What is your opening piece?" asked Scheel.

Not to be caught with another objection, I asked, "Well, what is yours?"

"*Mignon overture.*"

"Good!" I exclaimed, "I congratulate you, and I'll take *William Tell.*"

It was finally settled that Scheel should open the programme with *Mignon*, I should follow with *William Tell*; then the solos by Fritz Hell and Arthur Pryor; then I was to do the Feremors music, Scheel the Liszt *Rhapsody*, and the two finishing numbers would be *Tannhäuser*, by the combined bands, Scheel conducting, and *Rienzi* with myself as conductor.

The concert started brilliantly — a packed house and high prices! Scheel's orchestra played Mignon and played it very well. There was a polite patter of applause and he bowed himself off the stage, while my men filed in for their first number.

At the morning rehearsal, there had been an exhibition of studied indifference among the foreigners in Scheel's orchestra which was vigorously resented by my men; in fact, Henry Koch and others of my band had bluntly informed the offenders that there would be a row if they continued to show inattention when I was conducting. To make matters worse, one of the San Francisco papers had published a cartoon, depicting a big six-footer labelled "Scheel" leading by the hand a little two-footer labelled "Sousa," intimating thereby that the Sousa band and its director should feel highly honored to be allowed to play on the same stage with the Imperial Orchestra. This, of course, did not contribute to the tranquillity of my bandsmen, and they were a grim and determined lot when they marched on to the stage to begin the *William Tell Overture*. It was the most impeccable performance I have heard in my entire career! The clear-cut execution of all parts was a marvel. It swept the audience completely off its feet, and at the end of the number there came a thunder of spontaneous applause. I was forced to bow again and again; still the clapping roared on.

I then did the meanest thing in my life. I whispered to my band, "*The American Patrol*, boys!" and mounted the platform. We began almost inaudibly, working up to a great crescendo, and suddenly forsaking the *Patrol*, launched into *Columbia, the Gem of the Ocean*. The audience began to applaud, and as we swung into *Dixie* they yelled as if every one of them had been born south of the Mason-Dixon line. With *Yankee Doodle* we finished the number. But Scheel, like Bret Harte's Chinaman, was no longer interested in the subsequent proceedings!

It was a mean trick, but Scheel forgave me, and years afterward we laughed over it together. The rest of the concert passed off decorously. Financially and artistically it was a great success. We were compelled to give a second one, but like first love, no second concert could duplicate the thrills of the first. However, it was a good concert, and the only flaw was its abrupt termination, due to the sudden extinction of every electric light in the hall. No audience likes to sit in darkness!

With the end of our engagement in San Francisco we began the tour which wound up in New York, for our second season at Manhattan Beach, where I received a medal from Mr. Corbin for having broken the record of the Beach for concert crowds. From Manhattan we proceeded to St. Louis for our second year at the Exposition, and another medal was forthcoming for having broken the attendance record there also.

At this time the march which rivaled in popularity the far-flung *Washington Post* was *The High School Cadets*. I had written it for a company of high school cadet students in Washington and they had paid me twenty-five dollars for the dedication. At that time I had no adequate idea of the value of my compositions, and sold *Semper Fidelis*, *The Picador*, *The Crusader*, *The Washington Post*, *High School Cadets*, and several others, under a contract with Harry Coleman, the music publisher, in Philadelphia, for thirty-five dollars apiece, and I was also to furnish three arrangements, one for piano, one for orchestra, and one for band!

The Gladiator, my first hit in the march line, I offered to Stopper and Fiske, of Williamsport, Pennsylvania, for fifty dollars. They returned the manuscript, and nothing daunted, I sent it to Coleman, who took it for his usual price of thirty-five dollars. And that was the march that put me on the musical map! I really believe that every band in America played it.

It seems to me now that I had a very hazy idea of the value of money. When I was a boy in Washington, the pay for a fourth-class clerk in the Government Departments, eighteen hundred dollars a year, seemed as much as anyone should earn or require; in fact our neighborhood reckoned an eighteen-hundred-dollar clerk as something of a nabob. I believe that boyhood idea, derived from those about me, had much to do with making me a poor business man. Up to 1892 I sold all my compositions outright, some as low as five dollars. The highest price was fifty. Many of those marches became immensely popular and simply coined money for the publishers. In fact Coleman bought a reed instrument factory and a brass instrument factory entirely from the profits he made on my compositions. I was more interested in producing music which would appeal to the public heart than in gaining a fortune for myself.

I had understood from Mr. Blakely that he would undertake the publication of my compositions, since he had a large printing establishment in Chicago, so my first piece written after I went with Blakely was offered to him. This was the well known *Belle of Chicago March*. Blakely rejected it and when I questioned his decision, he wrote me:

> "My dear Sousa, a man usually makes one hit in his life. You have made two, *The Washington Post*, and *The High School Cadets*. It is not reasonable to expect you to make another, so I am willing to let Coleman publish *The Belle of Chicago*."

Coleman took it and *The Beau Ideal* as well, two marches which made another little ripple on the River of Success. But because they did not electrify the country like the two characterized by Blakely as "hits," Coleman believed that I had shot my bolt as a successful composer. When I asked him how the marches were going, his invariable reply was an unenthusiastic, "Well, they're moving along slowly."

Chapter VIII

THE COTTON STATES EXPOSITION — "EL CAPITAN" — EUROPE IN 1896 —
SHOWMANSHIP AND ITS VIRTUES — VENICE — THE COMPOSITIONS OF
"GIOVANNI FILIPO SOUSA" — ROME — BLAKELY DIES — THE HOMEWARD
VOYAGE AND "THE STARS AND STRIPES FOREVER"

THE year 1895 saw us touring again — Manhattan Beach for the season, then St. Louis once more, and on to Atlanta, where we were to play at the Cotton States Exposition. I had written "King Cotton" while on tour, and this was adopted as the official march of the Exposition and proved to be a great success. About a week before we were scheduled to arrive in Atlanta, Blakely received a telegram from the manager of the Exposition: "Impossible to carry out contract. Consider cancelled."

Blakely turned to me. "What's to be done?"

"Done?" I echoed, indignantly. "Telegraph them that you will open at the Exposition, precisely according to the terms of the contract."

We could not have done otherwise. We would have lost at least ten thousand dollars in bringing the band back, and rearranging our tour after Atlanta. Blakely sent his assistant ahead with instructions to explain to the manager the impossibility of canceling our contract, and to advertise our opening date with all the customary exploitation. Blakely's man informed us, when we arrived in Atlanta on the morning of our opening, that the board of directors had proved difficult indeed. They had two famous bands from New York, neither of which had drawn money. The board had been forced to borrow money from a public-spirited citizen in order to carry on the Exposition. The outlook was a dismal one.

We opened, however, and drew a splendid crowd, the second largest in the annals of the Exposition. The delighted Blakely announced, "Now watch 'em; they'll come around and apologize handsomely." As we went to dinner that night a bellboy handed Blakely a large, official-looking envelope.

"Bully," said he, "here's the apology."

He opened the envelope and his gladness changed to gloom. "Damn it!" was his only comment.

The note was from some petty official connected with the Exposition transportation department.

David Blakely,

Manager Sousa's Band.

SIR:

The Exposition paid three dollars to carry your large instruments from the hall to the band stand. Kindly reimburse us on receipt of this, and hereafter make your own arrangements for the transportation of your instruments.

After the concert that evening, Blakely introduced me to a lawyer named Glenn, whom he had engaged to look after our interests. Mr. Glenn knew the general manager and the board of directors of the Exposition, and had made an appointment with them to meet us and discuss the situation the next day. The board proved to be a group of fine men who were much distressed over their inability to carry out their contract. One of them told me that eighty per cent of their daily receipts had to be paid over to their creditors, leaving the Exposition but twenty per cent to carry on business. After considering various plans to have us remain, and arriving always at the fact that they simply hadn't the money to pay us, I made a proposition; we would release the management from the contract; we would give a series of concerts in the Festival Hall, charging an admission of fifty cents, all profits to revert to us; either side was privileged to terminate this agreement by a week's notice.

The board consented, and the next day we gave our first indoors concert in Festival Hall. I received a number of abusive letters, upbraiding me for charging the people for my music after they had already paid fifty cents for admission to the fair-grounds. One paper carried a cartoon, in which I was in a glass case, with the inscription, "Drop fifty cents in the slot and hear Sousa."

It worked beautifully. Although the public was indignant, still they came and filled the hall. We played the week out, and on Sunday gave a musicale at De Grive's Opera House. The Exposition was making money through us, at the gate, and it wasn't costing them a penny. The second week was as successful as the first, but on Saturday night the board of directors received the following notice:

> Sousa's Band will terminate its engagement with the Exposition next Saturday evening.
>
> Very respectfully,
>
> DAVID BLAKELY

The man who had written the "three dollar letter" was the first to expostulate. "What are you stopping for?" he demanded. "You're making money, and so are we, so why end the concerts?"

"I'll tell you. After we had come to an agreement to give these concerts, without any expense to you, Mr. Blakely sent his assistant ahead to book contracts for the band in various towns ahead

between here and New York. He has done so, and we open in
Spartanburg, South Carolina, a week from Monday," I replied.

Months before, B. D. Stevens, the manager of the DeWolf
Hopper Opera Company, had come to me with a libretto. He said
that Mr. Hopper retained a happy recollection of *Désirée* which I

MR. SOUSA AT HOME WITH HIS DAUGHTER PRISCILLA

had composed, and in which he had made his initial appearance in comic opera, and had said that if I saw enough in this libretto to write the music, he would produce it. I took the libretto, which was written by Charles Klein, and was called *El Capitan*. I read it carefully, liked it very much, and assured Stevens and Hopper that it was an excellent vehicle for musical treatment. Klein was not a lyric writer, so we called in Tom Frost, who enjoyed some reputation as a versifier. I marked out the places for music, and Frost and I wrote the lyrics. I wrote the words and music of the *El Capitan* song, *Sweetheart I'm Waiting, The Typical Tune of Zanzibar* and quite half of the lyrics of the piece.

There was a newspaper man on the *Constitution* whom I came to like and admire. His name was Robert Adamson, and he was very well known indeed during the time Mr. Gaynor was Mayor of New York. One morning he came to the hotel to see me and I said, "Hopper has asked me for a different song for his *El Capitan* entrance. He doesn't care for the one I've already sent him, so I've written a new one, words and music." I sat at the piano, and played the piece, and Mrs. Sousa sang it. Adamson was delighted.

"If that doesn't make a hit, I'll eat it!" he exclaimed. He never ate it!

In the third act there was a cumbersome and expensive change of scene. B. D. Stevens — who sometimes because of his inititals, was called Breakfast, Dinner and Supper Stevens — was a careful and thrifty manager. He saw no necessity of spending a large sum of money on scenery that might prove valueless, so he wrote me, "Hopper wants a knockout song for this act. Send as soon as possible."

I remembered some verses I had written a few years before for a now defunct magazine. They were called, *The Typical Tune of Zanzibar.* So, on my way from Omaha to Chicago I wrote music for them, and wired I would be in Philadelphia in a week to see Stevens. Both Klein and Stevens were enthusiastic when they heard the song. It has remained one of the many hits of the perennial *El Capitan.* Boston took an instant fancy to both the story and music; although the critics were not unanimous in their praise of the work. Indeed, Ben Wolf of the *Herald* whetted his knife upon it. Yet *El Capitan* is played almost every year, and vies in revivals with the Gilbert and Sullivan operas. When I last heard it, two years ago, the words and music seemed as fresh and tuneful as on the first night of presentation. The libretto is probably the best ever written on this side of the water.

After *Désirée* I had composed with Ned Taber a one-act piece called *The Queen of Hearts*, representing the nursery tale of the Queen who made some tarts and of the naughty Jack who ate them. It was produced in Washington, and met with moderate success. But it was *El Capitan*, my fourth opera, which captured the hearts of the public. The march of that opera stirred the country and is to-day one of the most popular of all my marches.

When we reached San Francisco on our next tour, our violinist, Miss Currie Duke, was ill, but, with the courage and good-sportsmanship characteristic of American girls, insisted on appearing. We were scheduled to be there a week. Miss Duke was anxious not to disappoint the audiences but felt able to play only one of her simpler pieces. Of course I acquiesced and on the first night she played a Hungarian Fantasie by Natchez, which she repeated at every performance thereafter. Since the programmes had all been printed a week before, it was impossible to alter the titles and we made no announcement to the audience. To my amusement, on the closing night, one of the critics of the San Francisco press came to my dressing room and said, mildly,

"Mr. Sousa, I haven't missed a performance since you opened, and I have thoroughly enjoyed every concert, but I *am* puzzled about the violin solos. The titles of the selections on the programme have changed for each performance, but the music remains the same!"

We started on our journey eastward. When we got to Missoula, after days of snow, we found that the Chinook winds had descended and melted the ice which had carried away the bridge. At last we were able to cross, but later in the day we found still another bridge swept away by the melting ice, and were obliged to wait until a plank walk was constructed. Instrument cases and music trunks were transported by hand, and leaving our Pullmans on one side of the river we took a day coach for our concert in Butte, Montana. We reached that city at ten thirty and found the theatre packed with people who had patiently waited for us since eight o'clock. The manager suggested that I announce our arrival. I took the stage, and said cheerily,

"How do you do, everybody? We have been fighting the Chinook winds all the way from Missoula, but if you will be patient with us for a few minutes, we will give you the best concert we have ever given!"

That long-delayed concert began at eleven o'clock and we played the last note at a little before one. As we waited for our train, heading eastward, a baggage porter spoke to me, and thanking me for a pleasant evening, inquired how I composed a march. I knew that the man's interest was genuine, and so I said slowly, "It is conceived; that is all I know about it. I know what you mean, of course, and I am afraid that I cannot answer your question more satisfactorily. The musician is actuated by a power beyond himself, so fleeting and intangible that it cannot be explained and I can only call it inspiration."

At the close of the 1896 Manhattan Beach engagement, I needed a rest, and so Mrs. Sousa and I sailed for Europe on the *Fürst Bismarck*. In London I was delighted to hear Hans Richter's orchestra. They gave a purely Wagner programme, with the exception of a Haydn symphony. Our own Lillian Nordica was the vocalist and sang exquisitely the Elizabeth song from *Tannhäuser*. When the first part of the concert was concluded the orchestra left the stage, and at the end of the intermission there appeared, for the performance of the Haydn symphony, an orchestra of the size employed by Haydn in his day, instead of Richter's great group of a hundred men. I counted six first violins, four second, four violas, three 'cellos, four double basses, two flutes, two oboes, two clarinets, two bassoons, two horns, two trumpets and tympani. This contrast between the heavier fare of Wagner, in the first part, and the delicacy of a delightful miniature orchestra in the second, pleased me exceedingly. It was rare showmanship on Richter's part. After all, that is effective in every walk of life. Men may object to being called showmen, but the history of mankind is a record of continual showmanship from the very beginning. The Queen of Sheba's appearance before Solomon was showmanship of the cleverest sort.

And a more modern example is the recent appearance of Henry Ford as super-showman par excellence. Did not Mr. Ford hush the country into a state of breathless expectation during the weeks immediately preceding the advent of the new model Ford car? The *Springfield Union* caught the drama of Mr. Ford's supremely knowing gesture and said appreciatively: "With the simultaneous 'unveiling' in all cities in the United States, as well as in many foreign cities, of the new Ford models, Mr. Henry Ford takes his place as the master showman of all times. The mystery with which the new car has been surrounded, the tremendous interest aroused in this and other countries and the huge volume of newspaper publicity which has attended the change of the Ford designs constitute an advertising feat which has never been equalled." It is indubitably true that suspense is essential to effective drama. To create a feeling of suspense is the aim of every dramatist who knows his art. Mr. Ford, like Mâkéda, Queen of Sheba, knew the value of surprise and used it.

After a pilgrimage to Paris and a refreshing tour through Switzerland, we went on to the equally marvellous beauties of Italy. Having been long an admirer of Giovanni Boccaccio, the father of the modern novel, I had looked forward to seeing a performance of Suppe's opera of *Boccaccio*, in Florence, but, alas, it was a horrible presentation in every way. One of my greatest delights while in Florence was to read again Machiavelli's life amid scenes familiar to him. I was especially impressed by one paragraph from his biographer, Villari, which made me wonder if we in America are not too lavish with education. It was:

"Accustomed as we are now to hear daily that knowledge and culture constitute greatness, and prove the measure of a nation's strength, we are naturally led to inquire how Italy could become so weak, so corrupt, so decayed in the midst of her intellectual and artistic preeminence." Isn't it possible, then, that a nation may educate certain of its people beyond their intelligence?

Our arrival in Venice was timed about midnight, and we hailed a gondola exactly as we would a cab in an American city. A porter placed our trunks in the gondola, and as we glided through the dark waters, the gondolier commented on the various buildings we passed. Most of the canals are very narrow and at that late hour were dark and forbidding. The gondolier, with the dramatic instinct of the Latin, would utter a human honk as we turned sharp corners. When we passed beneath the Bridge of Sighs, he halted his gondola and uttered a peroration which neither an Italian nor an Englishman could have understood, since it was a sort of mince-meat of both languages. With the Bridge of Sighs behind us, he seemed oratorically exhausted and soon brought us to the Royal Danielli hotel.

One of the many attractions in Venice was the series of concerts given in the Piazza of St. Mark by Castiglioni's band. Mrs. Sousa and I, with a group of friends, were attending one of these concerts, and listening with great interest, when, to our delight, the band struck up *The Washington Post*. At the close of the piece, we entered a music-store not far from the bandstand and inquired for "the piece the band had just played." A clerk went over to the bandstand and on his return volunteered the information that it was *The Washington Post*. "I will take a copy," said I. I was immediately supplied with an Italian edition by Giovanni Filipo Sousa!

"Yes," I said, "that is what I wanted. The title-page gives the name of one Giovanni Filipo Sousa. Who is this man?"

"Oh," said the shopkeeper, "he is one of our most famous Italian composers."

"Indeed! I am interested to hear it. Is he as famous as Verdi?

"Well, perhaps not quite as famous as Verdi; he is young yet, you see."

"Have you ever seen him?" I persisted.

"I do not remember, Signor."

"Then," said I, "let me introduce you to his wife. This is Signora Sousa!"

And she, in turn, observed, "Permit me to introduce my husband, Signor Giovanni Filipo Sousa, the composer of the

Washington Post." There was much explanation and laughter and then the shopkeeper nobly offered to charge me only the whole-sale price for a pirated copy of my own march!

We were in Rome when news came of the election of Mr. McKinley to the Presidency. The bellboys, who for a few years had not received an abundance of tips, because of the shortage of opulent American tourists, had evidently heard some fervent Republican say that prosperity would accompany the election of McKinley, for on that night they shouted, "McKinley and prosperity! Prosperity and McKinley!"

Rome offered us a thousand delights; for me there was the interest of observing a choir in the Vatican rehearsing from a large book of hymns whose notation differed absolutely from the Guidonian in use to-day; then there were the usual little contre-temps with lazy sons of Italy anent "tipping"; Mrs. Sousa drank in avidly every beauty of the Holy City, and when we went on to Naples she seemed to find a sort of Earthly Paradise in the Madonnas of the National Museum, one of which is described in my novel, *The Fifth String.*

Our preparations to leave Naples and visit Sicily were abruptly ended when I chanced upon an item in the *Paris Herald*, cabled from New York, saying that David Blakely, the well-known musical manager, had dropped dead in his office the day before. The paper was four days old! I cabled at once, and Christianer replied that it was indeed our manager who had died so suddenly and that I must now be responsible for the next tour of the band. We sailed on the *Teutonic* for America the following Saturday.

Here came one of the most vivid incidents of my career. As the vessel steamed out of the harbor I was pacing the deck, absorbed in thoughts of my manager's death and the many duties and decisions which awaited me in New York. Suddenly, I began to sense the rhythmic beat of a band playing within my brain. It kept on ceaselessly, playing, playing, playing. Throughout the whole tense voyage, that imaginary band continued to unfold the same themes, echoing and re-echoing the most distinct melody. I did not transfer a note of that music to paper while I was on the steamer, but when we reached shore, I set down the measures that my brain-band had been playing for me, and not a note of it has ever been changed. The composition is known the world over as *The Stars and Stripes Forever* and is probably my most popular march.

Following are the words I set to it — they are sung in countless American schools and by countless singing societies throughout the world:

THE STARS AND STRIPES FOREVER

LET martial note in triumph float

And liberty extend its mighty hand;

A flag appears 'mid thunderous cheers,

The banner of the Western land.

The emblem of the brave and true.

Its folds protect no tyrant crew;

The red and white and starry blue

Is freedom's shield and hope.

Other nations may deem their flags the best

And cheer them with fervid elation

But the flag of the North and South and West

Is the flag of flags, the flag of Freedom's nation.

Hurrah for the flag of the free!

May it wave as our standard forever,

The gem of the land and the sea,

The banner of the right.

Let despots remember the day

When our fathers with mighty endeavor

Proclaimed as they marched to the fray

That by their might and by their right

It waves forever.

Let eagle shriek from lofty peak

The never-ending watchword of our land;

Let summer breeze waft through the trees

The echo of the chorus grand.

Sing out for liberty and light,

Sing out for freedom and the right.

Sing out for Union and its might,

O patriotic sons.

Other nations may deem their flags the best

And cheer them with fervid elation,

But the flag of the North and South and West

Is the flag of flags, the flag of Freedom's nation.

Hurrah for the flag of the free.

May it wave as our standard forever

The gem of the land and the sea,

The banner of the right.

Let despots remember the day

When our fathers with mighty endeavor

Proclaimed as they marched to the fray,

That by their might and by their right

It waves forever.

Chapter IX

A S SOON as I reached New York, I called upon Mrs. Blakely. Feeling under a strong moral obligation to fulfil the dates arranged by her husband, I readily consented to her nominal assumption of the management, with Mr. Christianer as active manager of the band. It was an unfortunate agreement, destined to produce a good deal of storm and stress. Mrs. Blakely's true representative was a relative who endeavored to cut my salary a hundred a week and went so far as to instruct the John Church Company to tie up my royalties. This they declined to do, and I very naturally refused to take the drastic cut in my salary. My insistence upon what I believed to be my just share of the profits brought the dispute to a head, and I was accused of violation of contract. Christianer lost his position: I was unwilling to accept a substitute manager, and new dates made in Yonkers and Jersey, since I had agreed only to carry out the plans originally made by Mr. Blakely. Finally I took the entire responsibility upon my own shoulders, dismissed the entire Blakely outfit, and in view of probable litigation and threats by Mrs. Blakely's relatives to warn managers not to pay me directly, I made it a rule, under the exceptional circumstances of this tour, to require my treasurer to count up the house immediately after the concert began and to obtain payment before the second number was over. I let it be known that if he failed to receive payment I should be obliged to stop the concert and dismiss the audience. High-handed though it was, the rule proved effective, for the managers preferred to settle with me — with one exception.

In Waterbury, Connecticut, the local manager proved to be a very handsome young woman who was profuse with her compliments about my music and me! The house was packed, but the treasurer failed to report the money at the end of our second number. I took a chance, however, and continued the programme. After the concert, the treasurer appeared, crestfallen and apologetic.

"What was in the house?" I began, as usual.

"Nineteen hundred dollars," he said, "but I didn't get a penny of it."

"Why not?"

"That young Circe who runs the theatre did nothing but talk of you, your greatness, and her tremendous admiration for you. I listened, in a trance, and meanwhile the concert was going on to an end. When the last note was played, I said, 'I'll take our share, now.' She said, 'Oh, no, you won't. I have a letter from Mr. Blakely's lawyer asking me not to pay over any monies to Mr. Sousa, and I shall hold on to this money until the law says Mr. Blakely is right, or Mr. Sousa is. Of course I admire Mr. Sousa very, very much, but — business is business!'" And my poor treasurer wiped the sweat from his agitated brow.

I looked up a first-class lawyer and before midnight the enchantress disgorged, still protesting her respect and admiration for my musical ability. She even came to me the next morning, and quite undismayed, said, "I know you are dissatisfied with your management, and I should like to apply for the position."

"My dear young lady," I replied, "you would be far too sharp for an innocent little bandmaster like me. Good day!"

White Studio, N. Y.

MR. SOUSA WITH HIS DAUGHTER HELEN AND GRAND-
DAUGHTER JANE PRISCILLA ABERT

Ultimately the dispute with the Blakely group came into court — and to a settlement, but it was a very unpleasant affair both for our peace of mind and our several pocketbooks.

It taught me, however, a salutary lesson — that absolute cooperation and confidence between artists and their management is indispensable to the success of the enterprise.

Perhaps because of my own stab at lyric-writing for various comic operas, there was an entente cordiale between poets and myself. In 1896, a new version of Dixie was sent me by some admirer:

WHEN Sousa's Band's in de land ob cotton
Work and worry's all forgotten
Look away! Look away! Look away, Dixie land.
When de music plays and de coons am hummin'
It makes 'em think good times are comin'
Look away! Look away! Look away, Dixie land.
CHORUS
When Sousa's Band's in Dixie,
Hooray, Hooray!
Longside dat band, we'll take our stand,
An' sing an' dance in Dixie!
Away, away!
Away down south in Dixie!
More verse came rolling in!
WHEN SOUSA LEADS THE BAND
THE lover takes his sweetheart out to hear our famous band;
While listening to the music sweet, he holds her little hand,
He pictures to himself the day when man and wife they'll stand,
And life is all a blissful dream, when Sousa leads the band!
The people flock from far and near, to concert hall or beach,
That they may hear the tunes they love, the songs the heart
will reach.

Each voice is hushed, each ear attends, the leader takes command
And music floods the earth with joy, when Sousa leads the band!

CHORUS
Sorrow flies away when music fills the air,
Troubles fade and fail, forgotten every care;
Hearts are keeping joyous time to music sweet and grand
For joy has come and reigns supreme, when Sousa leads the band!

And this from some kindly member of the fair sex:

TONE PICTURES
(A tribute to John Philip Sousa)
As I listen, enchanted, when Sousa is playing,
My fancy, unfettered, and light-winged, is straying.
I airily drift on the rhythmical measures,
And revel in music's ethereal treasures.
He woos me to meadows where flowers are blowing,
To shadowy woodlands where brooklets are flowing,
To mirror-like pools where the moonlight is sleeping,
And flute-throated birds their love trysts are keeping.
I float upon rivers where sunbeams are glancing;
I wander mid bowers where fairies are dancing;
I hear plaintive winds regretfully sighing.
A requiem sad that the summer is dying.
I traverse strange lands 'mid scenes ever shifting,
'Neath azure blue skies where fleece-clouds are drifting.
I view Alpine heights, where the wind-flower is blowing,
And the haughty Jungfrau in the sunset is glowing.
A change comes over my fancy's creations —
The darkies are dancing on Southern plantations;
The 'Liberty Bell' bold, in triumph is ringing.
And its tones on the night air 'King Cotton' is flinging.

Then come vivid pictures, where passion is raging,
And love, unrequited, a tempest is waging.
The bugle's reveille the war-note is sounding,
And boom of artillery to echo is bounding.
Then dainty tone-poems of tenderest feeling
Into the heart come silently stealing —
Till passion and pain, and sorrow are ending,
And o'er the whole world the rainbow is bending.
Thou versatile weaver of musical rhyming!
Throughout the broad land thy sweet strains are chiming!
They come to the heart when twilight is falling,
Like whip-poor-will note through the dusky woods calling.
O, minstrel, to thee the multitude listens;
In eyes bravely calm, a tear often glistens.
And souls that are strengthened with hope for tomorrow
Will cherish and bless thee, thou healer of sorrow!"

On December 28, 1897, *The Bride Elect* for which I wrote libretto and music, was produced in New Haven, by Klaw and Erlanger. A number of New York critics attended that first performance. So great had been the success of *El Capitan* that naturally there was great interest everywhere as to whether "he could do it again." The piece soared completely over the top, although the cast boasted not a single star. At the finale of the second act, *Unchain the Dogs of War*, the enthusiasm of the audience was tremendous, and Mr. Bunnell, owner of the Hyperion Theater, came to my box and said, "Mr. Sousa, I'll give you a hundred thousand dollars for your opera."

"Thanks very much," was my reply, "it is not for sale."

Next morning, a newspaper man who had overheard our conversation bewailed in print the fact that poor Bizet died in poverty three months after the production of *Carmen* while I, a far lesser luminary, had been offered a hundred thousand dollars for *The Bride Elect*. I afterwards said to the sympathetic scribe,

"I do not know whether your remarks about *Carmen* were meant as a reflection on my opera or on Mr. Bunnell's judgment in offering me a hundred thousand dollars for it. I think the real reflection is on the French managers who failed to see the beauties of Carmen and to offer Bizet a huge sum for it!"

America is willing to pay for good music. Europe may call us an infant in musical art, but America to-day is the Mecca of every European musician who has anything to offer. Of course some theatrical managers drive close bargains, but there are many who display a gratifying generosity. My experience with Messrs. Klaw and Erlanger was a happy one. When I wrote *The Bride Elect*, the first opera I had ever done for them, a formal contract was drawn up, every provision of which was carried out to the letter. For the same firm, I wrote *The Free Lance* and *Chris and the Wonderful Lamp*. The day after I had played over a new score for them, there would be a ring at the telephone, and either Mr. Erlanger or Mr. Klaw would say, "Well, we're going to produce that opera of yours very soon. How much do you want for it?"

"The usual terms," I would reply, and I am confident that every dollar which should have been mine was given me to the last penny, by Klaw and Erlanger.

We started in 1897 under the management of Everett R. Reynolds, who had been the manager of the Long Island Railroad and the Manhattan Beach Hotel all the years I played at the Beach, and who came with me after Mr. Corbin's death.

When we reached Providence, "Bob" Fitzsimmons, the new world's champion, announced himself at the box-office.

"I'm Bob Fitzsimmons, champion of the world. I want a box to see this show."

"I'm awfully sorry, Mr. Fitzsimmons," said the ticket seller respectfully, "but all the boxes are taken."

"Then give me an orchestra seat."

"I regret to say that I haven't one left; in fact there is only standing room."

"Then give me a 'standing-room.'"

And Fitzsimmons attended the concert, standing! At its close, he said to my manager,

"Let me see that little fellow that led the band. I just want to shake hands with the man who can draw more people than the Champion of the World. I had a rotten matinee to-day!"

He was ushered to my dressing room and there we chatted of prize-fighting, past and present. We became so interested that the meeting finally adjourned to the Narragansett Hotel where Ed Corliss and Wallace Reeves joined in the conversation. Naturally we talked of the recent encounter between Jim Corbett and Fitzsimmons. Fitz could not forgive Jim the memory of the little playful rubbing of the laces of Jim's glove on his nose, which resembled raw beef for days afterwards. Ed Corliss, who weighed at least two hundred pounds, was much interested and wondered how Corbett had managed to do it. Eager to oblige, Fitz rose, pulled Ed close to him, placed one hand against his mouth (the first finger of his right hand pressing under Ed's nose) and with the other hand pressing against his victim's back, the champion raised him off the ground. Once released from the torture, poor Corliss immediately felt his nose, fearing that it had been torn off! Ed afterwards declared that it was so sore he could not bear to touch it for a month.

Not only did Fitzsimmons and I dine together, but we met after our respective performances, and had supper. Events were at that time leading up to the Spanish War, and nearly every conversation would either begin or end with an allusion to Spain or Cuba. It was not so many days previous to the destruction of the *Maine*.

I had imbibed much knowledge of Spanish history from my father, whose Spanish birth and love of study had made him an able teacher. So I began to recite the salient points of the history of Spain. Fitzsimmons was a most attentive listener. I finally got to the Saracens, and began to expound the glories of El Chico, the last Moorish king, more commonly known as Boabdil, who finally was defeated by Ferdinand of Aragon and forced to leave the land where he and the Saracens had been masters for half a thousand years. I dramatically intoned my story: "Whipped and disgraced, Boabdil, riding towards the mountains, turned to take a last lingering look at Granada, and cried in despair, 'Allahu akhbar!' (God is great!) and then burst into violent and uncontrolled sobs. His mother, standing beside him, said angrily, 'Do not weep like a woman for that which you could not defend like a man!' "

Fitzsimmons had shut his eyes during this recital. I thought he might be dozing. But suddenly he shook his head, looked around and said raptly, "Sousa, tell us again about poor Boabdil and his mother!" Someone started to make a joking remark, but Fitz stopped him sternly with, "Don't you say a word. Let the little fellow talk!"

About this time, Mr. Reynolds and I began to plan a European tour for 1898. We employed Colonel George Frederick Hinton to go over and make the necessary arrangements. Col. Mapleson, the well-known manager, became interested in the tour, but with the breaking-out of the Spanish War, we found it wise to change our plans. Col. Mapleson cabled that there was an anti-American feeling on the Continent, and advised the band not to try Europe for a while. So we made a tour of the States instead, which covered January, February, March and April.

I wrote a show-piece called *Trooping the Colors*, which started with a company of trumpeters proclaiming in a fanfare, *Liberty throughout the world!* Then each nation friendly to the United States was represented by a tableau — *The British Grenadiers* for England, the *Marseillaise* for France, then Cuba, Belgium, and many others, winding up with the entrance of Columbia, singing *The Star Spangled Banner,* with band and chorus. The effect was electrical and the performance proved to be a tremendous success financially.

I sent John Braham, the well-known Boston conductor, ahead to rehearse the chorus. Cuba was represented by a company of Cuban patriots protecting a pretty mestiza girl from the onslaught of the Spanish. Braham telegraphed from Louisville: "Fine chorus, but they refuse to appear if you have colored girl in production. I believe in holding out." John was born in New England; I, however, having been born south of Mason and Dixon's Line, knew that no Southern lady or gentleman would ever agree with his radical ideas, however well-disposed they might be toward the African race. I telegraphed back, "Request the prettiest girl in the chorus to make up for the colored girl, but be sure you get the prettiest one." When we gave our performance in Louisville, feminine Cuba was represented by a dazzling beauty, skillfully powdered to an Indian copper!

I had made no arrangements to spend my usual season at Manhattan Beach that summer, since I had expected to go to Europe, so I leased a farm up in Suffern, N. Y., and there wrote the lyrics and music of *The Charlatan*. It was produced in Montreal on August 29, 1898, by the DeWolf Hopper company. It did not make the prodigious hit that *El Capitan* had, but musically it was considered superior.

The Montreal opening accomplished, we then presented the piece to critical New York at the Knickerbocker Theater on September 5th. It was a night straight out of the Inferno, for suffocating heat! Why anyone chose to go to the theatre that night is a mystery. Of course it was a severe test for any new piece. The favorable reception accorded the piece in Montreal was lacking. Curiously enough, the comments of the critics ranged from ordinary praise to loud acclaim. Alan Dale, one of the best known of New York's critics wrote:

> *The Charlatan* is a comic opera of distinct merit and as I have been the howler at Hopper's buffoonery for a good many years, I am going to emphasize the fact that it has evaporated — vanished into atmosphere. You can now look upon DeWolf Hopper as a tall and rather rigid gentleman with a slight swelling to grand opera attitudes, and even a mild hankering for vocal fireworks. That this sort of work seems strange I am bound to confess, but that it is pleasant for a change nobody will deny. Still, the role of "Demidoff" might have been made a trifle funnier without any sacrifice to Hopper's dignity. There is a happy medium between severity and buffoonery which, although it is hard to hit, may in time be found. Under the circumstances, however, it is better to err on the side of severity, because this comedian can really sing in addition to being able to act.
>
> *The Charlatan* is chiefly interesting for its music, which is full of ginger and entrain. The music began rather simply, with melodies which resemble a *Child's Guide to the Piano*. But it woke up and v'la! biff! before we knew it we were revelling in Sousaism, affable waltzes, two-step affairs that made you yearn to get up and try it lightly — a jolly, rollicking ensemble. Sousa is always interesting. To commonplace people he is "catchy." To those who are not commonplace he has a twist that stamps

him with the luminous brand of originality. In The Charlatan he makes one or two efforts to be merely pretty that are not quite acceptable. Sousa is the comedian of music, and when he tries to be merely pretty he reminds you of Nat Goodwin attempting to be emotional, or Annie Russell starting out to be "strong." He has an individuality of his own, and although for the sake of comic opera he is anxious to be as versatile as possible, he is never quite happy unless he is Sousa.

The delightful finale to the second act and *The Seventh Son of a Seventh Son* song and one or two other musical instances hold you in complete admiration of this peculiar person and you feel that *The Charlatan* had a great many of the charms of *El Capitan* and *The Bride Elect*. I am one of Sousa's wildest admirers. His name alone is sufficient to capture my attention. His work in *The Charlatan* was no disappointment and those who miss hearing these humorous strains can blame themselves for their omission.

Although I wrote all the lyrics of *The Charlatan*, except the *Ammonia* song, I did not allow my name to go on the programme as the author of them, but Alan Dale, thinking it was Charles Klein, said, "Mr. Klein has written some lyrics which are extremely clever."

After *The Charlatan* had made a tour of the States, DeWolf Hopper went to England, and produced there successfully *El Capitan* and *The Charlatan* under the name of *The Mystical Miss*. On his return to America he continued the season with *The Charlatan*. The first reports that came from London were not unanimous in praise of *El Capitan*. I was worried, so I wrote to an English musical friend, in whose judgment I believed, and asked him if the piece really were a success there. He cabled back, "Don't worry. London endorses *El Capitan*." Nevertheless, every now and then, some paper would assert that Hopper was going to replace *El Capitan* with *Wang*, one of his former pieces, but as *El Capitan* and *The Charlatan* were the only two pieces that ran during Hopper's entire English season, evidently there was no necessity for a change, and no proposal to make one.

Some time after the initial performance of *El Capitan*, the Lambs Club invited Klein and myself to a dinner. Although Klein was an interesting raconteur when surrounded by a few friends and sympathetic listeners, it was an utter impossibility for him to "think on his feet." His brain refused to work when he was called upon to make a speech. At this dinner, after I had spoken briefly, the toastmaster called upon Mr. Klein. The poor fellow arose, looked about him helplessly for a moment, said, haltingly, "I am yours truly, John L. Sullivan" and stopped for a full minute. Then, in a voice full of real agony, he asked, "Will someone kindly hit me with a bottle?" and sat down.

Charlie Klein, after the production of *El Capitan*, shot upward to fame and fortune with unexpected rapidity. His *Lion and the Mouse*, *The Auctioneer*, and *The Music Master* enjoyed an immense popularity and brought to the playwright very substantial returns. Suddenly, Klein "got religion." He was an English Jew, but had paid little attention to the ancient Hebrew creed. He blossomed out, now, as an ardent Christian Scientist, and thereafter ascribed all his stage successes to his belief in the teachings of that faith. Dear fellow! At the height of his success God called him home; he sank with the *Lusitania*. Those who knew him loved him very much.

When war was threatening between the United States and Spain, I was touring the States and reached New York on April 10, 1898, for my concert at the Metropolitan Opera House. The war fever was intense, and the *New York Herald* described the unforgettable scene at my concert thus:

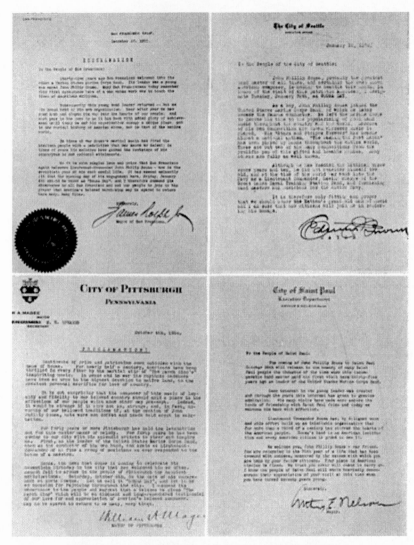

PROCLAMATIONS OF WELCOME FROM
AMERICAN CITIES

There had been some lively scenes in the theatres of late, when *The Star Spangled Banner* was played, but none of them equalled the extraordinary demonstration of last night at the Metropolitan Opera House, when Sousa's Band played the national anthem and then swung into *Dixie*.

During the playing of the former piece the demonstration kept up, and when it came to a conclusion with the final crash of music from the band, the scene beggared description. An encore was demanded, but Sousa stood calmly awaiting quiet before he would go on. Then when he could be heard he said,

"Ladies and Gentlemen: It seems the only appropriate encore I can give in these days is *Johnny, Get your Gun*. But stop! There's another air we all will cheer tonight." The musicians swung into *Dixie*.

If there had been orderly enthusiasm before, there was bedlam let loose now, and while the cheers went up as heartily as ever, there burst from certainly a thousand throats the famous rebel yell. It came from all parts of the house. For quite a time this continued, men and women joining in the uproar, the ladies leaning out of the boxes, and waving their handkerchiefs while the southern air was played.

The audience had hardly quieted when a man in one of the boxes leaped over the rail and yelled, "Who says we're not ready for war?" and the house went wild again, with another combination of Union cheers and Rebel yells. Then someone in the orchestra jumped into the aisle and called for three cheers for "our flag and our country, the north and the south — we're all ready," and the previous scene was repeated.

When *The Stars and Stripes Forever* was sung, there was still another demonstration, and then five thousand tired and hoarse individuals took themselves home.

These scenes were repeated in nearly every town we visited. In Chicago the *Inter-ocean* said:

The spectacular feature described as "Trooping the Colors" is a stunning affair, cleverly arranged in detail, calculated to arouse patriotic fire in the most phlegmatic. First came the trumpeters, "America proclaiming liberty to the world." Then came the invincible Continentals playing *Yankee Doodle*. The national allotment then procedes, *God Save the Queen*, *The Marseillaise*, *The Wearing of the Green*. The Scottish bagpipes playing *The Campbells are Coming*, enter the Auditorium through one of the tunnels, march down the aisle and up to the stage. The Cubans marched to the air *You'll Remember Me*. When the boys in blue and the Marines came marching to the front to salute the flag, the enthusiasm was uproarious. The *Star Spangled Banner* was encored three times. There were 200 young women in the chorus that made a striking background for the brilliant color of the fine costumes. "Trooping of the Colors" is one of the most remarkable displays of its kind ever seen on the local stage.

But with all this enthusiasm, in a very little while the country had virtually shouted itself hoarse. A victory was assured and expected; so when we returned to New York for our final concert, it was a very decorous and strictly music-loving public that greeted us, and not one intoxicated by patriotic fervor.

As I became more widely-known, a number of men began to do imitations of me — some of them clever, and some the rankest kind of burlesque. Walter Jones, a comedian with Rice's musical pieces during their stay at Manhattan Beach, was a constant attendant at my concerts and began giving imitations of me wherever he went with musical comedy. As his fame increased with this merry burlesque of my conducting, a host of others sought to emulate his success. Lafayette and Zimmerman took up the mimicry. On one occasion when Klaw and Erlanger's *Round of Pleasure* company was playing at the Knickerbocker Theatre in New York, they gave a benefit for the *Herald* Ice Fund, and I volunteered to bring my band up from Manhattan Beach to aid in the performance. Walter Jones was once more the comedian. After I had given my programme, and while the audience was still applauding, Mr. Jones walked in from the wings, made up in a perfect disguise of me. With great dignity he extended his hand, and said:

"Ah, Mr. Jones, I wish to congratulate you and your splendid band. I knew there was something in you when I saw the clever way you mimicked me last season in *In Gay New York* and I am glad to see you have gathered such a good band of your own. Go ahead, my dear Jones, go ahead!" And with another hearty handshake, the actor, still imitating my carriage and my walk, bowed himself off and allowed the concert to proceed. It was so well done that for a moment the audience was half-convinced.

Just after our declaration of war against Spain, I applied to General James H. Wilson to join the Sixth Army corps, requesting only that I be allowed to fulfill engagements already made for concerts, after which I would report at the headquarters of the Division at Chickamauga. Unfortunately I was destined never to see a day of service. I sent the General some data concerning the formation, cadences, and duties of army bands, but just as I was about to go to Chickamauga I was taken with typhoid fever, and for sixteen weeks kept my bed. When I was restored to health the war was over. Major-General Wilson, who had been informed by my doctors of my condition, later wrote me the following letter:

HEADQUARTERS

DEPARTMENT OF MATANZAS AND SANTA CLARA

MATANZAS, CUBA

May 19th, 1900

JOHN PHILIP SOUSA, *Esq.*

Paris, France

DEAR SIR:

Inasmuch as you accepted my invitation at the outbreak of the Spanish War to become the Musical Director of the 6th Army Corps, I now take pleasure in handing you the Headquarters Badge, which you are entitled to wear upon all occasions.

My idea, you will remember, in asking you to accept the above-mentioned position, was to utilize your great skill as a composer and director in securing uniformity in the music of the regimental bands, without which regularity of time and step in marching, especially in parades and reviews, is impossible. The necessity for this needs no demonstration to military men.

You will also recall that I recommended you to the War Department and the President for the commission of Captain in order that you might have proper rank and consideration in the performance of your duties, but for some reason not explained and much to my regret, the commission was not issued. It is understood that while this was a disappointment to me at least, if not to yourself, you were prevented by sickness alone from reporting for duty at Camp Thomas, Chickamauga.

Wishing you continued success, I am,

Very respectfully yours,

JAMES H. WILSON, *Major-Gen.*

In 1899 our tour stretched from coast to coast and from the St. Lawrence to the Gulf. While we were playing in Los Angeles I accepted an invitation to breakfast with friends in Pasadena. I am very fond of horseback riding and indulge in it at the slightest provocation. Accordingly I thought it an excellent plan to go to Pasadena, not by stuffy train or lurching trolley, but cross-country, on a saddle-horse.

Returning to Los Angeles, after my pleasant visit, and jogging along at a very slow trot, I turned into the main street, with a trolley car just behind me, containing a brass band. Suddenly the band struck up a tune and startled my horse. Instead of dashing away from the burst of sound, the animal shied backward, and the car struck him with sufficient force to make him plunge and rear and become well-nigh unmanageable. His antics were decidedly dangerous in that street of crowded vehicles. My glasses were knocked off in the struggle (sadly upsetting my dignity, which I cherish!) and I found myself clinging to his neck in great alarm. I called to a Chinaman standing near, "Catch the bridle! Catch the bridle!" With a face like a graven image, he stared at me, and said slowly,

"Me not do; not my horse."

Since the inception of my Band it had appeared three times on parade — at the dedication of the World's Fair, the departure of the Cleveland city troops for the Spanish War, and the return of the Pittsburgh volunteer regiment from that same war. While I was on the road my manager was approached in New York concerning the use of the band for parade purposes in honor of Admiral Dewey. The manager, without my knowledge, made a figure, and when it was quoted in the New York papers, there was considerable comment among musicians upon the size of it. I read the reports at the Pittsburgh Exposition, thus receiving my first knowledge of the affair, and immediately telegraphed my manager, "Tender my services and band free of charge to the committee. Admiral Dewey is an old friend of mine, and I desire to appear in the parade given in his honor."

I augmented my own band to 150 men and we headed the *Olympia* crew on that eventful September 30. The march began at Grant's Tomb, and we proceeded after the parade was dismissed, with the *Olympia* crew, down to the dock where the sailor lads re-embarked on their ship.

Just as I believed that there was never a venal President of the United States, whatever his predilections in seamy politics, and that the office invariably glorified the man, so, too, it seemed to me, as Admiral Dewey stood at attention under the Washington Arch at the close of the parade in his honor, that he was thinking: "They have made me great. I must be worthy of the tribute they are paying me."

A year later, when I dined with him, I spoke of that occasion and of my impression. He replied, "I felt keenly the honor that my country had bestowed upon me. I was awed and uplifted, and the event is one which will never lose its vividness. The proud thought that my people loved me because I had served them faithfully was a source of great pleasure to me."

It is a curious coincidence that when Dewey's squadron sailed up Mirs Bay to attack Manila, the *Olympia* band played *El Capitan*, and the march we played in passing the reviewing stand on his day of triumph was again *El Capitan*.

After the Dewey parade I finished my engagements and then went to Boston to give concerts at the Food Fair, where I gave the first public performance of *The Fairest of the Fair*, I was followed on the programme by Lieutenant Dan Godfrey, the famous conductor of the British Grenadiers Band. His advance man, who had intently watched my methods of concert procedure, and my habit of responding instantly to hearty applause, with an encore, conveyed to Lieutenant Dan the importance of a similar response on his part if he expected success. Godfrey listened and said, "What do they like for an encore?"

"Oh, one of Sousa's marches will knock 'em silly," the press agent replied.

"All right," said the Lieutenant, and turning to his men, when the performance was about to begin, he said, "Remember: immediately, immediately — now don't forget, *immediately* after the overture we will perform Mr. Sousa's march, *The Stars and Stripes Forever*; see that you are ready *immediately* to go into it."

At the end of the overture there was a round of applause. Godfrey bowed and sat down. Then rose and bowed again. The agent whispered to him, "Play the Sousa march." Lieutenant Dan got up slowly, asked each man if he had his part handy, and after rapping for attention twice, played the march. The audience had ceased applauding some time before, and "immediately" was fifteen minutes after the close of the overture!

Miss Hannah Harris, the manager of the then famous Star Course at the Philadelphia Academy of Music is the one who suggested the symphonic poem, *The Chariot Race*. After I had appeared with the Marine Band in Philadelphia, Miss Harris engaged me for a concert at the Academy. She wrote me the following:

> Now I know how easily and how charmingly you adapt any fancy to music, and will you think of this suggestion? It is that you prepare a piece of music and call it *The Chariot Race from Ben Hur*. No doubt you are familiar with the spirited description, and if you are not, a single reading will give you the inspiration, I am sure. You would have the preparation for the race, the start, the progress, with the applause, etc. of the vast audience. The unfair advantages of Messala, the blow to the steeds of Ben Hur, and after all this, the victory of Ben Hur, the Jew. There is opportunity for a grand climax, and anything with the name of Ben Hur draws.

At these Academy concerts, where *The Chariot Race* was generously applauded, I appreciated as never before how widespread was public familiarity with my marches. No composition of mine figured in the programme. Instead, there was a list comprising gems from Wagner and other standard composers. During the first half of the concert, regular numbers and encores were of the "classic" kind. During the applause that followed the first piece in the second half of the concert, an old gentleman rose from his seat in the audience, and holding up his arm, said, "Will Mr. Sousa play *The High School Cadets*?" The request was music to my ears.

As 1899 was drawing to a close the editors of the *New York World* asked me for an article on "Musicians of the Nineteenth Century." They had enlisted the pens of Cardinal Gibbons, Edward Everett Hale, Susan B. Anthony, Julia Ward Howe, and a number of others to write about their respective fields of endeavor. The article follows:

> To one standing on the threshold of the century now drawing to a close a cursory glance over the political field of the world must have clearly shown that old ideas and institutions were being swept away and the world was starting in with a grand sweep for newer and better conditions. As music is the most potent of all the arts to move and excite the emotions, it was natural that the revolution in the body politic should have been accentuated in the sphere of musical art. Nations just emerging from revolutions, from tyranny, from oppression and national degradation, looking into the sunlight of liberty and freedom, could find no better means of expressing their thoughts than in the heroic measures and loud acclaim of musical sounds.
>
> Perhaps the first of the writers of this century to impress his genius and to leave the imprint of his talent in the world

of popular music was Rossini. When it is realized that he was born in 1792 and that one of the most popular, if not the most popular, pieces of music in the world to-day is his *William Tell* overture, it speaks volumes for the brilliant opening of this century.

To-day the master minds of music have their own types; express their feeling both as nationalists and individuals, and impart to their compositions the typical characteristics of their nations, whereas before this century even men as great as Händel, Gluck and Mozart wrote in the style belonging to a nation the antipodes of their own. While all these masters, especially Mozart, made reforms or changes in operatic treatment, either the musical tyranny of the people would not permit them to depart so radically from the fashionable forms of their art as did their great successors, Weber and Wagner, or else they were unable to gain such a clear insight into the possibilities of the lyric dramas as those later masters of the art. The achievements of Beethoven's life, were made during the present century.

Of the great figures of the century in opera, I should name Wagner first, Verdi second, Meyerbeer third, Weber fourth, Rossini fifth, and then in places of honor among composers, Auber, Donizetti, Bellini, Herold and Flotow. The latter, while charged with being an imitator of other national schools, has written two works that still hold the stage of the world — *Martha* and *Stradella*. The century has developed a Schubert, a Schumann, a Mendelssohn, a Wagner, a Verdi, a Liszt, a Tchaikowsky, a Rubenstein, a Berlioz, a Chopin, a Brahms, a Gounod, a Massenet, a Saint-Saens, and a countless array of wonderful instrumental performers.

During this time four of my operas were on the boards: *El Capitan*, *The Bride Elect*, *The Charlatan*, and *Chris and the*

Wonderful Lamp. Besides these I was also represented by my band which was touring the country. At the close of the season Mrs. Sousa and I went South and then on to Mexico where we spent many weeks. I was serenaded by the famous orchestra of Carlos Curti and had many another novel experience — even witnessed a bull fight, my first and last, for as I told the editor of the *Mexican Herald* in an interview on the subject, it is, to me, a worthless and unfair sport.

Chapter X

NINETEEN hundred was a busy year for the band. After making a tour which ended April 22, we sailed on the 25th for Europe, our first tour outside the United States and Canada. There was considerable discussion as to the reception we would get in Europe. I remember meeting John L. Sullivan at Madison Square Garden two days before the sailing. He came up to me and said, "How do you do, Mr. Sousa? I hear you are going to Europe."

"Yes, we're going over and we hope to please them."

"Please them!" he exclaimed warmly. "Why, you'll knock hell out of 'em!"

Despite such kind assurances I left with a heavy heart, for only three days before sailing, Mr. Reynolds, manager of the band, withdrew both his services and his financial support. He refused to continue because I would not sign an agreement extending his contract, until after I returned from Europe. His contract still had a year to run, and I saw no reason why I should sign one with him just then. I told him that we were going into new territory, and if his management proved successful I should be very foolish indeed to refuse to sign a new contract with him; if it were unsuccessful, he knew me well enough to feel assured that

I would give him an opportunity to recover his losses with an American tour. But Reynolds was not satisfied and so we parted. I immediately paid him off, obtained two letters of credit, and sailed on the *St. Louis*.

The band's publicity agent, Colonel George Frederick Hinton, was then in Europe; we met him at Southampton and I appointed him manager of the tour. Our first engagement was in Paris. Mr. Ferdinand Peck, United States Commissioner-General, had chosen my band as the official American Band at the Exposition, and we gave our initial concert on May 6 in the Esplanade des Invalides. Among the very friendly and heart-warming comments from the press of that date I have this:

The distance between Washington and Paris seemed very short yesterday as I sat in the beautiful Esplanade des Invalides, and saw the familiar figure of John Philip Sousa leading his superb band with his own peculiar force and swing, while the stirring strains of *The Washington Post*, *King Cotton*, and *The Stars and Stripes Forever* filled the air. Around the kiosk in which the musicians sat, clustered thousands of people. Every number played by the band evoked great applause, nor were the listeners satisfied with less than a double encore for each. The climax of enthusiasm was reached when the heart-lifting melody of *The Stars and Stripes Forever* was given with the dash and precision of which the famous organization is capable.

The last note was the signal for a tremendous outburst of cheering, in which I saw persons of many nationalities join. A turbaned Arab sitting close to the kiosk gravely nodded his head in appreciation and loudly clapped his hands, while two Chinamen in flapping robes excitedly waved their umbrellas.

After the last number there was a wild rush for the kiosk by many of the audience, among them American ladies, who wished to shake hands with the popular composer. It was really an impromptu reception and the remarks of one expressed the sentiments of all. A stately middle-aged woman who was accompanied by two beautiful girls, apparently her daughters, grasped Sousa's hand and exclaimed, "I cannot tell you how proud we are of you and your band. I am from California." Another old gentleman came up, shook Mr. Sousa's hand, tears streaming down his cheeks, and said, "I'm Colonel Glenn of Galesburg, Illinois, and just think, you've played in my town, too!"

To say that Sousa was gratified with his reception in Paris would be to put his feelings in very inexpressive words. Indeed, he is enthusiastic over the way he and his men have been received. "Paris has given us a royal welcome," he said, "and I can hardly express myself in fit terms. A very delightful compliment was paid me by a famous musician from Vienna: 'You have not a band, but a living organ under your direction.' "

I had not been in Paris a day when I received a call from M. Gabriel Pares, the conductor of the Garde Republicaine Band, probably the greatest band in Europe. He graciously gave me a card to the Army and Navy Club, and invited me to lunch with him and a group of his friends on the following day. I gladly accepted. Hardly had the courteous M. Pares left the hotel when the card of an interviewer was brought up to me. I consented to see him and we were talking music and bands, in a pleasant impersonal fashion, when suddenly he asked, "How do you compare your band with the Garde Republicaine?"

Of course that was a thoroughly yellow journal question and one which no gentleman, a guest of France, would think of answering.

"Oh," I exclaimed, "we have the greatest possible admiration for the Garde Republicaine. When they came to America as the

Photo by J. C. Milligan

MR. SOUSA AND JACKIE COOGAN, 1922

representative band of France, for the Gilmore Jubilee in Boston, everybody was charmed with the perfection of their playing."

"But you have given me no information as to a comparison between your band and the Garde."

"No, I have not; but you may rest assured that no foreign organization was ever more welcome in America than the Garde Republicaine and its brilliant conductor, M. Gabriel Pares."

We talked a few minutes longer, and then the reporter withdrew.

Next morning his paper carried the following: "Mr. Sousa was asked how his band compared to the Garde Republicaine. He threw his arms upward, pointing to the French sky, and said, 'We are far superior to the Garde Republicaine!' "

At luncheon Pares was quiet and wore an injured expression. I could see plainly that he had read the article and his pride was hurt. So I said to a French gentleman at my side who spoke excellent English: "Please say to M. Pares that the article in the paper, which he must have read this morning, was a pure fabrication and a gross example of impertinent yellow-journalism!" I do not think, however, that he entirely recovered from the effect of the article, false though it was.

During our first engagement in Paris we played at the dedication of the American Pavilion and gave a concert in the famous Trocadero Concert Hall by invitation of the French Government.

On May 15 we were assigned to proceed to the American Machinery Building in the Vincennes Annex of the Exposition for another dedication. The American Ambassador, General Porter, chartered two Seine River ferryboats, known as "hirondelles" in Paris, and had them lashed together. On one were the officials and guests, on the other my band. A young society tad, with a great desire to become internationally famous, earnestly requested that I permit him to conduct the band in one of my marches.

Leading a band in a rhythmic piece like a march, waltz, polka, or a piece of jazz requires interpretation, and not time-beating, provided the men know how to keep together, for good orchestral and band players can mentally play a thing so strongly marked as a march or waltz without the aid of a baton. Grinding out music does not require much direction; interpreting does require intelligent and ceaseless effort.

I laughed and said, "All right, go ahead. But since we are rather cramped, suppose you take my baton and go over on the other boat and conduct the band from there." He climbed over the railings of the two boats, rapped for attention, and then, just as he started to conduct, some rascal cast off the rope which held the boats together. Of course they rapidly drifted apart while he frantically beat time sixty feet away from the band!

On that same day we serenaded the German Commission in the German Building, which they were dedicating. Quite naturally I played the favorite German patriotic song, *Die Wacht Am Rhein*. The Germans were terribly nervous about it; one of their officials even whispered to me to stop, but I continued the piece to the end. It was the first time the tune had been played in Paris since the Franco-Prussian war, but neither the French officials nor the populace seemed to mind it a bit. I had not wanted to resort to the Prussian national anthem, *Heil Dir im Siegerkrantz,* because the music is the same as the English *God Save the King*. But how the talk did buzz in German circles for days afterwards!

On May 20, Harry Thaw of Pittsburgh, who was destined to startle New York afterwards with the shooting of Stanford White, gave a party at the Ritz hotel which made even gay Paris sit up and rub its eyes. Mr. Thaw engaged my band to give one hour's concert, for which he agreed to pay fifteen hundred dollars. A large Hungarian orchestra was to play dance music. The guests numbered twenty-five. Someone of a mathematical turn of mind did a bit of addition and announced that the party cost eight thousand dollars, and set the facts down thus:

Number of guests	25
Sousa's Band	$1500
Price of entertainment	$8000
Cost per guest	$320

Thaw asked for none of the old masters, but he expressed a fondness for Wagner and Liszt and we played *Tannhäuser*, *The Second Rhapsody*, and a *Carmen* fantasie, together with some of my marches. He was a most attentive and enthusiastic listener and was loud in his praise of all but one number, that from *Carmen*. Designating a movement by singing a few measures of it, he demanded, "Don't you take that number a bit too slow?"

"I don't think so," I replied; "it is marked 'molto moderato.' "

"Well, I have heard Calvé sing it, and she sang it much faster than that."

"Ladies first," I amended; "the next time I play it for you I will adopt the lady's tempo!"

Since I had no evening performances, we went about Paris and heard nine important concerts by symphony orchestras, and the best of the French bands. Much to my surprise I found that in these nine programs, averaging seven or eight numbers each, there was just one piece which was not French. I concluded that the conductors were under the domination of publishing houses, or some narrow control that made them play only French music, though I failed to understand how any conductor who loved his art would consent to confine his programmes to the literature of one country, instead of making them eclectic. I felt so keenly on the matter that I wrote an article and used as my argument the idea that subsidy is the death of Art. It follows, in part:

NO STATE AID FOR ART

SAYS MR. JOHN PHILIP SOUSA

OPPOSED TO THE IDEA OF NATIONAL THEATRES, NATIONAL BANDS, AND SIMILAR SUBSIDIZED ORGANIZATIONS

DISCOURAGES ORIGINAL WORK

IMPRESSIONS OF MILITARY BANDS IN FRANCE AND GERMANY

THROUGH AMERICAN SPECTACLES

PLAY FEW FOREIGN WORKS

DOES NOT APPROVE OF THE USE OF STRINGED INSTRUMENTS IN A MILITARY BAND, EXCEPTING THE HARP

Although at a certain period of my life, I rather favored the idea of "national theatres," "national orchestras," "national bands" and "national conservatories," I have been converted completely by a comparison of the superior results produced by individual effort with those due to a governmentally-subsidized art.

I think French military bands are wonderfully good — considering the care the State devotes to them. An artistic organization that is fostered by State aid is like a hardy plant brought up in a hot-house. It may keep on living, and that's all you can say about it, for it will always be sickly.

The reputation of a band that is not based exclusively on public favor resembles the reputation for military genius earned by some generals in time of peace, which melts like snow in July in the first weeks of actual warfare.

If a musician, a writer, or a painter, has anything in him, he will dig it out of himself, if the State will only let him starve long enough.

When a bandmaster has nothing to pay his bandsmen with, save what the public thinks he deserves, he must do good work or go to the wall. But if he has the Government behind him, it is merely in human nature that he will quote the famous saying, "The public be damned!"

It is an old saying that love and art have no frontiers. There seems, however, to be a predilection for French music in French bandmasters. Other things being equal, they appear to prefer music by a native composer to music by a foreigner. I could understand this were they arranging programmes to be played outside their own country, when a desire to show the wealth of their nation from a musical point of view might justifiably warrant them in giving the preference to works written by their fellow-countrymen. But, it seems to me, a wider range of selection might easily be permitted for concerts in Paris, where Saint-Saens, Messenet, Gillet, Ganne are likely to run no danger of being eclipsed in popular affection were Wagner, Goldmark, Puccini or other foreign composers drawn upon a little more generously.

BAND PROGRAMMES IN PARIS

I have the programmes of military band concerts given in the Luxembourg, the Palais Royal and other places. At the Luxembourg, Massenet contributes two numbers out of five, Delahaye one, Saintis one, and Weber is represented by a selection from his *Freischutz*. At the Palais Royal there is not a foreign work on the programme. Yet there must be some number in international musical literature that might have been dropped into the concert, if only to flavor it with the spice of exoticism, as it were.

This, again, I attribute to the evil influence of Governmental support, which always creates a tendency to work in a groove, to stop in a rut. As it does not matter financially whether the public is pleased or indifferent, why should the bandmaster waste the gray matter of his brain in building programmes that will arouse interest, why should he grow old in going through veritable public libraries of musical works in the hope — alas! Too seldom rewarded — of finding some new or unknown gem with which to feed the unlimited repertory that a concert organization such as my own is compelled to possess?

I am convinced that military bands in France could be made something really marvellous. The evident artistic taste of the nation is displayed in the high average standard of excellence attained by executants who are not professional musicians, and who are in the military bands merely because they are doing their military service. The precision of their playing is soldier-like, if not particularly telling, for elasticity of "tempo" is the life of a musical composition.

It must also be admitted that military bands, both in Germany and France, are not perfectly adapted to the purposes for which they are used. In Germany their instrumental composition is admirable for military work, — that is, for parades, marches, and other purely professional duties of a regimental band. They are, thus, badly equipped for concert playing as the nice shades of tone-color are absolutely beyond their capabilities.

In France, on the other hand, greater care is devoted to the composition of military bands for concert use, which naturally destroys to a certain extent their effectiveness for military work, owing to their delicate instrumentation. In addition, the French bands are not shown at their best, even when heard in concert, as they so frequently play in the open air without a sounding-board to reinforce and concentrate the sound, and thus many of the nuances that would be wonderfully effective under proper acoustic conditions are lost.

AN ARTISTIC ATMOSPHERE

I have been impressed by the artistic atmosphere of France and Germany. Not only are the musicians brilliantly gifted, but the audiences are also very critical, discriminating and intelligent. At the same time, Governmental aid is a drawback rather than an assistance, as, although it may facilitate in the routine of artistic production, it is an impediment to the development of true artistic genius. If you look over the field of musicians, conductors and composers, you cannot fail to be struck with the fact that those who are most famous, most popular with the people, and whose reputation has passed the frontiers of their respective countries are precisely those who have been left untrammelled by Governmental or official bonds, and who have been compelled to put forward the best that was in them by the beneficent law of the survival of the fittest, which has forced them to be ever upon the alert to conquer competition.

I am convinced that many of the occupants of official positions in France and Germany would discover original genius of a high order in themselves were they to be left entirely to their own resources, while some who are first in the race might be limping in the rear. For the Juggernaut of public opinion and support soon crushes out the life of him who has nothing but Governmental influence to justify his occupancy of a given position in the artistic world.

I have heard during my visit here several of the military bands. As I said before, I have been impressed by the excellent artistic results obtained as a general rule, a detail that proves the genuine musical nature of the people. The Garde Republicaine band, for instance, is admirable, and others would be better under more favorable conditions.

So far as specific criticism is concerned, I do not care for the use of a string contra-bass in a military band. If a string-bass, why not a 'cello? And once granted the 'cello, why not the viola and divided violins? In fact, why not become a symphony orchestra at once? There is no room in a military band for stringed instruments, except the harp which has no simulating voice. The bass tuba does all and more than a contra-bass can do, is richer, gives fuller and sounder harmonic basis for the volume of tone, and can be played on the march — which a contra-bass cannot!

MIGHT BE IMPROVED

I think too, that French military bands would be improved if the alto-horn and valve-trombone were abandoned. They are only concessions to the laziness of instrumentalists, and are a poor substitute for the warm, effective and beautiful tone of the French horn and trombone.

Another thing; I fancy musicians still entertain a vague idea that a military band is inferior to the symphony orchestra; inferior it is not. It is simply different. There is no hierarchy in art. The artistic effect produced is the sole criterion of value. A simple folk-song may be a greater living musical truth than a symphony that calls for the united resources of all the musical instruments to perform. The melody that touches the heart of both the trained musician and the uneducated public is a musical thought that has been lying dormant in the hearts and minds of the people, and to which the composer has given expression at last. The form in which that thought is presented is of no importance. Yet composers will write for the symphony orchestra willingly, and for the military band with a certain sense of doing humbler work.

This feeling is absurd, and is rather a proof of ignorance or indolence upon the part of the writers than anything else, for it shows either that they have not realized all the resources of the wood and brass wind, or that they do not care to take the immense trouble necessitated in trying to reproduce the musical effect of some well-known orchestral work with the military band.

It is curious that this prejudice does not exist with regard to the orchestra. I attended one of Colonne's concerts to-day, and the second number on the programme was a transcription of Chopin's *Funeral March*, an orchestration of a piano composition. I may add that it was well-played and admirably conducted. The wood and brass wind are irreproachable, and the strings have an excellent quality of tone. In fact, I enjoyed the concert immensely. But if an orchestra may play transcriptions of piano works, why should not a military band play transcriptions of works for orchestras?

It may be this feeling that causes French bandmasters to limit themselves to overtures and operatic selections with little "genre" pieces instead of roaming over the entire world of music.

And, I repeat, they probably would if the State left them entirely to their own resources. There is nothing that develops individual initiative so much as the necessity of scoring a success. Literature in France has been left without a "Prix de Rome" yet it is flourishing, and will be so until it is given an annuity, when, like music and painting, it will become very conservative and tradition-loving. For there is nothing that encourages conservatism more than a position under the Government...."

Almost immediately my article was attacked by a man who signed himself "Musician" and claimed to be an American. I took his letter and incorporated it in my answer under the head of Exhibits.

UNMUSICAL WAR BETWEEN MUSICIANS
MR. JOHN PHILIP SOUSA REPLIES TO CRITICISM MADE
UPON HIS INTERVIEW
ARGUMENTS MISUNDERSTOOD
NO ATTEMPT TO INSTRUCT, BUT CRITICISM OF THE
SUBSIDIZING OF MUSICAL ART

To the EDITOR OF THE HERALD:

In the halcyon days, when I trudged the mountain paths of the wild and woolly West in quest of deer, or popped over the toothsome quail in the stubble below, it was my wont to sit around the campfire at night and listen to words of wisdom from the cowboys and mountaineers, my companions in the chase. At these nocturnal debates regarding religion, politics, war or art, it was generally conceded that when a fellow departed from the subject matter on tap he was indulging in conversation through the medium of his chapeau. And speaking of "talk and headgear" I cannot forbear pointing out the application of this truth to the letter published in the *Herald* of July 20 and signed "Musician," which has sadly shocked, not to say mournfully mystified me.

The writer takes pains to claim that he is an American, but I am a little skeptical on that point, for in his letter of half a column he reiterates the statement of his nativity (methinks he doth protest too much), a thing most unusual with the genuine "blown in the bottle" native of our country. The usual way, you may have observed, is to announce that fact to the world once, and it is known forever after. (*Vide* Washington at Yorktown, Jackson at New Orleans, Taylor in Mexico, Dewey in Manila, etc.)

I would like to inform "Musician," before taking up his letter *seriatim*, that vituperation is not argument and glittering generalities are not conclusive. "Musician" pays no attention to the points advanced by me in the recent interview in your columns relative to French bands, their masters, and their music, but in a soggy sort of way endeavors to show foreign superiority over all things American in music.

To quote "Musician":

EXHIBIT A

"It is very kind of Mr. Sousa to come over from America in order to instruct Americans and others in Europe about military bands, but are we quite as ignorant as we seem? In carrying his coals to Newcastle, would it not perhaps be more becoming to put ourselves in the rear instead of in the front of European military bands?"

In my interview there was no effort at instruction but only criticism of what appears to me to be the deplorable condition of musical art when under the patronage of the State. I maintain that the individual initiative is lost or weakened through Governmental subsidy, and "Musician" does not attempt to refute that argument, but tells what he thinks was my reason for coming to Europe. Bless his confiding nature, he is "way off." My purpose in coming to Europe was twofold. Firstly, I felt reasonably certain that an organization which for years had won the plaudits of the American public would have an excellent chance of duplicating that success here; and, secondly, I believed I could pick up a good collection of the Continental coins of the realms. In both surmises I was correct, for I have won both plaudits and shekels!

EXHIBIT B

"Does Mr. Sousa perhaps remember that when the citizens of Boston raised a large sum and lost $200,000 in importing all the best bands in Europe, the French band took the palm and Gilmore's Band wasn't in it?

"The German band also was marvellous. Does Mr. Sousa not know that there are no wood instruments in the world like the French? And such a flutist as Taffanel (now leader of the concerts at the Conservatoire) has never yet been heard in America?"

No, Mr. Sousa does not remember, nor does anyone else, for "Musician's" statement is but the "baseless fabrication of a dream." Possibly the absent-minded gentleman has heard somewhere during his sojourn in Europe that there was given nearly thirty years ago, in Boston, a "Peace Jubilee" under the direction of Pat Gilmore, and among the many attractions taking part were three foreign bands — English, French, and German. There was no band competition or contest at the Boston Jubilee, and each and every organization had its admirers for the excellent work performed. Certainly, I never heard of any Frenchman, German or Englishman who was in Boston at that time decrying the merits of the band of his own country, or calling attention to the fact that American musicians were the best on earth, or even asserting that Billy McGoogan of Bitter Creek was the finest bass drummer in four counties, and is now of the Boston Conservatory, which forever deprives Europe of the opportunity of hearing such a great artist. In passing, it is not inapropos to remark that Europe gave us the tallow candle, but like grateful children we sent in return the electric light; Europe gave us the primitive hand-power printing press of Gutenberg, and in our simple-hearted way we showed her the Goss perfecting press; Europe placed the goose-quill in our hands and we have added the typewriter to her resources; Europe put the bare needle in our fingers and we reciprocate with the modern sewing-machine. But why enumerate?

EXHIBIT C

"The literature of music for military bands is as limited as the music for male chorus. Composers who have written for male chorus have done so in their off moments — because the limit of about an octave and a half is too small. Only with the addition of female voices can a good chorus be secured. It is the same with military music. Stirring and inspiring as it is played at the head of a regiment, especially returning from a war, or at dress parade, it falls flat when a military band endeavors to interpret music for which strings are as necessary as female voices in a chorus."

What under the sun a male quartet or its literature has to do with a brass band is beyond me, although "Musician," with characteristic inaccuracy, is in error as to the compass of the male voice, for in God's country we have baritones and tenors who can sing two octaves or more. Of course, a chorus is better for the addition of the ladies, God bless 'em — and the more there are around, the better.

EXHIBIT D

"Colonne's orchestra can transcribe and play music with effect, which Mr. Sousa's band cannot transcribe and cannot play with effect — at least not to a musical ear."

As I am ignorant of the nicety of "Musician's" musical ear, I am unable properly to contest the point that military music falls flat on that part of his anatomy, but if it is as generally inaccurate as his statement he must be suffering from chronic auricular astigmatism.

EXHIBIT E

"As an American, I have not the faintest desire to detract from Mr. Sousa's efforts to come over here and impress Americans and others with his band, and no doubt it will give him a great réclame on the other side, and add to his laurels when he returns."

Here "Musician" again reiterates his claim to American citizenship, but the word "réclame" makes the statement sound fishy, for real Americans say "advertising!" I have travelled from the Straits of Northumberland to the Rio Grande, from the Atlantic to the Pacific, but I have never heard an American speak of "réclame.

EXHIBIT F

"I should have remained silent if Mr. Sousa had not told us in your columns what, to my mind, had better been left unsaid, and if his avowed purpose in coming over here had been to learn rather than to teach.

"I am only prejudiced in his favor and not against him, and I admire his energy, but when it comes to questions of art, I must protest against our assuming an attitude which to some minds may make us appear ridiculous."

For the life of me, I cannot tell under what banner the gentleman is living! My opinions were not addressed to Americans, but on the contrary, to the wide, wide world!

If anything I have said will make the gentleman appear ridiculous, I humbly crave his pardon, but I rather suspect he was an accessory before the fact. This self-constituted champion of French music and musicians reckons without his host, for many French artists coincide with the views expressed in my interview.

Far be it from me to belittle the great achievements of Frenchmen in music's realms. Many of them escape the Government appropriation and win international fame. Their number would be increased were there no subsidies from the State, and therefore greater chance for genius to soar. A people who have produced a Berlioz, a Saint-Saens, a Massenet, a Bizet, an Auber, and a constellation of musical brilliants, have not lived in vain. But these geniuses, being

untrammelled by governmental aid and official consider-
ations, went forth into God's sunlight of freedom and gave to
the world their best efforts.

To sum up: My sin, if it be a sin, in the eyes of "Musician,"
was in criticising the system that I believe detrimental to
the best interest of art! My sin, if it be a sin, lies in my not
accepting everything in Europe, including the people, customs
and arts, as superior to what we have at home. Gentle stranger,
do not decry the McCormick reaper because they use a sickle
in the grain fields of Europe; do not decry the Morse telegraph
because the donkey post still obtains in some places in the Old
World; do not decry the Washington monument because the
Luxor obelisk happens to be in the Place de la Concorde; do
not decry a Hudson River steamer because it would not have
room to turn in the Seine! Be big-hearted; be without prejudice; see good in all things, even if they are American, and let
us get together in friendship and amity, and be fair, even to
Americans. And then

The night shall be filled with music,

And the cares that infest the day

Will fold their tents, like the Arabs

And as silently steal away.

The letter was copied and was the subject of editorials in
many papers.

We were kept reasonably busy in Paris with our daily
concerts and on the Fourth of July we played at the dedication
of the Washington and Lafayette statues where we also serenaded General Porter, then paraded with the American Guards
through the Rue de Rivoli; in the afternoon we gave our concert
at the Exposition and at night a three hours' concert in the Place

de l'Opera, engaged by the California Commission. That was a holiday's work. On that occasion Mr. George W. Ochs presented me with a magnificent American flag on behalf of the Americans in Paris. The crowd at the concert that night was so great that it was almost impossible to move.

Chapter XI

AFTER Paris we went to Brussels and Liege and our receipts and criticisms were both very satisfactory. The *Gaulois* said, "The sonority of this remarkable phalanx is very agreeable, and the equilibrium between the various instruments is perfect."

La Gazette said, "America, which exports so many things, has now exported a band conducted by Mr. John Philip Sousa, a band very much above the ordinary. A single concert such as they gave here would suffice to place it above rivalry. The instrumentalists considered individually are persons who have nothing more to learn."

Le Mers said, "Sousa's Band gave its first concert at the Alhambra on Wednesday. Great power, a superb ensemble, with exquisite shadings. I have never heard pieces played with so much correctness, neatness and cohesion."

We went on from Liege to Berlin by special train, which was a nine days' wonder to the people who had never heard of a mere troupe of musicians travelling special all the way from Liege to Berlin. It was almost too much for their credulity. It was a bold stroke on the part of the management. Its publicity made every man, woman and child appreciate the fact that we would be in Berlin on the eighth.

At that concert we were honored by the presence of Mr. Andrew D. White, the Ambassador, and Mrs. White; Mr. John B. Jackson, Secretary of the Embassy, and Mrs. Jackson; U. S. Consul-General Mason and Mrs. Mason, and thousands of Germans, Americans, and men and women of other nationalities.

The *Morning Post* wrote: "Sousa is the Johann Strauss of the New World. When in his elegant non-chalance he indicates the beats of the kettledrum or at a pianissimo his white-gloved hand moves only to rise again to a veritable thunderstorm, he seizes his audience and carries it with him. Hit after hit followed each other. While the programme called for only nine numbers, Mr. Sousa was compelled to play thirty. He may well be satisfied with his success."

Occasionally, in our travels through Germany, we met critics who said things that were funny, rather than truthful, in order to satisfy their readers' appetite for the satirical, but, viewing German criticism in general, the treatment of the band as an artistic organization was entirely satisfactory.

While we were in Berlin, Count Hochberg, the intendant at the Royal Opera House, interviewed me about a command performance for the Kaiser at the Schloss. My experience in Washington had taught me that it was not considered good manners to inform the public that "the President is coming." It was however, both good business and good manners to spread the news afterwards! So, assured that the Kaiser would wish the same form observed, I resolved that, so far as I was concerned, no one except Count Hochberg, my manager and myself should know that we were to play the following Friday for the Emperor.

On Thursday morning a notice appeared in one of the Berlin papers saying that I had received a royal command to play for the Emperor. Before I was out of bed, a reporter called and asked to see me on an important matter. I told him to come up to my room and there he displayed the article underscored with blue pencil and asked me what I knew about it. I said that I knew absolutely nothing about that article and that it must have appeared by mistake, which was of course begging the question, but which also seemed necessary.

When we reached the Royal Opera House for rehearsal, Count Hochberg courteously informed me that, to his exceeding regret, the Kaiser had been called out of town and there would be no concert. I believe that the advertising fever had taken possession of the German theatre-manager, and he had noised abroad the news of the Kaiser's command, in the hope of filling his house to overflowing for that night; I also believe that the Kaiser considered it a breach of good manners, and so called it off.

The Washington Post was probably the most popular piece of music in the world at that time. It had re-popularized the two-step in America, a dance which, I was told by a famous dancing-master, had languished for years until *The Washington Post* proved a reviving influence. As I have previously remarked, in England and Germany they not only called the dance a "Washington Post," but European composers writing compositions for the dance called their numbers, "Washington Posts." For instance, Herr Diffendorfer wrote such a composition and gave to it the title: "Vorwaerts—"*A Washington Post.*

Throughout Germany I was never allowed to forget that march! I usually played it as an encore to the third number on the programme. Every member of the audience expected me to do so, faithfully. If I chanced to deviate from the custom, some gentleman with a gutteral Teutonic voice would shout, "Der Vashingtun Pust! Der Vashingtun Pust!" followed by a unanimous, "Ja! Ja!" and deafening applause. About the sixth number,

ON HIS FAVORITE ARAB, "ALLADIN"

another Teuton would cry out, "Der Vashingtun Pust! Der Vashingtun Pust!" and the scene would repeat itself. On more than one occasion I had to play that march six times.

We left Berlin to tour Germany and the manager of the German Musical Bureau who had previously conducted our affairs was superseded by Mr. Solomon Liebling, a fine musician and court pianist to the King of Saxony. The night we closed in Berlin, Liebling turned to me and said,

"Mr. Sousa, I have noticed that, when tipping waiters and others, you use very little discrimination. If you are pleased with them you tip too liberally, and if you are displeased you

show your displeasure too markedly. I should like the privilege
of doing your tipping for you on your tour. I have toured this
country and know it thoroughly. I will take charge and give you
a faithful account every week of the amount I spend."

I was delighted to be rid of a disagreeable task. Cassel was
the first town we touched, after Berlin. Liebling and I entered a
hotel; I approached the desk and stood there like a poor boy at
a huskin'. Mr. Liebling registered boldly for both of us and then,
looking about at the assembled porters, bellboys, waiters and
other employees of the hotel, observed seriously, "My good men,
look at him!" nodding towards me. "Look at him well. He is so
great that he never carries money. You must look to me for that
part of it. Only see that he gets the best of service. Mind you, the
best of service," and he strode pompously away. Although I knew
some German, no muscle of my face betrayed the fact, and so the
trick worked marvellously. If ever a man received perfect service,
and obsequious attention in a hotel, I did.

When the time came to depart, Mr. Liebling and I went to the
office, and he became paymaster. A line of those who had served
me was waiting with outstretched palms. Liebling searched diligently in his pocketbook for coins of a certain value, and handed
them judiciously to the waiting line. I do not believe that he ever
gave a pfennig more than the coldest custom had established. But,
strangely enough, whatever the prevailing opinion of his parsi-
mony, the waiters, bellboys and chambermaids never showed the
slightest feeling of resentment towards me or sought any redress
for his stinginess. I was an important stranger in the land, and I
had nothing to do with the prosaic matter of tips! I was too great
to carry money!

Of course I wished to show Liebling some appreciation of
this service for me. From the time of the cholera in Hamburg

in the eighties, Liebling had never touched a drop of water, but had substituted Moselle. Six times a week I invited Liebling to dine with me. I would ask the waiter for the wine card. My eye falling on the Moselles, I would ask Liebling if he were fond of Moselle? His answer was always, "I drink no other." Seeing a Moselle at twenty marks, I would ask solicitously, "Do you consider Fleckenburg a fit wine to drink?" "Oh, Mr. Sousa!" he would rapturously exclaim, "That is a very rare wine, drunk only by emperors on state occasions."

"I do not ask you, Mr. Liebling, if this wine is used by emperors on state occasions. I desire only to know if you consider it a fit wine for gentlemen to drink?"

"Oh, Mr. Sousa," here his eyes would grow large and his face assume an expression of utter felicity, "it is a delicious wine."

"You endorse it then?"

"Oh, Mr. Sousa, yes!"

"Very well. Waiter, bring us a bottle of Fleckenburg."

This dialogue was repeated daily, the only change being the name of the wine and the price.

In June, after my tour of Belgium, I received the following message:

"In recognition of the success of the concerts given in Belgium, the Academy of Arts, Science and Literature of Hainault has conferred on you the grand diploma of honor and decorates you with the Cross of Artistic Merit of the first class." I am still proudly wearing that decoration.

As a prelude to a confession I might say that I have always been extremely moderate in smoking and drinking. When I was twelve, my father treated me to a long talk on the subject of tobacco.

"You know," he began, "I am an inveterate smoker; it is seldom I am not smoking either a cigarette or a cigar, and I think you might inherit my love of tobacco. If you refrain from smoking until you are sixteen, you have my full permission to smoke then."

I gave him my hand on it, and I celebrated my sixteenth birthday by smoking my first cigar, and becoming deathly ill from the effects. With a few periods of abstinence, I have smoked steadily ever since. I did not touch any alcoholic drink until I was twenty-one, although wine and beer always had a place on the family table. After I left the Marines, I made a resolution never to smoke until after lunch, and never to drink between meals. I have kept that resolution inviolate. Up to 1898 my only drink was a little wine or beer at lunch and dinner. In that year, on the advice of a humorous physician who maintained that Scotch whiskey contained only *one* poison, while other alcoholic beverages contained many, I dropped wine and beer from my list, and took a well-diluted highball of Scotch whiskey, sometimes for lunch and always for dinner. After the Volstead measure went through, I had to amend my custom for there is so little pre-prohibition Scotch in the cellars of the people who invite me to dine, that I have been compelled to return to pure, cold water.

My confession concerns a stay in the proud and aristocratic city of Hanover, Germany. We were booked to give three concerts in that lordly town, an evening, a matinee, and another evening. The American consul called on me at my hotel, but showed a strange attitude toward the coming of my band. It seems he was doubtful of our success. He had been consul for twelve years and naturally knew many people in Hanover. His acquaintances, on hearing of our concerts, had greeted him with such sarcastic bits as: "Why doesn't America send us a pork butcher? She knows more about pork than music. We don't want to hear any American band." This continual ridicule of American music had worked sadly upon his nerves!

I did my best to reassure him. I told him that we had played in Paris, Berlin, and Brussels, and other sizable villages of the Continent, with complete success, and I saw no reason why we should not be equally well received in Hanover. Despite the consul's gloom, we played to a remarkably enthusiastic audience. There were even more encores than usual, and band and soloists were greeted with every sign of approval. At the end of the concert, the consul approached, radiant with joy. He and I went to his apartment, flushed with triumph, and enjoyed a glass of Rhenish wine. He discussed every piece on the programme, claiming each was better than the preceding one and all of them excellent. Placing his hand on my shoulder, he exulted:

"This is the happiest night of my life. Sousa, we are Americans! Let us celebrate this great American victory. I have a bottle of Kentucky whiskey. We will take it to the café, select a private room, and drink to your success!"

We asked his wife to join in our jubilee, and took the precious whiskey down to a small private room. The happy official mixed two highballs. We drank to each state in the Union. We drank to the President, to the Cabinet, to every man, woman and child in the United States of America and its insular possessions! We refought the Revolution, switched to the War of 1812, awarded a couple of sips to our activities in Mexico in 1846, and then took a long drink to the flag and the war with Spain. Still burning with admiration for my country, I addressed my companion:

"We have whipped everything on this planet; bring on another one!"

His poor wife was fast asleep by this time, and the dawn was beginning to creep through the window. After a final drink, and the lighting of a fresh cigar, I bade him an affectionate goodnight and asked him to make my adieus to his wife when she woke! I went to my room, never more wide awake in my life. Indeed, I felt not the slightest suggestion of sleepiness. I sat on the edge of my bed for ten minutes, thinking deeply, then rang for a waiter. The waiter who had attended us on our triumphant orgy, and who was loaded down with tips (we had given him one every time he filled the glasses) entered and I said, "I think I have what is known in this monarchy of yours as a katzenjammer. What would you, out of your vast knowledge, advise me to take?" He suggested a large glass of Munich beer, but the very thought was repugnant to me.

"Then take some cognac, mein Herr."

The suggestion of any spirituous drink was frightful.

"No, no, not that, either! Bring me four quart jugs of seltzer."

I drank that seltzer, quart by quart, and the proceeding occupied the entire morning. By mid-day my system was thoroughly diluted. I bathed, ordered some soup and toast, dressed and went to my matinee where a large and appreciative audience received me. The matinee was followed by a dinner worthy of a hungry laborer. A pint of champagne, a good cigar, and I was at peace with the world. The evening concert was one of the best yet given!

At the hotel, a bedraggled and woe-begone consul awaited my return from the performance. His first words were, "What did you do to-day?"

"Just what I intended to," I replied.

"But did you go to the matinee?" he asked.

"I'm not here for my health," I smiled, "of course I went to the matinee, but why do you ask?"

"Man, don't you realize what we did last night?"

"Of course. We sat downstairs and had a few drinks, celebrating the success of the concert; that's all."

"All!" he echoed, holding his head. "All! Why, we drank an entire bottle of Kentucky whiskey. I've been in bed all day with a towel around my head. I've been so thoroughly knocked out that I couldn't even sign important official papers."

"My dear consul," said I impressively, "you have been here twelve years. You have grown soft. Go back to America, my dear sir, and be a man again!"

When we left Paris for our second tour through Germany our first stop was Mannheim. I took an earlier train than my bandsmen. When their train reached the frontier, the manager, the baggageman and the entire corps were fast asleep. Either through ignorance, stupidity, or pure cussedness the three cars containing the band were shunted to three different trains going in as many different directions. One was going to Mannheim, the other two to points in France. The baggage car was finally located at Ems and reached us in Heidelberg.

When the carful of American musicians reached a village far to the north at the end of the line, the boys got off and inquired where they were; they were told the name of the town. At length an American was found in the village who offered to interpret for them.

"Well," he asked, "who are you?"

"We are members of Sousa's Band," answered Arthur Pryor, the solo trombonist.

"Sousa's Band?" queried the American, "I never heard of it!"

"You never heard of Sousa's Band?" shouted Pryor, "Stranger, I don't know what part of America you come from but I'll bet ten dollars to one that your town isn't on the map!" The bet was not taken.

One third of the men reached Mannheim about eight o'clock, but only those who played clarinet, flute or oboe had their instruments with them, the rest of the band paraphernalia being in the strayed baggage car. We hoped against hope until eight-thirty that the missing instruments and men would arrive, but luck was against us. We were obliged to dismiss the audience and refund the money. I made the announcement through an interpreter, assuring the assemblage that they were the artistic centre of the universe and that I fervently hoped I might be able to return later and give them a concert. One little sawed-off fellow mounted a chair and shouted that all this was very true, but he had come fifteen miles on the railroad and who was going to pay his fare?

It is impossible to argue with an angry mob, so I retired and left them to disperse. The theatrical manager, equally unreasonable, swore out a warrant for damages for non-appearance and collected twelve hundred dollars before I could leave town. I have warm memories of Mannheim!

At last we were reunited — in Heidelberg. There we gave a concert in the municipal garden. There is a peculiarity about the terms of payment in Germany. In the summer months when we played in the famous gardens we usually received anywhere from 85 to 90 per cent of the "gate." But when we played indoors in the winter months (as we did in 1905) we would have difficulty in getting 70 percent. That was because in the gardens the proprietors look to food and drink for their profit and since we were a strong attraction, were willing to give us nearly all the entrance money. In Heidelberg the management seemed singularly indifferent whether the public paid an admission fee or not. I noticed a pole across the road and a stream of people stooping under it, thus gaining entrance without any tickets. I sought the intendant (always a very grandiose person in Europe, either a count or a duke!) and complained to his Nibs that people were crawling under the pole, sans payment. "Impossible!" he said, and becoming angry at this reflection on Teuton integrity, wanted me to understand distinctly that no German would think of doing such a thing.

"Doubtless true," I replied, "but please remember there are Americans, Frenchmen, Englishmen, Italians, Spanish, Portuguese, and Senegambians at large in the world. In fact, they all seem to have concentrated on my concert to-day. I want them to pay as well as the honest Germans."

"Nonsense!" he was shouting now; "I will do nothing about it."

"Very well. If in five minutes there are not proper guards placed on that road, I shall march my band out of here, sue you for breach of contract, and then report you to the authorities at Berlin for neglect of duty, and limited capacity." I drew out my watch and held it ready in my palm. The magnificent intendant suddenly became remarkably tractable. He got busy, and in three minutes he had placed guards at the pole, who, I really believe, would not have allowed the Kaiser to enter without his ticket! Authority, real or assumed, is a valuable weapon in Germany.

In Dresden, we found a beautiful city and a wonderful public. The famous pianist and composer, Emil Sauer, called on me in my dressing-room at the close of the concert. German girls kept us busy for an hour, writing our autographs on post-cards. The importunate maidens' pleading, "Bitte! Bitte!" filled the air. When the last card was signed and the last blonde damsel had departed, we talked. Sauer praised our performance with gratifying warmth. I had played an overture, two suites, a valse, and several marches all my own, and he remarked upon the difference existing between German and French composers and myself.

"We," he said, smiling, "travel along a musical path that is rough, full of cobblestones and ruts. It is sometimes even discordant. But you seem to have discovered a delightful little path of roses in music which you hold entirely for yourself."

It was a charming compliment and I told him so.

"A successful man receives many compliments, but the sincerity of yours touches me deeply. It reminds me of one other which seems to me the only one to approach it in simplicity. I was travelling on horseback from Hot Springs, Virginia, with a companion, and one night we stopped for shelter at a farmhouse known to my companion. The farmer's little daughter, an exceedingly bright and pretty child of twelve, came with her father to meet us. She gazed at the horses with intense admiration. She had never seen a bitted horse, nor a beautiful saddle. Her knowledge of horses was confined to old farm hacks, heavy and cumbersome and in no way comparable to our splendid mounts. After supper, she rolled out the phonograph and surprised me greatly by calling out the names of twenty of my pieces and then insisting on playing every one of them. The next morning, when we went out to mount our horses, the little girl followed us. The horses were freshly groomed, saddles and bridles shining. As I got into the saddle, she stroked the mane of my horse and looking shyly up into my face, said, 'Do you know my idea of heaven?' 'No,' I said, 'I don't, but I should like to.' 'My idea of heaven is — horses and you!' "

After Dresden we played Nuremberg and then Munich. George Lange, the proprietor of the hall we played in, had guaranteed us sixteen thousand marks for four concerts and advertised the fact as widely as possible! To be sure, it was a large sum for the times, but the countryside and Lange hammered home the fact with great persistency.

The young and lovely Olive Fremstad, a great favorite with Munich music-lovers, and later one of the most famous of the prima donnas at the Metropolitan, attended the first concert and told me afterwards that she had been compelled to stand up during the entire programme. She added that she wouldn't have stood up for any one in the world but an American musician.

The day after the concert Mr. Lange and I lunched together. We were interrupted by a tall, cadaverous individual in a somber black suit who addressed me in German: "Herr Sousa?"

I nodded and he handed me a large envelope. It informed me that a law passed in the Pleistocene period required that any stranger giving a concert in Munich should pay a tax of ten per cent of his receipts.

"This doesn't concern me," I said. "This is a matter for Mr. Lange to adjust. We are guaranteed and our expenses are guaranteed for this concert. No doubt all taxes will be borne by Mr. Lange."

Mr. Lange intervened, "Don't worry; I'll fix it up." He said something to the mournful-looking intruder who, bowing low, withdrew.

Just before the last concert of the series I was dining once more with Lange and the same individual appeared, armed with the same old envelope.

"What does this mean?" I asked Lange, handing him the envelope.

"It is a demand that you pay ten per cent of sixteen thousand marks."

"But I understood that you were to arrange the matter."

"I did. The original order gave you until four o'clock today to pay it; I persuaded the authorities to extend the time to six."

"But the debt is yours," I protested.

"That's what I thought," he regretfully replied, "but the tax officer tells me that it reads, 'any *stranger* coming to Munich' and of course you know I am not a stranger, so the law requires that you pay. I hope to have the law changed later on!"

After we had made the rounds of the German cities we went to Holland. At the close of our first concert in Amsterdam I was approached by the Queen's musical director who told me that he had been requested to attend all our concerts in Holland. In our next town we lunched together most amicably and he introduced me to the grandfather of all cocktails. I accepted one and drank the health of Queen Wilhelmina and all her future children but I was obliged to refuse a second for I could never have survived it. The musical director was, however, a doughty man. He drank eight during the course of that meal and emerged as sober as a judge.

From Holland we took the boat for Queenstown and sailed the following Saturday on the *St. Louis*, for New York. We touched shore September ninth, 1900, in gala array, for the boat was decked with the colors of Germany, France, Holland and Belgium. On the forward deck we played American airs, and finished up with *Home, Sweet Home*. I told the reporters that I was delighted with the success of our tour abroad and especially happy that our Americanism had aided in it. "We found many a town where they did not even know the American colors, but they know now, and they are familiar with the strains of *The Star Spangled Banner* and *The Stars and Stripes Forever*. They loved every bit of it and we are now known throughout Europe. I cannot speak too highly of our reception abroad."

I received hundreds of telegrams and letters of congratulation. There was one from a lady who had been prima donna of a company which I conducted, but who was now retired and spending all her charms on her husband. She enclosed a note I had sent her when she was singing Josephine in *Pinafore*.

This Josephine had the unforgivable habit of singing sharp, and the equally unforgivable one of being careless in her dress. One night she came on the stage with her petticoat showing fully two inches below her gown, — and she began to sing a shade above the pitch. I hurriedly scribbled a note,

DEAR MADAM:

Please raise your petticoat two inches, and lower your voice one inch.

J.P.S

Women are strange creatures, anyway, particularly the warm-hearted, golden-throated, temperamental singing women. There was dear Nella Bergen who became the wife of DeWolf Hopper. I think it was Hopper's fourth try at matrimony. Nella was singing *La Pastorella* in my *Bride Elect*. The opera had been on the road for months and was fulfilling an engagement at the Knickerbocker Theatre, playing to capacity audiences. In fact that opera achieved the high price record at the Knickerbocker. Nella loved Hopper devotedly, and was dejected when she was obliged to be away from him. When Hopper had to go on the road and leave Nella alone in New York, he wrote to her, "How has *The Bride Elect* been doing?" She answered, "We are playing to packed houses. I have never seen greater enthusiasm in my life. The same people came night after night; they never seem to get enough of the opera. But I don't know whether it is a success or not!" Poor singing girl! Your heart and your eyes were for your husband alone, and you could see nothing that stood between him and your love!

Strange to say, all Hopper's wives — that is to say, his earlier ones — appeared in operas of mine. The second one, lovely Ida Mosher, appeared with him in *Désirée* under McCaull's management. McCaull had a habit of interjecting sarcastic remarks during rehearsal, especially when the company was slow to catch the stage manager's idea of how a certain scene should be played. On one occasion when the poor stage manager was trying to make them register ecstatic joy, McCaull appeared and shouted, "What would you do if I raised your salary?"

A musical but shy little voice behind Hopper said, "I should drop dead!"

The remark attracted Hopper's attention, and not long after, they were married.

Hopper's third wife, and the second to appear in one of my operas was Edna Wallace, who sang in *El Capitan*, and afterward in *Chris and the Wonderful Lamp*. Nella Bergen, the fourth, a charming and devoted woman, appeared in *El Capitan*, *The Bride Elect*, *The Charlatan* and *The Free Lance*. She had a glorious voice, bore herself like a queen and earned the respect and admiration of everyone who knew her.

Chapter XII

SECOND EUROPEAN TOUR OF THE BAND, 1901 — THE GLASGOW
EXHIBITION — LONDON LUNCHES ME — THE ENGLISH GRENADIERS
— A ROYAL CONCERT AT SANDRINGHAM — A CARPING NEWSPAPER
— INTELLIGENCE OF ENGLISH AUDIENCES — GUINEAS AND POUNDS —
THE RIBBON OF THE FRENCH ACADEMY — EDWARD BOK — "THE FIFTH
STRING" — I SEDUCE A WHOLE LEGISLATURE — WILLOW GROVE — THE
PAN-AMERICAN EXPOSITION, BUFFALO, 1901 — "NEARER MY GOD TO
THEE" — EUROPE AGAIN — "IMPERIAL EDWARD" AND HIS BRACE OF
ROYAL PHEASANTS — A CONCERT WITHOUT A SCORE — THE EARL OF
WARWICK'S CIGARS — A SECOND COMMAND CONCERT AT WINDSOR
CASTLE, AND A SOUSA CONCERT IN THE ROYAL NURSERY — JAMES
WHITCOMB RILEY — ST. LOUIS WORLD'S FAIR — PALMS AND ROSETTE OF
THE FRENCH ACADEMY

IN SEPTEMBER, 1901, we sailed for a second tour across the
Atlantic, having signed a contract with the directors of the
Glasgow International Exhibition to appear there for four
weeks. I had already received an invitation for October fourth
to be the guest of honor at a luncheon given by music-loving
London at which Sir Lewis McIver, Bart., M. P., was to be toast-
master and chairman, and the musical, artistic, and professional
world had promised to be present. Members of the reception
committee were: the Earl of Kinnoull, the Earl of Lonsdale, Sir
Henry Irving, Clement Scott, Anatole France, W. H. Stephens,
John Hollingshead, Henry J. Wood, George Ashton, Colonel
Probyn, H. S. J. Booth, Charles Morton, Philip Yorke.

Our steamer was a day late in arriving at Southampton and
so I did not reach London until the morning of October fourth.
When I finally sat down in that brilliant assembly, I was tired,
preoccupied and dejected. Sir Lewis McIver delivered a very

witty introductory speech. I knew while he was speaking that all this was designed to bring me to my feet but when I tried to formulate some kind of a reply my mind absolutely refused to work. I wished ardently that the floor would open and swallow me up. Came a final grand burst of oratorical eloquence from Sir Lewis all in praise of my achievements (which he had only read about and never witnessed) and it was my moment to respond. As I pulled myself to my feet, I thought how grateful, how beautiful, sudden death would be in such a crisis. I had not the faintest idea of what I was about to say. I knew only that Sir Lewis had just uttered these words: "We will now hear from the guest of honor, Mr. John Philip Sousa." Like lightning, the whole scheme of a speech flashed into my head. I began:

"Mr. Toastmaster and Gentlemen: I cannot recall a time when I have addressed an intelligent audience feeling as I do to-day. I once believed that a Britisher could be trusted at all times. I fear my belief was unwarranted. In regard to my speech I feel that an explanation is in order before I finish.

"I arrived this morning, a day late from Southampton, and while I sipped my breakfast tea, a card was brought to me bearing the legend, 'Sir Lewis McIver, M. P.' I could not at first determine what the 'M. P.' represented unless it meant 'Metropolitan Police.' I referred the card to my valet, asking if I had committed any breach of the peace since arriving in London. He considered it carefully and said he thought not.

"'Then why should an M. P. call on me?' I asked.

"'Mr. Sousa,' said my sage valet, 'in this bloomin' country "M. P." means either Metropolitan Police or Member of Parliament. I would advise you to take your choice after you see the gentleman, but, meanwhile, I'll lock up everything that isn't nailed!'

"The gentleman made his appearance, and my valet seemed glad that he had locked up everything! Sir Lewis began, 'Mr. Sousa, after a heated campaign I was elected, by a substantial majority, chairman and toastmaster of the luncheon in your honor. It is necessary in these days of more or less strained diplomatic relations between our respective countries that I consult with you on the subject matter of your oration. I trust that your speech will not prove offensive to any loyal Englishman, therefore I have come to ask you to allow me to read it and blue-pencil anything that might conceivably endanger the international peace.'

"I, with the utmost innocence, quite free from any suspicion of guile, went to my trunk and brought forth the manuscript of my speech. Sir Lewis assured me that he would take it to his office and return it to me at the luncheon. I even called his attention to the trend of the address — the love existing between Great Britain and the United States — how we as an ex-daughter still loved our former mother and felt for Britain much the same affection as do Canada and Australia, which seemed to please him very much.

"Imagine my surprise and consternation when Sir Lewis delivered his speech, or rather *my* speech, for what he has said is, word for word, all, all my own! I knew my speech was a good one, but I never realized how magnificent it was until the honorable member from Scotland delivered it to us. It was a great speech, if I say so who wrote it. I congratulate you all on having heard it delivered by so consummate an artist as Sir Lewis!"

When I sat down, Sir Lewis said, mildly, "Y'know, at first I was puzzled, and then I realized you were spoofing. I enjoyed every bit of it!"

That night, the next afternoon and the next night we appeared in Albert Hall. We played the concerts to 27,000 people. The critics were very complimentary and one said: "For two hours and a half Sousa and his band thrilled an Albert Hall audience. Rapturous applause greeted the performance at every opportunity. Several of the band did some remarkably able execution with most difficult instruments. The whole audience was perfectly charmed with Sousa's style of conducting. It is very modest in its characteristics — speaking of self-suppression; all the same it is most remarkable in its effectiveness as well as in its gracefulness."

From London we went to our four weeks' engagement at the Glasgow International Exposition. His Majesty's Grenadier Guards Band was there also and, after a period of looking offishly at each other, a friendship sprang up between the two bands and we gave a dinner to the Grenadiers which was almost immediately reciprocated by them in the same week.

Musicians as a rule are either very loyal to their organization or horribly indifferent. At the very beginning of our engagement at the Exposition our men might easily have become enemies owing to the rivalry existing between the two bands. Mr. Hedley, the manager of the Exposition, read me a note from the leader of the Grenadiers complaining that we were assigned a better place to play than that given to his band. He intimated that Hedley was favoring the Americans.

"What would you do?" Hedley asked.

"Simplest thing in the world," I answered. "Just write and tell him the stand where Sousa's Band plays is to be his without change during the time he is playing at the Exposition and that you will assign the American band to the despised point now occupied by him."

And if the people afterwards flocked in greater numbers to our stand, *I* had no reason to complain.

But this dinner smoothed everything out and brought the two bands into close companionship. Of course, we toasted his Majesty, King Edward, and the President of the United States; then I proposed the health of the Grenadier Guards: "It is thirty years since the Grenadiers and the Americans have had a drink together. Thirty years ago the Grenadiers took part in Boston in what was believed to be the greatest musical festival ever organized, under the direction of that great bandmaster, Patrick Sarsfield Gilmore. Three thousand of the best players in the world appeared and the three leading bands of the world, — one from France, one from Germany, and the Grenadier Guards from Great Britain. At that festival American bandsmen acknowledged one father and three brothers. The father was Gilmore, the man who knew that music was a universal language and believed that no geographical lines could separate musicians. The brothers were the English band, the French band, and the German band. Still speaking that universal language of music, I take great pleasure in asking you to drink to the health of the Grenadier Guards and their distinguished conductor."

We gave a farewell performance on November 4 to 152,709 people. According to the *Record and Daily Mail* it was the second highest turnstile count of the Exposition and scarcely had the last notes of the British National Anthem faded away when a cheer went up that could be "heard round the world."

At the close of our Glasgow engagement we toured the provinces and returned to London, playing six afternoons at the Empire and six nights at Covent Garden. Mr. Albert de Rothschild gave a reception to Mrs. Sousa and myself. Among the guests were Mr. and Mrs. Arthur Bouchier, Mr. and Mrs. Gordon Lennox, Mr.

and Mrs. Herbert Beerbohm Tree, Mr. George Grossmith, Mrs. Patrick Campbell, Mr. Brown Potter, Mr. George Edwards, Miss Fay Davis, Miss Edna May and Miss Ethel Matthews.

Madame Melba sang for us that evening and Mr. Ysaye was the violinist.

Mr. George Ashton called on me; he was the director of the entertainments for the royal family. After dismissing my valet from the room he said, "His Majesty desires a command performance. He wishes it to be a surprise for the Queen on her birthday."

We quickly arranged matters. I told the bandsmen we were going to Baron Rothschild's on Sunday to give a concert, and asked them to gather in the Liverpool street station at six o'clock. An Englishman in the band immediately complicated matters by reminding me that the proper way to reach Rothschild's was by the Euston Street station. I replied only, "That was the station given me and no mistake about it."

When we took the train, so well had we enforced secrecy that only Ashton and myself knew where we were going. The band dined on the train, and we reached Sandringham about 8:45. The concert was to begin at ten. At that hour their Majesties entered the great ballroom which had been converted into a temporary concert hall. The Prince and Princess of Wales, Princess Victoria, the Prince and Princess of Denmark, Lady de Grey and a few others were present. The programme ran:

1. SUITE, *Three Quotations*   *Sousa*
2. MARCH, *El Captian*   *Sousa*
3. TROMBONE SOLO, *Love's Thoughts.*   *Pryor*
   MR. ARTHUR PRYOR
4. COLLECTION OF HYMNS OF THE
   AMERICAN CHURCHES   *Sousa*

	MARCH, *Washington Post*	Sousa
5.	SOPRANO SOLO, *Will You Love when Lilies are Dead*	Sousa
6.	CAPRICE, *Water Sprites*	Kunkel
7.	MARCH, *Stars and Stripes Forever*	Sousa
	COON SONG *The Honeysuckle and the Bee.*	Penn
8.	VIOLIN SOLO, *Reverie "Nymphalin"*	Sousa
	MISS DOROTHY HOYLE	
9.	PLANTATION SONGS AND DANCES	Clark

The King demanded no fewer than seven encores and in most cases stipulated what they were to be. At the end of the concert he presented me with the medal of the Victorian Order and congratulated me on a fine performance. The Prince of Wales (the present King George) and the Queen joined in the felicitations. The Queen remarked graciously on Mrs. Sousa's unusual beauty and the Prince of Wales took the casket from my hand, drew out the medal and said, amiably, "Where shall I pin it?"

"Over my heart," I replied.

"How American!" he smiled.

I told his Majesty that I should like to have the honor of composing a march dedicated to him. He replied that he would be delighted to accept the dedication. This led to my afterwards writing *Imperial Edward*. Which reminds me that the day after the King's concert I met an Anglomaniac who said to me, "You must have been overwhelmed at the honor of leading your band for his Majesty." "Possibly," I replied, "but I have conducted for gentlemen before."

Your true-born Briton is a man who will fight an injustice, if only for the satisfaction of squelching the knocker. When we played Birmingham, one paper was so manifestly unfair that the president of the syndicate which managed my appearances came to me and showed me a clipping which was the quintessence of vituperation and abuse.

"What are you going to do about it?" he asked.

"Let it die in its swaddling clothes," I cheerfully replied. "It is so absolutely at variance with the manifest opinion of the audience that the public will know it is absurd."

"*I* don't propose to let it rest. I propose to take legal proceedings. Do you wish to contribute to the fund?"

"Yes," I said, "how much do you want?" and gave him ten pounds to hearten his battle!

In England a lawsuit is inaugurated most politely with a note from solicitor to defendant, who was, in this case, Mr. Alfred Harmsworth (afterwards Lord Northcliffe), and perhaps the most powerful newspaper man in all England. He was the proprietor of a string of papers, among them the *Birmingham Gazette* which had printed the offensive item. In answer to the solicitor's letter, the *Gazette* replied that they had the utmost confidence in their musical critic, in his honesty and capability, and that the paper would endorse any conclusion of his. They refused to withdraw any of the remarks which had been made concerning our band.

Now came the second stage — calling in a barrister. The barrister entered suit against the *Gazette* for a hundred thousand pounds. His contention was that the syndicate, the conductor, and every bandsman from the piccolo to the bass drum had been grievously offended and woefully mortified and grossly libelled by the false statements in the Gazette, and that a hundred thousand pounds could not hope to compensate for the ignominy which the offended had suffered at the hands of the offender! I added that I personally did not so much desire money as a full retraction in their paper. The paper retracted thus:

MR. SOUSA AND HIS BAND

We learn with regret that Mr. Sousa is deeply hurt by the criticism of the performance in Birmingham which appeared in the *Daily Gazette*. Mr. Sousa considers that our critic very far outstepped fair criticism. That was certainly not the intention. Our critic has strong preferences — they may be called prejudices in favor of other bands, and the interpretation they give of classical music, but the superlative excellence of Mr. Sousa's band in the treatment of American music, has, undoubtedly, been proved by his great popular success throughout his British tour, terminating in his performance by royal command before the King, Queen, and royal family. We regret, therefore, that the publication of our article gave pain to Mr. Sousa, whose tuneful genius has been a source of infinite delight to thousands.

This was the *amende* honorable, and we let it go at that.

After a week more of concert playing we sailed from Southampton for New York on December 13, 1901, on the ship *Philadelphia*.

I had found English audiences highly satisfactory. They are the best listeners in the world. Perhaps the music-lovers of some of our larger cities equal the English, but I do not believe they can be surpassed in that respect. Reputation-building in the musical world would be a pleasant task among the educated English. In England audiences were always fair and often wonderfully enthusiastic. It is wholly natural that this should be so. They have received their musical education through oratorio and organ, the two severest forms of vocal and instrumental music. They are particularly fond of fine orchestral music and of light music as well. Since their society is not maintained by the standard of wealth, grand opera does not assume the overwhelming importance that it enjoys in America. An educated Englishman has so keen a musical perception that it is a delight to play for him; he knows values and at once places a composition where it belongs. An inspired waltz or march will receive applause from him when a dry-as-dust symphony is met with silence. On the other hand, an inspired symphony is given its due of spontaneous applause and an inane march or worthless waltz falls perfectly flat. He judges a composition according to its musical worth alone.

I had a merry time in England, giving interviews. Occasionally, a "Constant Reader" or "Vox Populi" would arise and write a complaining letter to the press taking exception to my "quips and cranks and wanton wiles" over contacts in Great Britain. I could not help it — some things simply insisted on appearing funny to me. There is the matter of English money. I told one of the reporters who talked with me:

> "A great deal more money than they imagine is being spent by American visitors in buying things cheap. The guinea is only a snare and a delusion. There is no such coin in England outside the museums and yet goods are continually priced at so many guineas. Many Americans think 'guinea' is another word for 'sovereign' and make their purchases accordingly. The other day I bought thirty guineas' worth of clothes and, after doing a sum in mental arithmetic, discovered that I had paid thirty shillings more than I thought I had paid. 'Why do you call them guineas?' I asked the attendant, 'instead of pounds?'
>
> " 'In dealing with gentlemen we always call them guineas!'
>
> " 'Well,' I declared, 'in the future, I shall certainly receive money as a gentleman and dispense it as one of the Great Unwashed! It is apparently the only profitable way to do business in this country!' "

On the 26th of April, 1901, I received a cable from Paris informing me that the French government had conferred upon me the ribbon of an officer of the Academy, an honor reserved for those who attain distinction in the field or art and letters.

On the 17th of May, the French ambassador, M. Jules Cambon wrote me thus:

Washington le 17 Mai, 1901

AMBASSADE DE LA REPUBLIQUE FRANÇAISE AUX ÉTATS UNIS

Monsieur, J'ai l'honneur de vous faire savoir que M. le Ministre de l'instruction Publique vient de vous décerner les palmes d'Officier d'Academie pour votre concours gracieux aux cérémonies officielles d'inauguration à Paris au mois de Juillet 1900 des statues de Washington et de Lafayette.

Je suis heureux de vous informer de la bienveillante decision dont vous avez été l'objet et je m'empresse de vous faire parvenir ci-joint le brevet et les insignes de cette décoration.

Recevez, Monsieur, les assurances de ma considération très distinguée.

L'Ambassadeur de France

JULES CAMBON

In the spring of 1901 I received a letter from Mr. Edward Bok of the *Ladies' Home Journal* offering me five hundred dollars and the copyright if I would make a new setting for S. F. Smith's *My Country 'tis of Thee*. I immediately declined the offer on the ground that the public was wedded to the music which had been used for so many, many years, and added that in my opinion no music, good, bad, or indifferent could take its place. Mr. Bok would not take that for a refusal and came to Manhattan Beach to repeat his offer. After dinner, as we sat on the porch of the Oriental Hotel and argued the point pro and con, I still maintained my position in the matter.

At last I said, "If you really want my name in the *Ladies' Home Journal* why not buy a story I have?"

He threw up his arms with a laugh, and said, "Stick to music, Sousa. Let others write stories."

"I have been listening to your arguments for two hours as to why I should write music for you, which I know could not supersede that already in use. Now why not listen to me for a half hour, while I unfold the outlines of my story? That's only fair," I told him.

I outlined to Mr. Bok my novel, *The Fifth String* and when I concluded, he said, "Have you written it out?"

"Not a word, I have been carrying that story around for twenty years, talking baby talk to it, and hoping that some day some one would see fit to buy it."

"Get it on paper at once, and then let me know," was Mr. Bok's parting sentence.

I went to work the next morning and tried to dictate my story to a stenographer; it didn't work, so I sat down and wrote it out slowly in long hand, and then, still, haltingly, dictated it again. I then read it to two critics, had it copied again, and wrote Mr. Bok that the story was finished and he might have it for five thousand dollars.

He requested me to send the manuscript to him for examination but I never did.

Ten days afterwards, the band reached Indianapolis. Mr. Barnes, our treasurer, told a friend of his, connected with the Bobbs-Merrill Company there that I had a good story in my trunk. Mr. Hewitt Howland — at that time the editor of Bobbs-Merrill

— immediately called at my hotel and offered to read the story. I read it to him myself and he telephoned to Mr. Bobbs, who asked me to dine with him at the University Club and discuss terms of publication. He made me a very liberal offer for the novel and so became the publisher of the *The Fifth String*. It was a best seller for quite a while — why should it not have been, since it was illustrated by Howard Chandler Christy?

When we reached Olympia, capital of the State of Washington, I noticed a man peering out from the wings for the first twenty minutes of our concert. I asked an attendant to find out his errand there and to ask him not to stand where he could be seen by the public. At the intermission he came to me himself and said,

"I beg your pardon, Mr. Sousa, but I'm the sergeant-at-arms of the Legislature and we couldn't transact any business there this afternoon because we lacked a quorum, and I've been hunting all over town for the members. When I came here, I was able to count in your audience the legislators of both Houses, almost to a man! I have been wondering whether I ought to round up the absentees but I guess I won't." I invited him to remain and put him in a box.

Presently we opened at Willow Grove, a well-known amusement park outside of Philadelphia. It is unique of its kind, for its first consideration is music and the management endeavors to obtain every year the best the country affords. Such organizations as the Chicago Symphony, the Damrosch Orchestra, the Russian Orchestra, and famous bands like Conway's, Pryor's, Creatore's and Banda Rossa have played there. All this can be heard without paying a penny.

For twenty-eight years the park has maintained its rule of "no liquor." On the opening day I dined at the Casino. I asked a waiter for the wine card. He said, "We do not serve any wine or liquors."

I scribbled a note to the manager, "Please send me a bottle of claret."

The manager came himself with the note in his hand and said, "Mr. Sousa, as a true Philadelphian I am devoted to you and your band, and I am ready to do for you whatever is in the range of possibility. I can give you the park, if you want it, but I can't give you a bottle of claret for there is no such thing in the place."

I always thoroughly enjoyed myself in Pennsylvania. In one of the towns, I received a note written on the edge of a program, just as I was about to conduct a concert. It ran: "I came forty miles over the mountains to see the man who makes twenty-five thousand dollars a year out of his compositions. Kindly oblige me by playing them all."

Other requests ran like this:

"*Bandmaster Sousa:* Please inform me what is the name of those two instruments that look like gas pipes." "A colored lady would like to hear a cornet solo by your solo coronet."

Perhaps the best bit of all was this ingenuous request: "Please play *The Ice Cold Cadets.*"

At the close of the Willow Grove season we left for Buffalo and opened there on June 10, 1901 for a month at the Pan-American Exposition. I noticed at our first evening concert that the lights were suddenly dimmed until the grounds were shrouded in darkness; then a little light appeared, the illumination grew steadily, till, brightening and brightening, the full blaze was restored. It was new at that time and had an almost supernatural effect on the watchers. When you burrow deep into the heart of the real America you will discover an intense affection for the old hymn tunes of the churches. Whatever a man's religious convictions, a hymn tune reaches his heart quicker than any other burst of music. Remembering this, I contrived the next evening, when the illumination began to wane, to have the band softly begin, *Nearer my God to Thee*, and as the lights grew the band crescendoed and swelled out its power to the utmost. The effect was thrilling! It was afterward the subject of much editorial comment. One paper said, "It was left to a bandmaster to discover the meaning of the illumination. The music was inspiring and beautiful."

I received hundreds of letters of congratulation, and the crowds flocked to the bandstand.

After several days, someone in authority sent me an order to substitute *The Star Spangled Banner* for *Nearer My God to Thee*. Now patriotic songs are inspiring only on patriotic occasions; at other times their appeal is purely perfunctory. But, having been trained to obey orders, I played *The Star Spangled Banner* the next night. Morning brought a number of written protests. In three nights the order was revoked and I was requested to resume *Nearer My God to Thee*. The official had doubtless found out the real preference of the public.

At the end of the week Mr. Barnes, my manager, received a check for the week's work, amounting to several thousand dollars. He asked me to go to the bank to identify him.

"Are you Mr. Sousa?" asked the teller of Mr. Barnes.

"No," I interrupted, "I'm John Philip Sousa."

But the teller looked at me coldly and handed back the check. "You'll have to be identified," he said.

Turning my back to the teller's window, I raised my arms as if preparing to start off my band and began to whistle *The Stars and Stripes Forever*, bringing my arms up and down in the manner familiar to those who attend my concerts. The clerks in the room broke out in laughter and applause, and one ran over to whisper in the cashier's ear; he beckoned for the check and cashed it without a word!

After the Exposition closed its doors we went to Manhattan Beach for the season. That year I wrote *The Invincible Eagle*, a march commemorating the Exposition. Manhattan Beach was rapidly changing. The crowd, though appreciative, was not a wealthy one and I saw the writing on the wall which proclaimed, "This is the end." When we closed there, we started to fulfill an engagement in New England and, as I was getting off the train at a station to stretch my legs for a few minutes, an excited woman rushed up to me and demanded frantically, "Has the nine-three train pulled out?"

"I really don't know," I replied.

"Why don't you know?" she shouted. "Why do you stand there like a log? Aren't you a conductor?"

"Yes, I'm a conductor."

"A fine conductor you are!" she exclaimed contemptuously.

"Well, you see," I humbly replied, "I'm not the conductor of a railroad train, I'm the conductor of a brass band."

On September third we opened at the Pittsburgh Local Exposition where we drew an audience of ten thousand people in the Music Hall. Mentioning Pittsburgh reminds me of a good friend, Thomas Preston Brooke, the bandmaster. One season, at the Pittsburgh Exposition, both his band and mine were engaged, Brooke and his Chicago Marine Band to open and play the first half, Sousa's Band to follow immediately and close the Exposition.

During the last week of Brooke's engagement both bands were well featured in the press but each notice was printed just above the announcement of some other attraction — no less important — and the "ads" were more or less run together. Brooke clipped these "ads," pasted them on one of his letter-heads and addressed it to me. The following is a copy of his letter:

"Hell, John — How about this?"

EVERY RESIDENT OF THE CITY SHOULD HEAR
SOUSA

THE WONDERFUL EDUCATED HORSE

"It is almost as good as this, eh?"

BROOKE AND HIS CHICAGO MARINE BAND AT THE
EXPOSITION

A WONDERFUL TROUPE OF TRAINED ANIMALS

Yours faithfully,

TOM BROOKE

We sailed once more for Europe, this time on the twenty-fourth of December, 1902, on the *St. Louis*, and opened in London on January eighth, 1903. King Edward paid me a graceful compliment, a few days after a concert which we gave in honor of her Majesty's birthday, by sending me four beautifully marked pheasants, accompanied by a card, "To John Philip Sousa, from his Majesty, at Sandringham." I had them mounted and hung in my dining-room. I had written "Imperial Edward" before leaving America, and my manager had received the following letter from General D. M. Probyn, Keeper of his Majesty's Privy Purse:

Buckingham Palace

23rd June, 1902

DEAR SIR:

In reply to your letter of the 21st instant, I write to inform you that I have had the honour of submitting to the King the copy which you have brought from America of Mr. Sousa's march, *Imperial Edward*.

His Majesty has commanded me to ask you to convey his thanks to Mr. Sousa for the march and to acquaint you with the fact that his Majesty has given directions for the music of the march to be transposed so that it may be played by several of the principal Military Bands of England.

Yours faithfully,

D. M. PROBYN

On the 18th of January, 1903, I gave a matinee at the Shakespeare Memorial Theatre at Stratford-on-Avon and that night we were to play at Leamington. We had just arrived from America when the Countess of Warwick (the former Lady Brook, whom ribald, whispering London had, after the Baccarat affair, christened "The Babbling Brook") called on my English manager to arrange a concert at the famous Warwick Castle. My manager regretted exceedingly that no open dates were left us, but the Countess was a very beautiful and charming specimen of English womanhood and quite used to getting her own way.

"Well," persisted the lady, "you are to play in Leamington on the 18th. Why not play for me after the Leamington concert? Give me a midnight concert, and I'll announce the hour to my guests."

I consented to the arrangement. It was a tempestuous night. The many conveyances which were used to bring the band to the castle arrived in good time but the driver of the vehicle which contained our music lost control of the car in the storm and the thing went catapulting downhill, twining itself around a lamp-post at the bottom. The music, therefore, did not appear until the concert was over. The band played the entire programme from memory.

After the concert, the Earl of Warwick, Mrs. Sousa, Maud Powell, Miss Liebling and myself, together with the guests, went to supper. I sat with the Earl who presently addressed himself to me:

"I know you come from a land where they smoke the very finest tobacco, but I am going to offer you a cigar which I believe is better than anything you can produce in America."

"Ah," said I, "don't hurt my feelings! Criticise my band — abuse my compositions, express a distaste for the red, white and blue; I can accept those opinions without serious resentment. But do not, oh, do not say that you have a cigar superior to those I import from the great Fonseca of Cuba."

The humidor was rolled in and I selected a most fragrant cigar, and puffed it critically.

"This is all right; but when I return to London, my dear Earl, I shall send you a cigar that *is* a cigar."

We returned to London not long after, and from there I sent him a box of twenty-five Fonseca McKinleys. Fully two weeks passed before I received this letter:

We are far North in Scotland, hunting and having a grand time. Only last night your box of cigars arrived. I opened it and gave one to each of my four companions. We sat around the ingle puffing away, and I now desire to say that your remark about your cigars was modesty itself.

WARWICK

On January 30 we played a second command performance for the King. There is considerable misunderstanding on the subject of an alleged command from the English court. To me it seemed to come in the form of a most courteous request, "I am commanded by His Majesty to ascertain if it is convenient for you to give a concert at Windsor."

There were about forty people present at the Windsor performance. Just before the band struck up, Lord Farquhar came to me and said, smilingly, "Mr. Sousa, we are having two Sousa concerts at Windsor tonight! When the children heard you were coming they had the gramophone rolled into the nursery and now they have selected a programme of your compositions and, while you give your concert in the Waterloo Chambers, they are giving theirs in the nursery, following your programme as far as the records permit them." I imagine the present Prince of Wales was master of ceremonies at that affair!

Since the King's equerry had informed me that the King was very anxious to hear, at the end of our performance, the American national anthem, I instructed my bandsmen to play *The Star Spangled Banner* and then to go into *God Save the King*, beginning just as softly as possible and then gradually growing louder. I brought my band to a standing position, the assemblage rising with us, during the rendition of *The Star Spangled Banner*. The King was every inch a ruler as he stood there, decorated with the sash of a Knight of the Garter. Almost inaudibly we began the British anthem. I was facing his Majesty and had the full pleasure of seeing the change in his expression. As the music swelled it seemed to me that I could read his thoughts: "These aliens are asking God to protect me and my country," and in the splendor and solemnity of the moment he seemed to be glorified.

At the end of the programme he came up to me and shook hands cordially, told me how much he had enjoyed the concert, and added that he had invited the band of the Scottish Guard to sit in the gallery and hear American music as it should be played. The King and Queen chatted for some time with Mrs. Sousa and me on that never-failing theme, America and Americans.

While we were travelling in England I was taken ill at St. Leonard's-on-the-Sea and the distinguished medical adviser diagnosed the complaint as "a chill on the liver." We do not recognize that malady in America — at least not under that name — but it was evidently rather serious, for the physician at once called a trained nurse. She was a conscientious, whole-souled, hardworking girl of thirty or so, who, after the fashion of her kind, briskly took possession of me, body and soul. My liver occupied my attention to such an extent that I did not notice whether she was beautiful or not, but later on I realized that she was extremely pleasant to look at.

At night my anxious little nurse moved her cot next my bed. The next night, since I had shown improvement during the day, she moved it to a distance of about two feet from the bed. I still gained, and on the third night the cot was placed about six feet from my bed. On the fourth night, it moved three feet further. Presently it was removed to the next room. Had I been there a month and improved as rapidly as I did the first week, the nurse would probably have been sleeping in the next block!

I deeply appreciated the devotion of that efficient young woman and was anxious to reward her appropriately. She often read to me and, one day, after reading an account of a dinner given to me at a famous restaurant for successful musicians and artists (the famous Pagani's in London) she sighed that the one desire of her life was to eat dinner at that holy of holies. I replied, "Very well, young lady. If I live, I shall certainly invite you to dine there!" On my recovery, I journeyed to Weymouth, still accompanied by my nurse, according to doctor's orders, and we stopped in London to have dinner at Pagani's in the artists' room, which we had entirely to ourselves. It made a deep impression on the hero-worshipping little nurse, for when I returned to England

Windsor Castle.

Consommé Printanier à la Helen
Potage à la Saxonne
Mousse de Homard à la Meunière
Cailles Polies à la Diane
Selle d'Agneau à la Niçoise
Bécasses sur Canapés
Poulets Rôtis à la Casserole
Salade à la Rachel
Cardons à la Moelle
Timbales à l'Espagnole
Croûtes au Jambon
Brouettes Garnies de Glaces Variés
Petites Merlitons

31 Janvier 1903.

MENU OF DINNER AT WINDSOR CASTLE
THIRD EUROPEAN TOUR

on my next tour, she sent me a prayer book, in remembrance of what she called the happiest day of her life.

During the season in Great Britain we played again in Glasgow and I gave a banquet to friends who had entertained me a great deal when I played at the Exposition there. This was my first opportunity to reciprocate. I sent out invitations to some sixty people for this banquet, which was given in the Windsor Hotel. The guest of honor was the Lord Provost of Glasgow, the Hon. John Chisholm, a splendid old gentleman and a very patriotic Scotchman.

Among my guests was Mr. Hedley, who had been the General Manager of the Exposition. When he was called upon, he spoke of the great success of my band, of the splendid music we had discoursed, and how much Scotland had profited by our appearance there. I thanked him for his kind words and said that I would like him to understand that we in America had taken to our hearts and nurtured many of the beautiful folk songs of Scotland; that the songs of England, Ireland, Scotland and Wales had become American by adoption, and that I thought Scotland had given the world the most beautiful of all folk songs — *Annie Laurie*, a piece of undying inspiration, which we Americans cherished as we did *Old Folks at Home*. One of our great poets, I added, had immortalized himself by writing a poem around that ballad. I referred to Bayard Taylor's *Song of the Camp*. It is the story of the night before the bombarding of Sebastopol by the British in the Crimean War. While the soldiers are entrenched before the city one of them takes up the ballad of *Annie Laurie* and gradually another, and another, until the entire army is singing it. The poet says "Each heart recalled a different name but all sang, *Annie Laurie*." Then the poet gives a description of the battle and after the battle, towards the closing verse, he says:

> AND Irish Nora's eyes are dim
> For a soldier grim and gory
> And English Mary sighs for him
> Who sang of Annie Laurie.

As I repeated this verse, the Lord Provost jumped to his feet and, smashing his fist on the table, rattling the china, sang out at the top of his voice, "Nay, nay! Not *English* Mary! *Hieland* Mary! *Hieland* Mary!" The sixty guests, springing to their feet, men and women alike, shouted at the top of their voices, "Not English Mary — Hielan' Mary! Hielan' Mary!"

I motioned to them to sit down and I added, "The author of the poem has gone to his long home, but I am very sure if he were here to-night he would change the lines to say,

> AND Irish Nora's eyes are dim
> For a soldier grim and gory,
> And Hielan' Mary sighs for him
> Who sang of Annie Laurie.

After touring the cities of Great Britain, we sailed for America again. I went south for recreation and clay-bird shooting, and from there to Willow Grove. During the younger days of my life I was very fond of playing baseball. The band boys had organized a club and were having matches; they sent a challenge to the nine of the Marine Corps stationed at League Island Navy Yard, Philadelphia, and I surprised the boys and myself by pitching a no-hit first inning.

On August 30, 1903 we started the season at Willow Grove, then went to the Cincinnati Fall Festival, and from there to the Indianapolis Fair. At the first matinee they had a chorus of children, some fifteen hundred or two thousand, dressed in white, with white jockey caps that had very large peaks. At the close of the matinee a mite of a girl, who had evidently already developed the autograph mania, tendered me her cap.

"Please, Mr. Sousa, will you write your name on the peak of my cap?"

"With pleasure," I said, and did so. That set all the others a-clamoring. I worked on those peaks for two hours. I began with "John Philip Sousa," then I wrote "John P. Sousa," then "J. P. Sousa" then "J. Sousa" and at last when I got very tired, I scribbled just "Sousa." A diminuendo dictated by necessity! My hand ached for a week thereafter.

My novel, "*The Fifth String,* attracted so much attention that when I reached Indianapolis I was given a dinner by the firm of Bobbs-Merrill, where I met for the first time the great Hoosier poet, James Whitcomb Riley. On my return to New York I sent Mr. Riley some medicine and a box of Havana cigars, which elicited the following letter:

JAMES WHITCOMB RILEY

INDIANAPOLIS

Aug. 4, 1904

JOHN PHILIP SOUSA, *Master of Melody*

Dear Mr. Sousa:

The promised box of medicine is received most gratefully — likewise the box of exquisite Havanas. And now, in consequence, like the lordly old Jew Longfellow draws,

"My presence breathes a spicy scent

Of cinnamon and sandal blent

Like the soft aromatic gales

That meet the mariner who sails

Through the Malaccas, and the seas

That wash the shores of Celebes."

In return all inadequate, I sent you two favorite books of
mine, together with last photograph, that I may beg the latest of
your own. The Child Book you may hand on to your children,
but I charge you, *do* most seriously ransack the other. Still we
talk you over delightedly at *our publishers* ever agreeing that
you're our kind of man. God bless you!

Most gratefully and truly yours,

JAMES WHITCOMB RILEY

We opened at the St. Louis World's Fair in May 1904 for a
several weeks' engagement. During our stay there the French
ambassador, M. Jules Jusserand, presented to me on behalf of
his Government, the rosette of Officier de L'Instructeur Publique
of France, which gave me the golden palms and rosette of the
French Academy.

We volunteered to play at a reception and dinner given
to Miss Alice Roosevelt, and I was the recipient of a beautiful
bouquet of flowers from "Princess Alice."

After St. Louis I went to Mitchell, South Dakota, to play at
the Corn Palace Exposition. A company of vaudeville artists
were there and entertained the public a couple of times a day in
the same hall where we gave our concerts. One of the actors had
a comedy scene in which, among his properties, were about two
hundred hats that were kept in a net; at a certain cue these were
freed and came tumbling onto the stage.

We were holding the stage and, in response to an insistent
demand, the band struck up the "Manhattan Beach" march. Just
how it happened, I don't know; but in the middle of the number

someone cut the rope that held the hats in the net, and we were the most surprised lot of men you ever saw when a shower of hats descended upon us. In the bells of the Sousaphones they were piled nearly three feet deep. The laughter that overwhelmed the audience was so tremendous that you couldn't hear the band at all, although they valiantly continued to play!

We pressed on westward and when we got to Vallejo, Captain Bull of the U. S. S. *Solace* wined and dined me in commemoration of my approaching fiftieth birthday. Late September found us at the Pittsburgh Exposition and then came our return to New York for a final concert at Carnegie Hall on October fourth. While we were at the Pittsburgh Exposition, I selected September 29 for a Pittsburgh Composers' Concert. The pieces were to be chosen by postcard request. Curiously enough, I received a thousand cards for *The Monongahela Waltz*. I made inquiries and discovered that no one had ever heard of it. I sent a note to the composer and asked him to call on me and bring a band arrangement. He appeared, a miner who worked in McKeesport, and brought a composition written in an almost indecipherable hand on a single sheet of soiled paper.

"Have you no parts for it?" I asked.

"No, I figured you could play it from one part."

"How can sixty men play from one sheet of music? They cannot all look on at once."

I finally extracted from him the information that he had bought ten dollars' worth of postcards and had asked his friends and acquaintances to send in requests for the piece, hoping that I would then arrange it for my band. I did.

Chapter XIII

FOURTH EUROPEAN TOUR IN 1904 — BAND SOLOISTS — MUSICAL
PIRACY — ENGLISH CRITICS WHET THEIR KNIVES — PARIS, BERLIN, THE
BELGIAN CITIES — ST. PETERSBURG — TRIALS OF A RUSSIAN CONCERT —
THE NATIONAL ANTHEM — POLAND VIENNA AND "THE BLUE DANUBE"
— DENMARK, HOLLAND, ENGLAND — "RIGHT AND LEFT SOCKS"
— MALARIA

W E BEGAN our fourth tour of Europe in December, 1904, and opened in Liverpool on January 6, 1905. The new march for the occasion was *The Diplomat* which I had completed while we were playing at Mitchell.

When I recall European experiences, inevitably there comes to mind a host of pleasant memories clustering about the names of the splendid group of American girls who accompanied us on our tours, as singers and violinists. Amy Leslie, the famous critic of the *Chicago News*, in reviewing one of our concerts declared that she wondered how we succeeded in presenting so much beauty and talent at the same time; that every girl who sang or played with us was an able musician and delightful to look at. There were a great many of them and almost without exception they all married and led happy, successful lives. The band got the reputation of being a sort of matrimonial bureau! Even if the girl were disinclined toward matrimony, the moment she sang with our band marriage came her way. Among the first of our prima donnas was Marcelle Lindh, who married, after singing with us, and later became one of the famous artists of the German stage. Beautiful Leonora Von Stosch, who was our violinist, married Sir Edgar Speyer and is now the well-known Lady Leonora Speyer. Then there were two Kentucky beauties, both wonderfully talented young women

— Miss Currie Duke and Miss Florence Hardman. Myrta French, a talented soprano, married in Philadelphia, Elizabeth Northrup is resting on her laurels in Washington, Martina Johnston and Blanche Duffield have been married some years. Charming Bertha Bucklin married in Syracuse, and died several years ago. The Hoyt Sisters, duetists, are still playing for a devoted public. How many, many of them there were — Elizabeth Schiller, the German opera singer, the famous little harpist, Winifred Bambrick — sweet and lovable Jeanette Powers who left us to marry Carl Block, the Wanamaker of Peoria, Marjorie Moody, the great Boston soprano, Lucy Ann Allen, a truly statuesque beauty who became Mrs. Haviland, and the Misses Rickard, Rocco, Jenkins, Gluck, and Caroline Thomas who, bless them, never miss a concert when I am playing in their towns.

The record in appearances with us, goes, however, to Miss Estelle Liebling, who sang in a thousand concerts with the band. Miss Liebling toured Europe twice with us, and her companion on the tours was that remarkable violinist, the late Maud Powell, who was one of the best-loved soloists in America.

The artists on our first European tour were Maude Reese Davies and Dorothy Hoyle. On the trip around the world Miss Virginia Root sang with us, and the violinist was Miss Nicoline Zedeler. Both those artists are now married and mothers. Their conductor will always remember them as splendid women and splendid artists. Others who contributed happy hours to the public with the band were Miss Mary Baker, and Miss Nora Fauchald. They were a noble band of women, and I recall with delight all our associations.

Reaching London in 1905 I was immediately greeted by a caller — Mr. Willie Boosey, General Manager of the music-publishing house of Chappell and Company, who had come to bewail the epidemic of musical piracy. He deplored the fact that no new composition by a popular writer could hope to escape the thievery of the music-pirates. They would print the piece and send out hawkers to sell it on the street for tuppence a copy. If they were arrested, only the mildest punishment followed; the copies were taken away from them and they received a light fine. Publister and composer were the real sufferers.

Mr. Boosey said, "You're a great favorite in England and if you will write two letters, one dignified and the other satirical, the *Times* and the *Daily Mail* probably will publish them and it may influence Parliament to make the stealing of a composition a felony."

I wrote a letter which was published in the *London Times*:

ANOTHER PHASE OF THE PIRACY QUESTION

INTERNATIONAL OBLIGATIONS

To the EDITOR: *The Times.*

Sir, — The question of music piracy has been so fully exploited that it is not my desire to enter upon any general discussion of the case, but if you will permit me to encroach upon your valued columns, I should like to call your attention to the international aspect of the question. The British government participated in the Berne conferences of 1885 and 1887, and the International Copyright Convention which resulted was adopted in full by English orders in council, which were intended to afford foreign authors and composers protection for their works, in Great Britain, in return for reciprocal advantages for British authors and composers in the other countries parties to said agreement. In 1891 the United States of America agreed upon terms of international copyright with the countries comprising the Berne Convention, including

Great Britain. As far as Great Britain is concerned, this international copyright agreement has proved a delusion and a
snare, because no foreign author or composer is protected in
his rights here.

To the best of my belief, music piracy does not exist in
any country where there is an international copyright law in
force, except Great Britain. Certainly it has been unknown in
the United States since 1891, and when a British subject has
complied with the copyright laws of my country he is immediately clothed with clearly defined legal rights which are
protected for him by the strong arm of the American law. I know
that my compositions, after having been entered for copyright
in Germany, France, Belgium, etc., are not stolen, and only in
Great Britain do I fail to receive the complete protection for my
music which was clearly the intent of the Berne Convention and
the subsequent copyright agreement with the United States.
Reciprocity is of no value if it does not reciprocate.

I have before me a pirated edition of my latest composition
which was printed and hawked about the streets of London,
within a few days of the authorized publication of this march, at
a price at which my publishers could not afford to print it. And
this has been the case with all my compositions in England for
several years. Piracy has had the effect of practically stopping
the sale of my genuine publications, thus depriving me of the
substantial income from that source that the popularity of my
music in this country gives me every reason to expect.

I am informed that the opposition of one of the law-makers
of this country has heretofore prevented the enactment of
proper legislation to remedy this evil. Whatever reason this
gentleman may have for refusing the British composer the
legitimate return for the work of his brain, I certainly deny his
right to say that the American composer must come under the
same ban, when the international copyright treaty guarantees

to the American composer the same protection in Great Britain which he enjoys at home. Is it reasonable to suppose that any country would have expended the time, trouble and money to establish an international copyright agreement with Great Britain except with the full belief that she would faithfully fulfill the terms of that agreement?

If, subsequently, Great Britain discovered that her laws were too lax to give the foreign composer the protection guaranteed him, I submit that it then became incumbent upon his Majesty's government to enact such legislation as would protect the foreign composer in his rights under the Berne Convention.

In short, when other countries are honorably carrying out the terms of a treaty to which Great Britain was a party, it seems to me that the national honor and pride demand that immediate steps be taken to fulfil the treaty obligations of this country in the matter of international copyright.

Yours truly,

JOHN PHILIP SOUSA

After a few days I followed that letter with this one in the *Daily Mail*:

To the EDITOR OF THE *Daily Mail*:

Sir, — With an avidity worthy the cause, I have read during my sojourn in these tight little islands everything that has come my way which has borne on the subject of music piracy.

Because of the laxity of your laws, and because of the perseverance of your music pirates, my royalties have gone a-glimmering. To use an anatomical expression current in my own country, I have been "getting it plump in the jugular."

One or two of the arguments I have noted, which were in opposition to the publisher and composer, have not struck me as hilariously humorous or even faintly facetious.

To elucidate: I read in your journal some days ago a communication in which the writer places the blame for the deplorable condition of the music trade here on the publisher, and points with argumentative finger to the fact that if the publisher had heeded the cry of the masses — whoever that nebulous body may be — and had sold his wares for less money, the music pirate would never have budded into existence. *Inter alia*, it would appear that the music pirate was called into the arena of activity to fill a long-felt want — to supply music at a cheaper price than the one at which the publisher cared to sell it — whether he could afford to or not.

It would appear under those conditions that the music pirate had a philanthropic mission. This mysterious and mercenary Messiah, noticing the dire distress of the tune-starved masses, whoever they may be, said, "I will save them. I will fill their melodic little Marys with music at 2d. a meal, I will gorge them with gavottes, build them up with ballads, and make muscle with marches. They shall become comely with comedy conceits, and radiantly rosy with ragtime rondos — and all at 2d. a throw."

And this beneficent pirate has waxed fat and saucy as he has hawked in the highways and byways spurious editions of him who is the favored of Melpomene and the boon companion of Orpheus. And I beg to ask, in words tinged with doubt and despair, where does the favored of Melpomene and the boon companion of Orpheus come in? The royalties of the "f. of M.," and the "b. c. of O." are like angels' visits — few and far between.

Shall the sunlight depart from the soul of the sweet singer of melody? Shall the fount of the muse dry up, as it were? Is there no balm in Gilead? Is there no surcease from sorrow for royalties that never materialize? Behold, O Starry-Eyed Britannia, a suppliant at the bar of public opinion, asking for justice, for your own, and for your friends' own.

The law was amended some time afterwards, and the pirate, like Othello, found his occupation gone.

It was only fair that, after my temerity in rushing into print, some of the English critics should take a fling at my Band and me. We enjoyed reading, in the *Pall Mall Gazette* and the *London World* that:

> There is always a sort of excitement in the musical atmosphere when Sousa is about, not, indeed, because his art and the art of the men under him is of a particularly high and unattainable kind, but it is a sort of atmosphere of thunderstorm and electricity. When you go into the hall where Sousa's Band is about to play, it is with the certain expectation that you are going to hear something very special in the way of the big drum, and in the clash of brassy sound. Once this impression is turned into a conviction it is possible to listen to Sousa for quite a long time! …
>
> To sum up, Sousa is an admirable tonic and need do no harm to the most highly developed musical sensibility. Only we must not imagine that there is more in him than there really is.
>
> Sousa's concerts are admirable and unique of their kind — and that kind is not far removed from the music hall.

We left England and began playing the Nouveau Theatre in Paris. Among the various medleys which I had concocted and arranged for my band there appeared one that year called, *In the Realm of the Dance,* in which I had linked waltz themes which were at that time very popular. I placed it on the Paris programme and on the opening night I noticed three distinguished-looking men sitting together in the front row. When I started the number they manifested, one by one, an unusual degree of interest. At the end of the concert the three gentlemen sent in their names: M. Paul Linke, M. Bosc and M. Danne, the three composers whose themes I had molded into my fantasy and who, strange to say, had come to my concert together and were pleasantly surprised by the number.

After the Paris engagement we played Lille, Brussels, Ghent, Antwerp, Liége, Cologne, Berlin, Königsberg and finally opened in St. Petersburg May 16th. The audiences at the Cisnicelli, where we played, were (with the exception of boys from the Westinghouse Brake Company) Russian officers, their wives, and civilian officials. The royal box, however, was draped in such a way that the occupants could not be seen. I imagine that the Czar was present several times. We gave nine performances.

Before reaching St. Petersburg, I had received a telegram from my advance man, "The police authorities demand copies of the words to be sung by your vocalist. They must be forwarded immediately." Miss Liebling sang coloratura songs in which there were many "Ahs." I did not know the lines, aside from the fact that those "Ahs" did occur frequently. Of course I couldn't send a telegram stating that the words were simply "Ah," so it looked as if a Russian concert would be more difficult to give than an American one. Having to submit all programmes and advertisements to an official censor creates some awkward situations, especially when the songs are sung in half a dozen different languages. It was clear that something had to be done, so I telegraphed the words of *Annie Rooney* and *Marguerite*. Miss Liebling then overcame the difficulty by singing the words of *Annie Rooney* to the tune of the *Pearl of Brazil*.

Yet another annoyance awaited me in St. Petersburg — I found the city plastered with the name of some rival who seemed to have come at the same time and whose name was Cyza. I wondered who this Cyza could be, and remonstrated with my advertising agent for not seeing that I was billed as prominently. I found out that "Cyza" was the Russian way of spelling Sousa!

In every country where I have played the national anthem I have awakened at once an intensity of patriotic enthusiasm, but I can remember no instance where the song of the people was received with more thrilling acclaim than in Russia. We were in St. Petersburg on the Czar's birthday. When I entered my dressing-room in the Cirque Cisnicelli, which is the equivalent of our New York Hippodrome, I found awaiting me there the secretary of the prefect of the city, who had come to request that I open the performance with the Russian national anthem.

"And" he added, "if it meets with a demonstration will you kindly repeat it?"

I assured him I would.

"In fact, sir, if it meets with several demonstrations, will you repeat it again?"

I said that I would repeat just as long as the majority applauded!

The audience consisted almost entirely of members of the nobility and the military, with their wives, sweethearts, sons and daughters. At the playing of the first note the entire audience rose and every man came to a salute. At the end of the anthem there was great applause and I was compelled to play the air four times before the audience was satisfied.

On retiring to my dressing-room at the end of the first part, I was again visited by the secretary who told me it was the wish of the prefect that I begin the second part of my program with the national anthem of America, and that he would have an official announce to the public beforehand the sentiment of the song.

Before we began our second part, a tall Russian announced to the public the name and character of the words of *The Star Spangled Banner* and we were compelled to repeat it several times; I have never heard more sincere or lasting applause for any musical number, nor do I believe that it was ever played with more fervor, dignity and spirit than by our boys in the capital of the Russian Empire.

At the end of our St. Petersburg season we went to Warsaw, Poland, and opened there on May 22, 1905. I stopped at the hotel built by Mr. Paderewski and I want to congratulate the gentleman, for he had evidently admired many appointments in American hotels and installed them in his Warsaw house for the comfort of his guests.

I had my troubles in Poland, however. During the intermission of my Warsaw concert, M. Jean de Reszke came back-stage with Godfrey Turner, treasurer of our organization. Mr. Turner had with him a statement of the receipts which amounted to about five thousand rubles or twenty-six hundred dollars, American money, and indignantly pointed to various items charged against the whole. There were so many hundred rubles for police tax, so many for the orphans' tax, so many for a school tax, and so on ad infinitum. I turned to M. de Reszke and said disgustedly, "Just read this."

But de Reszke smilingly handed it back to me, saying, "Forget it, Sousa. You're not in America now."

From Warsaw we went to Vienna for eight concerts. After the first matinee, Mr. Emil Lindau the dramatist and brother of Paul Lindau, the poet, came to my room. We began to talk of

Viennese composers and their work and I asked, "*Is The Blue Danube* still popular in Vienna?"

"Mr. Sousa, *The Blue Danube* will endure as long as Vienna exists!"

"I am glad," I answered, "for I'm going to play it to-night as an encore."

It was certainly received with tremendous applause. One of the Viennese papers was kind enough to say that the performance of the waltz by my band was the first time it had really been heard since Johann Strauss died.

I invited Mr. Lindau to dine with me and we were both pleased to discover that his wife, a Washington girl, had lived in the next block to mine and was a schoolmate of my sister, Tinnie. She was Emma Pourtallis, daughter of Count Pourtallis, the man who made the first survey of the Atlantic coast, and I remembered the family very well. An opera of Mr. Lindau's, called *Frühlingsluft* was being performed in Vienna at that moment.

Before leaving St. Petersburg I had bought a black slouch hat, much like those used by officers in the Civil War. The Vienna newspapermen all made a note of that hat. In their accounts of my arrival they described my uniform minutely and dwelt especially on the American hat I was wearing, one which, so they said, was doubtless unknown in any country except America. On looking inside the hat for the name of the maker, I found that it was manufactured in Vienna!

From Vienna we went on to Prague where I played in the conservatory hall where Dvorák had been a professor. We played the Largo from the New World Symphony, and the professors were kind enough to congratulate me on my interpretation of the famous composition.

From there to Dresden; from Dresden to Leipsic. At Leipsic my programme was largely Wagner and Sousa. We opened with the *Tannhäuser* overture and, just as the applause began to die down, and I started to give an encore, a man seated in the first row emitted a vicious hiss. I glared at him and played my encore. With the rendition of the next Wagner piece the same vicious hissing was heard. At the intermission one of the bandsmen, stirred to anger, volunteered to go out and thrash the hisser, but I forbade him to leave the stage. When we resumed the concert, the two remaining Wagner numbers were just as vigorously hissed by the same individual. As I left the platform I encountered the local manager and asked him, "Do you know that man in the duster and straw hat?"

He replied that he did not but would bring him to my dressing-room. He jumped down from the stage and soon had the man confronting me.

"May I ask why you hissed every Wagner number we played this evening?" I said coldly.

The man's face distorted with anger and bitterness as he blurted out, "I hissed Wagner music because I hate the Wagner family."

Our tour now took us to Hamburg, Copenhagen, Kiel, Dortmund, Amsterdam, The Hague, and finally to our favorite England. After a few concerts in Great Britain, we sailed on July 31, 1905 from Liverpool on the *Cedric*, which arrived in New York August 8th. Before we left Liverpool, Mr. John Hargreaves honored me with a luncheon at the City Hall, at which Lord Mayor Rutherford was master of ceremonies. I was delighted when they presented me with a volume printed in 1604 and written by a distinguished ancestor of mine, Louis de Sousa.

Once more in America, I made a short tour of Virginia and Ohio and then went south for a long hunting trip and a well-earned rest. It was my custom every year to take a few weeks from my "musicking" to shoot quail and deer in North Carolina. At first I went as the guest of Governor Glenn on his plantation; later I stayed with Mayor Richard Southerland in Henderson, North Carolina. If ever there was a genuine sportsman it was Dick Southerland, Mayor of Henderson. Our scene of action was June Clement's plantation twenty-five miles from the city.

On one occasion Dick suggested after a week at June's place that we go over to the Roanoke River and spend a week with a friend of his, a Mr. James Tanner, who had invited him many times to come and enjoy some *real* quail-shooting. So Dick and I hitched up our teams and made the trip across country to the Tanner plantation. We travelled all day, arriving at twilight. Mr. Tanner was a true Southerner, full of hospitality and an eager desire to make our stay a pleasant one. After supper he told me, "Mr. Sousa, I have selected a boy to wait on you who will doubt-less take excellent care of you, for he is used to Northerners, having been North himself. Come here, John Henry," he shouted; and a most insolent-looking colored boy sidled into the room.

"John Henry," my host went on, "take the best of care of my friend and see that he has whatever he wishes."

"Yaas, boss," muttered the darky, and disappeared.

I grew sleepy and went to my room. John Henry came in shortly. His first outburst was unexpected.

"Mister, I ain't no common nigger. I been North. Been to Richmond and to Washington."

"Yes? Well, build a fire," I replied.

"Don' fash yo'self, boss. I'll build it, if'n you gimme time." I began to undress and prepare for bed. It was cold and I needed the log fire at once if I needed it at all. But the boy was more than

IN THE PUBLIC EAR
From the New York Musical Courier, April 25, 1906

leisurely in his movement and built it very reluctantly. At last I jumped into bed and dismissed him.

"All right, mister. If'n yo' want mo' fire, just get up and put some logs on. I ain't goin' to stay here all night, mister; I been North and I know how they does things up there, specially in Richmon' and Washington." Out he walked. I found his manner irritating. I did not mind what he said, but I did take offense at his way of saying it. I finally fell asleep and my darky woke me about five with the information, "If yo' wants to go huntin' yo'd better kick off them covers, an' get up."

He started a fire and I jumped up and indulged in a bird-bath at the washbowl. I pulled on my underclothing and motioned to him to get my socks and boots from the fireside. I was wearing at that time some German socks that were made for different feet — rights and lefts. I offered him my right foot, and he began to put on the left sock. I immediately stopped him and then, addressing the air, I began to spout:

"I ask of what avail is the intellectual development of Europe, the so-called progress in America, when we have produced a human being who does not know a right sock from a left!"

"Boss, what-all's eatin' yo'?" he interrupted.

"To think that I should come here to this Southern home, steeped in the traditions of hospitality, and find a servitor so ignorant that he does not know a right sock from a left. Would he," I thundered, "put a left shoe on a right foot? Go to! poor, deluded being; stand aside and let me put my right sock on my right foot and my left sock on my left foot. Oh, just Heaven! This is too much — too much!"

John Henry was completely bewildered by my senseless tirade. I took the left sock and adjusted it properly and then put on the right while the boy, awed and silenced, looked on with the sweat gathering on his forehead.

"Now, put on my boots; but be sure that the left boot goes on the left foot and the right boot on the right foot."

He obeyed me humbly, then, still kneeling, assured me, "'Fore God, Mister, I never heard tell there was a right an' left sock!" He finished lacing the boots and I went down to breakfast. Mr. Tanner was at the head of the table and a half-dozen darkies scurried about, serving breakfast. John Henry joined them. Winking at Mr. Tanner, I solemnly began: "It's a painful thing for me, Mr. Tanner, to report any member of your entourage for dereliction of duty, but it's the first time in my life that I have had a servitor who didn't know a right sock from a left. John Henry is the ignorant one, and it shows, alas, that when he lived up 'North' in Washington, he did not associate with presidents, cabinet officers, congressmen and justices of the Supreme Court, but probably with the ignorant trash of the town. God help him — let us hope he may reform!"

For the rest of that week poor John Henry was the butt of the plantation. The whisper that followed him everywhere was: "Don't know a right sock from a left!" He became unbelievably humble.

In this same year — 1905 — Bobbs-Merrill Company brought out another novel of mine, *Pipetown Sandy* — for younger readers. It was partly auto-biographical, for *Pipetown* was the vernacular for that region of the city of Washington in which I grew up; and by the way, I have found that name on an official map. Although I have already quoted *I've Bin Fightin'* from that book, perhaps I shall be forgiven if I take one more thing, *The Feast of the Monkeys*, nonsense verses which have served to amuse my own grandchildren and may possibly win a smile from the children and grandchildren of my readers.

THE FEAST OF THE MONKEYS

IN days of old,
So I've been told,
The monkeys gave a feast.
They sent out cards,
With kind regards,
To every bird and beast.

The guests came dressed
In fashion's best,
Unmindful of expense;
Except the whale,
Whose swallowtail
Was "soaked" for fifty cents.

The guests checked wraps,
Canes, hats and caps;
And when that task was done,
The footman he
With dignitee
Announced them one by one.

In Monkey Hall
The host met all,
And hoped they'd feel at ease.
"I scarcely can,"
Said the Black and Tan,
"I'm busy hunting fleas."

"While waiting for
A score or more
Of guests," the hostess said,
"We'll have the Poodle
Sing *Yankee Doodle*,
A-standing on his head."

And when this through,
Good Parrot, you
Please show them how you swear."
"Oh, dear; don't cuss,"
Cried the Octopus
And walked off on his ear.

The Orang-Outang
A sea-song sang,
About a Chimpanzee
Who went abroad
In a drinking gourd
To the coast of Barbaree,

Where he heard one night
When the moon shone bright,
A school of mermaids pick
Chromatic scales
From off their tails,
And they did it mighty slick!

"All guests are here
To eat the cheer,
And dinner's served, my Lord."
The butler bowed;
And then the crowd
Rushed in with one accord.

The fiddler-crab
Came in a cab,
And played a piece in C;
While on his horn
The Unicorn
Blew, *You'll Remember Me.*

To give a touch
Of early Dutch
To this great feast of feasts,
I'll drink ten draps
Of Holland schnapps,"
Spoke out the King of Beasts.

"That must taste fine,"
Said the Porcupine,
"Did you see him smack his lip?"
"I'd smack mine, too,"
Cried the Kangaroo,
"If I didn't have the pip."

The Lion stood,
And said: "Be good
Enough to look this way;
Court Etiquette
Do not forget,
And mark well what I say;

My royal wish
Is ev'ry dish
Be tasted first by me."
"Here's where I smile,"
Said the Crocodile,
And he climbed an axle-tree.

The soup was brought,
And quick as thought,
The Lion ate it all.
"You can't beat that,"
Exclaimed the Cat,
"For monumental gall."

"The soup," all cried.
"Gone," Leo replied,
"'Twas just a bit too thick."
"When we get through,"
Remarked the Gnu,
"I'll hit him with a brick."

The Tiger stepped,
Or, rather, crept
Up where the Lion sat.
"O, mighty boss,
I'm at a loss
To know where I am at.

I came tonight
With appetite
To drink and also eat;
As a Tiger grand,
I now demand,
I get there with both feet."

The Lion got
All-fired hot
And in a passion flew.
"Get out," he cried,
"And save your hide,
You most offensive *You*."

"I'm not afraid,"
The Tiger said,
"I know what I'm about."
But the Lion's paw
Reached the Tiger's jaw,
And he was good and out.

The salt-sea smell
Of Mackerel
Upon the air arose;
Each hungry guest
Great joy expressed,
And, "sniff!" went every nose.

With glutton look
The Lion took
The spiced and sav'ry dish.
Without a pause
He worked his jaws,
And gobbled all the fish.

Then ate the roast,
The quail on toast,
The pork, both fat and lean;
The jam and lamb,
The potted ham,
And drank the kerosene.

He raised his voice:
"Come, all, rejoice,
You've seen your monarch dine."
"Never again,"
Clucked an angry Hen,
And all sang *Old Lang Syne*.

After a season at Willow Grove my groom and I started off on a horseback journey to Washington, where two friends joined us on a trip to the Patuxent River in southern Maryland for some rail- and reed-bird shooting. The mosquito was, beyond a doubt, the original settler on the marshes of the Patuxent and had not deserted his birthplace at our advent. In my boyhood I had been bitten by every mosquito on the Potomac Flats, and never escaped malaria in the fall, but the swamps of old Patuxent were even worse. Before I left the River, I was thoroughly infected. When I reached New York I was greeted by Mr. Quinlan, the London manager who had contracted with me for a world tour and who wished to discuss with me a change of route. We had planned to sail from England on the *Anchises*, a brand new ship, but labor troubles interfered, and so we decided to sail on the *Tainui*, with Teneriffe for our first stop. Mr. Quinlan and a group of friends were dining with me when that deadly Patuxent malaria took me in its grip and shook me ruthlessly. My guests, alarmed at my quaking and quivering, insisted that I go home at once and call a doctor. Rest and much quinine enabled me to arise for our farewell concert at the Metropolitan Opera House, and the next day we left for New England and Eastern Canada. Malaria still dogged my footsteps. In New Haven I left the Yale Concert Hall on a stretcher. Two weeks in the hospital, and further stoking of quinine resulted in my finally joining the band in Montreal.

Chapter XIV

WE SAIL IN 1910 ON A WORLD TOUR — ENGLAND, IRELAND, SCOTLAND, WALES — AFRICA — AN AMERICAN KAFFIR IN KIMBERLEY — JOHANNESBURG — PRETORIA — FAREWELL CONCERT — TWENTY-TWO DAYS TO TASMANIA — MELBOURNE, SYDNEY, ADELAIDE — THE CRUEL HUNTSMAN — I TALK SHOP — AUSTRALIA LURES US — THE NATIONAL DIRGE OF AMERICA — NEW ZEALAND — MUSIC AND THE DRAMA — HAWAII — VICTORIA — HAS ANYBODY HERE SEEN KELLY?

WE SAILED the 24th of December, 1910, sixty-nine of us, on the *Baltic* for Liverpool.

On this tour, we opened in London January 2, 1911, and visited all the principal cities of England, Ireland, Scotland and Wales. At Myrta-Tydvil the stage had evidently suffered some amateur carpentering, in order to enlarge it to accommodate the band, and when we struck up *The Stars and Strips Forever*, that piece (always the climax of any programme) was the signal for catastrophe! My conducting stand collapsed and I was buried seven feet beneath it. It is a breath-snatching sensation to fall seven feet below the floor with nothing to catch on to. I went down in a cloud of dust and debris and the prima donna, Miss Root, on hearing the crash, believed I had been killed and rushed out on the stage, screaming. I quickly righted myself, however, crawled up out of the depths, bowed to the audience and said, "We will now continue." Calmly we finished the programme.

The news of my mishap spread throughout the kingdom and nearly every day some anxious person would come and ask if I were injured. I believe that among these solicitous callers who seemed so delighted to learn that I was whole and uninjured there were agents sent by their various cities to inquire so that the concert dates might be called off in plenty of time!

We left Europe for South Africa on March 4th and gave our first concert at Capetown on the 24th. It was there that I met Lady Gladstone, whose famous husband was on a mission in South Africa at the time. Capetown was a pleasant place for music. They were delighted with *Tannhäuser* and *The Ride of the Valkyries* and all our marches and popular fancies. We played to an enormous house. Next came Kimberley.

Kimberley's naïveté did not please me. When I arrived I found that we were advertised to give our concert in a public park, with no way of controlling the ingress or egress of the audience. That honest-hearted South African representative believed that the dear public would hunt up the ticket-seller, buy tickets, and wait in line to pass the proper entrance, even though the park was quite unfenced and the whole world might have crowded in. Said the simple manager to me, "There is only one hall in town and that holds but eleven hundred people."

"Get that," I directed.

He engaged the hall, and we filled it. There were, however, thousands of swarming, protesting people outside who had come in from the surrounding country, hoping to hear the band without cost. They were loud in their complaints over our meanness in expecting money for our efforts. But, since our expenses were $2500 a day on the tour and we were certainly not touring for our health, we felt no compunction.

One night at dinner in Kimberley, the East Indian head waiter came to my table and said, "Mr. Sousa, there's a Kaffir outside waiting to speak to you."

"A Kaffir? I don't know any Kaffirs."

"He says he met you in America, sir."

"Oh, all right, send him in. I'll see him."

My black friend could not reach my side soon enough; he rushed over to me, and cried, "How d'do, Mr. Sousa! Don' yo' remember me? I'm Jim Nelson f'om Henderson, Nor' Ca'lina!"

"How are you, Jim? And what are you doing so far from home?"

"Mr. Sousa, I ain't nothin' but a fool nigger. I meets a man in No'folk who says I ought to see the home of my fo'fathers, an' I gets it into my noodle that I gotta see that home o' my fo'fathers. That man gets me a job on a ship comin' over here an' it sailed an' sailed, and fo' de Lord, I'll never do it again! This ain't no place fo'an honest cullud man. These yere Kaffirs do me up at craps. Lord, how they-all can play craps! Now they got all my money an' I ain't got no place to lay my haid. Mr. Sousa, I begs you to take me along with the band. I'll work until I drops in my tracks, only take me, Mr. Sousa, fo' God's sake, take me!"

I told him he could come along on the African tour and help with the baggage. He was with us for several weeks, but the story ended like a good many others of similar import; the homesick one fell for a dusky Basuto belle and for all I know, remained in "the land of his fo'fathers" forever after.

The division of the Africans into tribes is very much like the division of our Indian tribes in America. The generic name for the African is "Kaffir" and this is the word most commonly used. In Africa practically no one says "Negro" or "nigger." In the larger towns there are Zulu policemen who are employed entirely for the purpose of governing the Kaffirs. They are usually magnificent specimens, six-footers, barefooted, dark, shining men, as strong as bulls.

Johannesburg kept us happy and occupied for two weeks. Then came Pretoria, the capital of the Dominion, and Krugersdorp, where I had an odd experience. I was lunching at one of the famous roadhouses in the vicinity, when suddenly the proprietor moved his Victrola out on the front porch and made ready to play some fifteen or twenty of my compositions! With the strains of the first record a crowd of Kaffirs immediately surrounded the place. When I had finished lunch (the crowd now numbered hundreds) the man asked me to come out while he addressed the natives. He spoke in their own tongue and then played *The Stars and Stripes Forever* on his Victrola. Whether he had declared that I was the composer of the march, or the inventor of the Victrola, I know not but I do know that I was alarmed by the worship I received. One by one those natives stole up, felt my coat, and salaamed until their noses nearly touched the dirt. They followed me to my motor car and shouted loud acclaim till we vanished from sight.

A Sunday morning visit to the Cinderella Mine at Boxburgh, one of de Beer's diamond mines, proved to be full of color and interest. The various tribes that work in the mines were to perform their traditional dances in the compound. Each tribe seemed to keep aloof from the others and to avoid interference in any way with the dances of another tribe. One of their musical instruments must have been the great-great-grandfather of the xylophone. It had no definite scale and consisted only of four or five pieces of wood grouped in such a way that hammering on them produced an indefinable sound not worthy the name of music! One of the surprises of that memorable Sunday was a meeting with W. J. Kelly, so well known to vaudeville audiences as the "Virginia Judge."

We played Grahamstown and Elizabethtown and then went to the Natal country where in Pietermaritzburg and Durban we found the finest town halls imaginable. In Capetown again, we

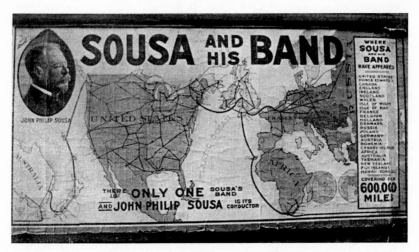

AROUND THE WORLD, 1910–1911

gave our farewell African concert. The night of the concert the boat which was to bear us further on our journey, the *Ionic*, made harbor. But in the morning, an ominous yellow quarantine flag was flying from her mast. I was scarcely out of bed when a telephone message arrived from Captain Roberts assuring me that there was no smallpox aboard. An arbitrary harbor inspector had insisted on putting the vessel in quarantine because a couple of stupid immigrants had gorged themselves sick with fresh pork, a senseless thing to do in that hot climate. Captain Roberts was confident that the boat would be permitted to sail that afternoon. We did sail, but the ship's physician was taken ill almost immediately and our band physician, Dr. Low, had to assume charge of the ailments of passengers and crew.

We were twenty-two days making that dreary trip across the Indian Ocean south to Tasmania and did not once see the sun. The boat tossed like a peanut shell, and when it wasn't raining it was snowing, and when it scorned to snow it incontinently hailed. Not a vessel did we meet until we were near Tasmania.

We were a day late and so lost our concert in Hobart much to the disappointment of a sold-out house. It was, therefore, in Launceston that we gave our first concert in Australasia. The critics were enthusiastic. One wrote: "It would be a strange audience that could not be pleased with the band and its conductor, for he gratified the vociferously expressed wishes of those present with well-nigh a dozen encores. The organization is superb; the versatility is remarkable, and its perfect rendition of the most difficult compositions, alike combine in compelling admiration."

The *Rotomahana* bore us to Melbourne, and from there we set out for Sydney. Sydney met us with seven of their largest bands, blended into one great harmonious group under the leadership of J. Devlin. At the Town Hall I was given a rousing reception. There the Professional Musicians' Band, conducted by Mr. O'Brien, played my suite, *Looking Upward* and *The Stars and Stripes Forever*. When I was called on to address the assemblage, I said:

"It isn't every fellow who comes thousands of miles with his band, and is met by a band of a thousand, a rattling good one too, and then, entering a hall, hears another band play his own music faithfully and beautifully. At the present time a splendid friendship exists between America and Australia. Our fleet has been here and returned home full of admiration for Australia and Australians. With your mother, Great Britain, to the West of you and your cousin, America, to the East of you, you can sleep o' nights without a sentry. One of your poets has said that you are the 'Empress of the Southern Wave' and I pray Heaven that you may reign forever!"

In the newspaper accounts of the first concert in Sydney, it was said: "Mr. Sousa, whose style as a conductor is entirely free from the absurd exaggeration humorous writers had prepared Australia to expect, advanced rapidly to his place, was warmly welcomed by the audience and at once cut short the applause by raising his baton. This concise manner of getting to work without delay characterized his system throughout the evening."

Sydney had its share of reformers, too, and some of them evidently thought I needed reforming. The *London Sketch* had published an article of mine on clay pigeon shooting; it had attracted the attention of editors all along our route and most of the Australian papers had reproduced it. I had been in Sydney only a few days when I received this letter from a well-meaning clergyman:

MY DEAR SIR:

I read your article on pigeon shooting, and I am horrified at the thought that you, a musician, a member of a profession giving to the world the sweetest tones of nature, should stoop so low as to shoot God's beautiful creatures. Repent, sir, ere it is too late. Give up your murderous practice of killing the beautiful feathered denizens of the fields, I beseech you.

It seemed cruel to spoil so choice a bit of crusading, but I bought a half dozen clay birds at a gun store and sent them to the soft-hearted cleric, with the following letter:

REVEREND SIR:

Your letter received and noted. Before I received it I went out and in my sinful way bagged the enclosed pigeons. I am sorry I didn't hear from you earlier, but I enclose the pigeons as evidence of my accuracy as a shot. Please have them broiled and let me know how they taste!"

But, alas, he wasn't sport enough to write and apologize!

It was while we were in Sydney that I met, after many years of epistolary acquaintance, Mr. J. C. Williamson, the famous theatrical manager. We talked of the time he was in New York in 1879 and heard my instrumentation of *Pinafore*. He had bought the Australian rights of that opera from Gilbert and Sullivan, and he told me genially,

> "When I obtained the Australian rights I heard a performance of the opera at Daly's theater, New York, by a Church Choir company, where the singing was the dominant feature. I was so delighted with the chorus and the orchestration that I inquired who had executed the latter and learned that the conductor of the company had orchestrated the music himself. He was glad to let me have a copy to take to Australia. You, Mr. Sousa, were that obliging conductor and doubtless recall the incident."

Gilbert had just died and Mr. Williamson and I discussed the operas which he and Sullivan had so happily conceived.

"Gilbert," remarked Mr. Williamson, "was terribly excited and worried at the final rehearsal for *The Mikado* when it was being prepared for production in London. Apparently he could not obtain the desired results from the company. It seemed to me that his method of explaining his conception made them more mechanical each time he had them repeat a scene. Of course at the dress rehearsal the thing limped horribly. From a brilliant gathering of professionals, society leaders and press representatives, there came scarcely a ripple of applause. The only thing which seemed to awaken much interest was the Mikado's song, and that they had been planning to cut out. However, since it received a little encouragement from the audience it was suffered to remain. But the dress rehearsal was in every way disappointing and the wise ones were shaking their heads and prophesying a failure for *The Mikado*. I was present at the first performance the next night, and it was an overwhelming and triumphant success. Gilbert was not in the audience. He was nervously pacing up and down the Embankment during the entire performance! Ah, there was a brilliant fellow. He was tremendously popular socially and one of the greatest wits the English social world ever boasted. London will miss him; and when London misses a man, he must be brilliant indeed."

It was a heartfelt tribute to a gallant gentleman and a great writer, who won his place with clean comedy and pure wit and kindly satire.

On June third we closed our Sydney season after fifty-six concerts and matinees in that interesting city of 600,000, of a character half English, half American. We opened June fifth in Melbourne at the Glaciarium, where we were met by the massed bands of Melbourne and vicinity and marched in triumph to our hotel. Winter was coming on apace and the advertisements read, "The Glaciarium will be especially heated for the Sousa season." For in Australia, July is the coldest month and December the hottest!

On the closing night in Sydney I made probably the shortest speech on record. As we finished *Auld Lang Syne* there were cheers and pleas for a speech. I bowed and backed off but the applause continued, so I advanced to the front of the platform and when I had obtained silence I called out, "Can everybody hear me?"

"Yes!" came from all parts of the house.

With a broad smile I shouted back, "Good night!" and scampered offstage.

TIME TABLE.

Day	Date	Town	Depart.	Arrive	Hall	Grocers	Box Office	Time	Time of Concert	Remarks
Friday	MARCH 24th	Cape Town			City Hall	Dyment Ground	La Quesne & Smith	Aft. 4 Even. 3 and 8.15	3 and 8.15	
Saturday	25th	"						Aft. & Even. 3 and 8.15		
Sunday	26th	"	11.30 a.m.							Travel
Monday	27th	Kimberley		5.52 p.m.	Town Hall	Gardens	Leo Simons	Even. 3	8.15	
Tuesday	28th	"	8.45 p.m.				Leo Simons	Aft. & Even. 3		
Wednesday to	29th	Johannesburg		9 a.m.		Wanderers Ground	Mackay Bros.	"	Even. Aft. & Even. at 3, 8, 8.15. m. Sunday Aft.	Sacred Concert, Aprl 2, evening Wanderers Grounds.
Sunday	APRIL 2nd	"							To be arranged	
	3rd		3.30 p.m.							
Monday	3rd	Pretoria		8.45 p.m.	Marion, Opera House	Town, Zoo, Gardens	"	Aft. & Even. 3 and 8.15	Aft. & Even. 3 and 8.15	
Tuesday	4th	"					"			
Wednesday	5th	"	8.15 a.m.				"			
Wednesday	5th	Johannesburg	8 p.m.	3.51 a.m.	Marion, Wanderers		"	Aft.	3	
Wednesday	6th	Krugersdorp		7 p.m.		Wanderers	W. B. Harris	Even.	8.15	
Thursday	6th	Johannesburg	11.30 a.m.	12.30 p.m.		Wanderers	Mackay Bros.	Aft.	3	
Thursday	6th	"	3 p.m.							
Tuesday	6th	Boksburg		7 p.m.	Femsled Hall		Gouldie & Co.	Even.	8.15	
Friday	7th	Germiston	11.30 a.m.	12 noon.		Boschum Ground	W. Jennings	Aft. & Even. 3 and 8.15	Aft. & Even. 3 and 8.15	
Friday	7th	Johannesburg	11.30 p.m.	11.45 p.m.				To be arranged		
Saturday	8th	"	1.30 a.m.							
Sunday	9th									
Monday	10th	Maritzburg		8.30 a.m.	Town Hall		Vause, Slatter & Co.	Aft. & Even. 3 and 8.15	Aft. & Even. 3 and 8.15	
Tuesday	11th		8.45 a.m.							
Wednesday	12th	Durban		1.30 p.m.	Even., Town Hall	Maison, Lurde Co.	Jackson Bracken	Aft. & Even. 3 and 8.15	Aft. & Even. 3 and 8.15	Sunne
Thursday	13th	"	1.30, 8.30. Sail							Sacred
Good Friday	14th	East London		Boat, 6 a.m.	Town Hall		Good & Grant.	Aft. & Even. 3 and 8.15	Aft. & Even. 3 and 8.15	
Saturday	15th	"	1.30 a.m.							
Saturday	16th	King Wm's Tn		4.10 p.m.	Town Hall		Randells	Even.	3 and 8.15	3 Matinee.
Sunday	16th	"	11.30 a.m.							
K'r Monday	17th	Grahamstown		6.10 a.m.	Town Hall	Fellies Green	Grocer & Sherry	Aft. & Even. 3 and 8.15	3 and 8.15	Easter Monday.
Tuesday	18th	Port Elizabeth	2.35 p.m.	2.45 p.m.	Feather Market	"	" Afternoon."	Even.	8.15	
Wednesday	19th	"				To be arranged		Aft.	3	
Wednesday	19th									
Thursday	20th	In train	8 p.m.							
Friday	21st	Cape Town					Sail S.S. IONIO for HOBART.			

ITINERARY OF SOUTH AFRICA TOUR, 1911

We played Ballarat and Adelaide, where an inquisitive reporter approached me with a copy of my programme in his hand and said:

"From what I have heard of your organization, it is so splendidly equipped that I should think you would play only the most majestic music of the masters. Why do you mix it up with lighter stuff?"

I answered him thoughtfully:

"When I left Washington to gather together my own organization I had four distinct bodies comprising instrumental combinations well suited to interpret my ideas of the entertaining and the educational. The lover of poetry would never scorn *The Ode to a Skylark* because it happens to be shorter than *The Vision of Sir Launfal* nor did I wish to confine myself to the ponderous symphony, the long-drawn-out overture or the massive prelude, banishing from my repertory the fanciful waltz, the stirring march and the tender ballad.

"Believing then and — even more strongly now — that entertainment is of more real value to the world than technical education in music appreciation, I would not accept the symphonic orchestra as my medium. Of course the cabaret orchestra's limitations were too great to bother with that; the military band was too vague in its instrumentation, but a new combination, unhampered by tradition, which could get at the hearts of the people was my desideratum. I wanted to avoid those musical combinations governed by certain laws as enduring as those of the Medes and the Persians, and institute one which I felt would cater to the many rather than the few. And the outcome is the combination which I have at the present time."

"What superiority do you claim for it?" asked the reporter.

"I claim a splendid balance of tone. Also, a multiplicity of quartettes; a virtuosity of execution, and my freedom to be absolutely eclectic in my programmes. I realized in the beginning that those composers known as the classicists would not lend themselves at all times to my scheme of orchestration. Therefore very little is heard at my concerts of Beethoven, Haydn and Mozart. The progress in complexity of orchestration and harmonic device, together with melodic charm is being supplied by the big men of to-day — such as Wagner, Richard Strauss, Elgar, Dvorák, Tschaikowsky, and others. And a combination of the instruments which constitute my organization gives an admirable rendition of the lavish tone coloring in modern music. Take the drama: it is not incongruous to see a comedy scene immediately follow a tragic one; in fact it is a favorite device of Shakespeare and many other master dramatists. It does not shock me to see laughter follow tears in the romantic drama. So it is that I have no hesitation in combining in my programme tinkling comedy with symphonic tragedy or rhythmic march with classic tone-picture."

The erudite men and women who usually buy tickets for symphonic concerts no doubt prefer that form of musical pabulum to any other. One feature is certainly in its favor; the symphonic orchestra is the same everywhere, be it Buda-Pesth, London, Paris, Madrid or New York; the same instruments and the same literature are in use. It is sad, however, to these same erudite men and women that the only addition to the resources of the symphony orchestra since the days of Haydn, with the exception of the harp, has been a wind instrument. Sometimes excellent judgment is displayed by the potentates of symphony when they enlarge an orchestra from sixty to seventy or ninety to a hundred players, in increasing only the string department and leaving the wood-wind and brass at exactly the same ratio for a hundred men as there had been for seventy. This idea of having four oboes for two parts gives the extra players more opportunity to think of home cooking than of playing. Two parts for two players seems to me to be correct. But a good deal of talent is lost in doubling men for each part. It reminds us of the lazy man and the diligent man who were called upon to lift a fat woman who had suddenly fainted. The lazy man said to the diligent, "You lift while I groan!"

The first of the classic orchestras dating from Haydn consisted of one flute, two oboes, two clarinets, two bassoons, two horns, two trumpets, tympani, and the strings. The additions to-day used by the moderns are piccolos, English horns, contra-bassoons, heckle-phone, saxophone, cornet, an array of French horns, trombones, tubas, euphoniums and Sousaphones. In the issuing of new orchestral compositions the publishers include these parts and know that players will be found for them. Here is where the symphonic orchestra has an advantage over the wood-wind band, for no two nations have the same instrumentation for the latter. It seems almost as if some committee had convened and decided on the instrumentation of a military band — and the bands of all countries had lined up accordingly, although, in the case of the Garde Republicaine, one notices a greater variety in wood-wind than the German band possesses. The Germans have plenty of brass and this makes them desirable for outdoor concerts.

Gilmore might be taken as an example of perfect organizing. His band went to Europe in 1878 equipped to a greater degree of musical perfection and artistic merit than any known organization of that day. It numbered about sixty-six musicians, divided thus:

2 piccolos

2 flutes

2 oboes

1 A♭ clarinet

3 E♭ clarinets

8 first clarinets

4 second clarinets

4 third clarinets

1 alto clarinet

1 bass clarinet

1 soprano saxophone

1 alto saxophone

1 baritone saxophone

2 bassoons

1 contra bassoon

1 E♭ cornet

2 first cornets

2 second cornets

2 trumpets

2 Fluegel horns

4 French horns

2 altos

2 tenor horns

2 Euphoniums

3 trombones

2 E♭ tubas

2 B♭ tubas

3 battery

My organization in 1924 included:

6 flutes

2 oboes

1 English horn

14 first clarinets

6 second clarinets

6 third clarinets

1 alto clarinet

2 bass clarinets

2 bassoons

4 alto saxophones

3 battery

2 tenor saxophones

1 baritone saxophone

1 bass saxophone

4 first cornets

2 second cornets

2 trumpets

4 horns

4 trombones

2 Euphoniums

6 Sousaphones in B♭

In the instrumentation of these two bands, it may be observed that sixteen of Mr. Gilmore's instruments had no place in mine.

Foreign conductors, after touring America with their bands, went back to Europe and made some rather ridiculous comments. One of them, who brought a fairly good band to the St. Louis World Fair, complained that America demanded a cheap type of music. That is arrant nonsense! I played in fourteen different countries and I gave Europe and America precisely the same musical fare. America evidenced much the same musical taste as all the other countries, and American appreciation of music played in an inspirational manner is exactly as great as that encountered in any part of the Old World.

It is, however, absolutely necessary that music should not be rendered in a prosaic or stereotyped manner, if it is to combine an inspirational with an intellectual appeal. With no wish to be egotistical, I believe that music often fails of a response, not because of the music or because of the players, but owing to a lack of ability in the conductor. Berlioz, in speaking of conductors, says:

"The performers should feel what he feels, comprehend his mood. Then his emotion communicates itself to those whom he directs; his inward fire warms them; his electric glow animates them; his force of impulse excites them; he throws around him the vital undulation of musical art. If he be inert and frozen, on the contrary, he paralyzes all about him, like those floating masses of the polar seas the approach of which is perceived through the sudden cooling of the atmosphere."

In an Australian hotel I was descending in the elevator when the man at my side suddenly turned to me and said,
"I'll bet you a hundred dollars to ten that you can't tell me where I saw you last." Concluding that he was an American because he had said "dollars" instead of "pounds" I replied,
"Doubtless in the States."

"Yes," said he, "between Parkton, Maryland, and York, Pennsylvania. It was raining 'cats and dogs' and you were soaked to the skin. I saw you leading a lame horse and shielding your face from the storm as you walked. I wanted to stop and ask you to join us in the car but my companion said, 'It's useless to attempt that. Any man who has trudged thirty odd miles through the rain is not going to abandon his horse as he nears the end of his tramp, for the sake of riding in an automobile.' " I remembered the occasion and Marguerite's lameness. The mare and I had reached York at ten o'clock that night.

There is an Australian saying, "Sydney for pleasure, Melbourne for business, and Adelaide for culture." I met a mighty fine Australian in Adelaide — a station-owner. Stations, in Australia, are much the same as our American plantations. He was sincere in his admiration for the simple bushmen of the island continent and recounted to me an incident which had greatly impressed him a few days before. He was walking over the station to inspect his sheep and cattle, and one of the bushmen, a young chap whom he often summoned to him, was following at his heels. When they returned to the bungalow this black boy threw himself at his employer's feet and cried, "Master, Master, whenever you take me out, make me walk ahead."

"Why, what's the matter?" asked the station-owner.

"Oh, master, when I walk at your heels something says to me, 'Kill him, kill him,' and it is all I can do to resist. Master, kill me now if you want me to walk at your heels hereafter."

Australia is a "crust" country. Its towns are usually on the seashore, and little is known of the interior. The "Laughing Jackass" is perhaps the most interesting bird in Australia. He is a member of the kingfisher family and a great snake killer. When he espies a snake he darts down, grabs it by the back of the neck, takes it far in the air, and then drops it to the ground; like the Irishman's explanation — it is not the fall that kills it but the sudden contact with the ground. During the descent of the snake the bird laughs wildly and delightedly. I have heard his laugh many times, and certainly it is a happy, satisfying sort of sound. Another bird found in immense flocks in Australia is the sulphur-crested cockatoo. When a thousand of them are flushed at one time the sky is a veritable scintillation of glimmering yellow and white.

On the Fourth of July I was playing in Melbourne in Exhibition Hall. I planned a programme that overflowed with American music, and tacked on the national anthem for good measure as a fitting wind-up. I had noticed a soldierly-looking man around the building and it occurred to me that it would be a good idea to have him bring on our flag when we played *The Star Spangled Banner*. The arrangements were made and he understood his instructions as follows: as I gave the sign he was to march down the centre of the stage, stop in front of me and wave the flag continuously until the music ceased. He was an amazingly conscientious man and arrived fully a half hour before the performance, although the national anthem was two hours and a half away.

At length we reached the next to the last number and Miss Zedeler entered for her violin solo. As she began, a note was handed me. It was from Sir George Reed, High Commissioner of Australia:

MY DEAR MR. SOUSA:

I am here with a party of friends and enjoying every moment of your concert. Some of my party heard your beautiful rendition last night of Chopin's *Funeral March*. May I ask that you repeat it? We are most anxious to hear it.

GEORGE REED

I instructed my band to have the music for the *March* ready to play immediately after the violin solo. The violinist made her bow and retired, and we began. When we reached the trio of the dirge I turned to the saxophones as the score indicated their solo. Facing them, I was in a direct line with the flag bearer. To him this was the supreme moment of the concert. Thoroughly oblivious of my signs of negation he marched forward, waving the flag, until he was directly in front of me — and he kept on waving that flag until the funeral march was finished!

A Melbourne paper observed next morning that it was indeed strange that wide-awake America should have so funereal a piece of music for its national anthem.

We visited Toowoomba and then Brisbane, which was as far North as we penetrated on the Australian tour. The papers there were most appreciative. One said: "If Sebastian Bach is the musician's musician and Carl Czerny the student's musician, emphatically John Philip Sousa is the people's musician."

In my address I thanked the audience for applauding so long because it would shorten my speech. I told them how I had met a Queenslander in New York who said, "I see you are going to Australia. Don't miss Brisbane. Adelaide is all right. So are Melbourne and Sydney, but Brisbane — well, it's just next door to Paradise. You have only to look over the fence and there she is, Paradise. The only reason they don't call Brisbane 'Paradise' is because Paradise patented it first!"

At my final concert in Sydney I said:

"I say goodbye with sadness in my heart. In the long experience of a man who has travelled over the greater part of the civilized world, I find that ideas of the countries visited often undergo a change. One is apt to possess preconceived notions of a place, which personal observation is bound to revolutionize. Australia seems to me a young country like my own land and consequently before the bar of public opinion. Interest is always keen in the young, whether nation or individual. Since we have been here we have covered the territory from Adelaide to Brisbane and I have gathered a very fair idea of the genius of your people and of their hopes for the future of the country. Australia has been modest in telling the world about herself, but with your climate and the tremendous amount of raw material you are producing, you are bound to become one of the important countries of the world. I have met some gifted musicians during my stay and the Australian audiences have endeared themselves to me because they are splendid listeners. No praise is more grateful than that of faithful attention. You have every reason to feel that you have a seat with the rest of us at the table of artistic endeavor."

We sailed on the *Ulamaroa* for Invercargill, New Zealand, the most southerly town in the world. In my walks about town I came upon two interesting pieces of jade. On one was carved "N. Z." and on the other, "V. R." The letters caught my fancy, for I foresaw a pleasant use for them, and, buying both pieces, I returned to the hotel and called on Miss Nico-line Zedeler, our violinist. I presented her with the jade marked "N. Z.," saying, "You seem to have made a great hit out here; they are already selling jewelled souvenirs with your initials on them." Miss Zedeler was delighted and so was Miss Virginia Root, our songstress, to whom I presented the jade marked "V. R." I didn't tell them that the shopkeeper who sold them said that the initials stood for "New Zealand" and "Victoria Regina." But they were bright girls and I have no doubt that they soon found out for themselves.

From Invercargill we proceeded to Dunedin, then on to Christchurch and Wellington. At Wellington I struck up a pleasant friendship. Mr. Hargus Plimmer, a celebrated New Zealand author, met our vessel at the dock and introduced himself to me, saying that the editor of the *Dominion* had directed him to ask me for an interview. We went to my hotel and talked an hour. Finally we lunched together. And then I invited him to dinner. In fact, our entire stay in Wellington was punctuated with pleasant dinners *en famille* with Mr. Plimmer's family or similar entertainments given by mine. In the course of the discussions I had that week with Mr. Plimmer, there was one on the music of the drama.

From the days of Arion and Thespis down to the present, I do not believe any of the arts of the theatre show a progress equal to music. The application of electricity has helped the stage immeasurably but its effect on the mind of the auditor is not so lasting as the influence of music. Among the various forms of theatrical entertainment music is paramount as a mode for expression and as a companion of another art. In tragedy and comedy, music is used to heighten the effect of a dramatic situation; in pantomine, to make clearer the intention to be conveyed by the actor. Music's fascination makes the ballet enduring and possible. Grand opera is the most powerful of stage appeals and that almost entirely through the beauty of music. Opera is drama for the sake of music, while in the spoken tragedy and comedy, music is for the sake of the drama. In the spoken drama the definite classes are the farce, the comedy, the romantic play and the tragedy. These are paralleled in melody by the musical comedy, the comic opera, the romantic opera and grand opera — each independent of the other and all judged by a standard set for its kind.

The introduction of music into the theatre (I use theatre in contradistinction to opera house) was brought about by accident. In the beginning there were no reserved seats, no press agents, no critics. Therefore the audiences had to come to the play to judge for themselves. It was a case of "first come, first served," and consequently, to secure the best seats there was pushing and shoving, snarling and bickering, and even fighting — which reminds us that we do the same thing to-day during the rush hours in the subways. After the audience was housed, the dimness of the candle light and the strain of waiting a whole hour for the performance to commence would bring about rows and riots and sometimes the stage itself would be invaded by an unruly mob, ready to demolish anything handy. The managers realized that something had to be done, and the C. B. Dillingham of his time solved the problem. He inaugurated preliminary orchestral music before the play. It was a concert of three numbers and was known as the first, second and third music. These musical numbers were played at intervals between the time of the opening of the doors until the rising of the curtain. The second selection was the longest and principal one and the third was the "curtain tune."

As time went on, the audience assumed the privilege of calling for their favorite tunes, or popular compositions of the day. But this did not work out satisfactorily, for at times factions

A SOUTH AFRICAN TAXI IN DURBAN

would insist on some political, racial or sectarian tune and if the orchestra played it, there would be a fight because they did play it and if the orchestra didn't play it, there would be a fight because they didn't play it; so these tunes were bound to start a fight anyway and consequently the custom fell into disuse. Imagine what would have happened if, just after our Civil War, someone in a theatre south of Mason and Dixon's line had called for *Marching Through Georgia!*

As the critic, the press agent and reserved seats became an established fact, the first, second and third music preliminary to the performance gradually retired and there came in their stead what is known to-day as the overture. Even the overture, now that we are so firmly established by law and order in our theatres, is disappearing from the houses devoted to the drama without incidental music.

With the development of the orchestra in symphony and operatic performances, and theater is calling more and more on music for help — the picture-houses have found it necessary to have orchestral equipment of greater than primitive type. Musical comedy and comic operas, romantic and grand operas, and productions depending on music, employ more musicians than ever before. Therefore the progress of music in connection with the drama shows a healthy growth.

I believe that where music is not essential to the spoken drama, it is the least interesting part of an evening's entertainment and therefore never will be missed; where it is essential it leaves its sister arts far in the shadow. Poetry, painting and music, properly mixed, have an overpowering fascination for the normal man, and when he sees and hears them produced in perfect proportion he feels he is near the God who created the poet, the painter and the musician.

After Palmerston we went to Wanganui and from there to Auckland, our last stand in Australasia. When I was called upon for a speech I described my first introduction to Auckland. When I was five hundred miles from New Zealand I had received a wireless asking me how I like it. I answered, "I reserve decision until I see it." I went on, "Now that I have been here I can truthfully say it is a fine country and that I like it very much. It is the cheapest country for a poor man — and the dearest country for a rich man — in the whole world. From my own observations I should say you were a nation of multimillionaires. Well, as to my own condition in life, I am happy in the thought that I am a march writer for, after all, what is life itself but a perpetual march? Perhaps the musical dramatists like Wagner looked upon life as an ever-changing succession of dramatic situations — all of us symbolizing our own points of view."

We sailed for Suva in the Fiji Islands September first, on the *Makura*. We spent a day there and then steamed for the Hawaiian Islands which we reached on the twelfth. We played in Honolulu to one of the largest houses since we had left Sydney. At the end of the concert a host of charming Hawaiian lassies (and some not so charming) showered me and my band with *leis*. I was decked with so many of these garlands that my ears were hidden! We took ship again immediately after the concert and set out for Vancouver, ten days away.

When we reached Victoria, we found the Canadian elections going at high pitch. One politician named Kelly seemed to be the storm centre of the day, but of course my thoughts were more on the concert than on any election. I was delighted to play to a packed house. In my journey around the world I had often played as a popular number the song, *Has Anybody Here Seen Kelly?* On election night in Victoria, I played it as a matter of course. Now just before we struck up that piece the information was passed around the hall that Kelly had been "snowed under" in the election. Apparently my audience rejoiced in the tidings, for the moment the boy put up the sign, announcing the title, *Has Anybody Here Seen Kelly?* and the band swung into the melody, a loud yell arose that shook the rafters. At the end of the concert a number of people surged backstage to congratulate me, believing that I had written the piece for the occasion. It would never have done to disillusion them. Audiences resent correction.

Chapter XV

NEW YORK and home again! I could not gather together my horse, dogs and guns quickly enough! It was no time before I was off on a long jaunt, following the shooting tournaments as far west as Des Moines.

We came to a Western town which boasted one of those excellent railroad hotels originated by Fred Harvey. The hotel table set forth, temptingly enough, a very large plate of spring onions. Mrs. Sousa is inordinately fond of spring onions, an odd hankering in a pretty woman and in violent contrast to my own tastes, though, rather than live on the roof or in the cellar when she indulges in the succulent genus *allium cepa*, I partake in self-defense. So Mrs. Sousa eyed these particular onions longingly and presently they were no more. Dinner over, my wife, with the ever-present feminine love of "picknickles and bucknickles," lingered about a little curio shop in the hotel where they sold Indian blankets and trinkets. Finally she strolled in. Behind her walked a Mexican laborer, and they reached the counter simultaneously. The proprietor, eager for an order from my wife, suddenly sniffed suspiciously, shot a furious glance at the Mexican and sniffed again. There was no doubt about the plebeian scent. The curio dealer indignantly ordered the Mexican from the shop.

"How in the world these Mexicans expect to be endured after gorging onions and garlic is more than I can see," declared the offended merchant. Mrs. Sousa discreetly backed towards the door, saying that she would return in the morning!

There is an interesting analogy between man and music. We say that an instrument is in tune when the several strings or chords are of that tension, which, resounding, gives the proper vibrations at due intervals. So it is with man. When his heart is filled with courage, happiness, love, ambition and general goodness, the adjustment is so perfect that he is in tune with all Nature and with the Infinite. But let weariness, disappointment, envy or illness creep in — then the balance is lost and the chords of life jangle.

The peculiarities of musical instruments have their counterparts in the characteristics of humankind. The queen of the musical family is the violin, an instrument which is sensitive under all conditions, capable of the most minute gradations of sound and pitch; now sentimental, now brooding, now brilliant, now coquettish, now breathing low, ardent notes of passionate love; for all the world like a lovely woman, high-strung, capable of all the emotions and an artist in every harmony of affection and sympathy. The bass drum with its eternal "thump, thump, thump" is like the heavy, stolid, slow-thinking man whose life is a round of breakfast, luncheon, dinner and sleep. Then there is that unfortunate man in life, who, like the instrument in the orchestra, may never rise above second position. A third alto horn man may envy a solo alto man but he remains a third alto forever. The second trombone may cast jealous eyes at his brother in the first chair but it availeth him not. If instruments were created equal, all would be sovereigns, and if men were born equal, all would be leaders.

And how the human disposition is reflected in the shrilling and cooing and wailing of the musical instrument! The shrieking fife and the hysterical woman can both become nuisances. The golden nuances of the oboe's tone are as sweet as the voice of a shy girl. The noble tone of the trombone has all the pomp of an emperor. The languorous rhythm of an Andalusian guitar is the very echo of a deep contralto. And so we run the gamut — with a love proposal embodied in the impassioned melody sung by the 'cello, and the giggling-fit of the coquette reflected in the fickle flights of the piccolo. We even have the man who never deviates from his chosen ordinance in the positive "umph" of the bass horn, and the never-can-make-up-his-mind individual in the hesitating "pah" of the second alto.

Here, however, the analogy ends, for, once out of tune, man and instrument require a different treatment. The tuner, the adjuster, the bridge-and-sound-post expert, the reed maker and the mandril maker are called in when piano, organ, violin, wood-wind or brass require tuning. But when the balance of life is lost and its chords jangle, no tuner can restore harmony. Like a tired child Man must turn to Mother Nature and live in her bosom until he fits once more into the eternal symphony. There is strength in the hills, solace in the plain, healing in the forest and immortality in the embrace of sky and ocean. There is a constant soft murmur of music in the breezes of a calm day and a weird harmony in the roar of a storm. From spring's overture to winter's dirge the motif ever varies and always the wide range of Nature is rich in melody.

There was no snapping of the strings of Life in my family until I had reached maturity. I was fortunate enough to keep my father with me until he was seventy years old. He died April 27, 1892, when I was giving a concert in Duluth. At the end of the programme my manager came backstage holding aloft a telegram, while I was still bowing to the final applause. As the curtain was lowered, I took my telegram. It was from my brother: "Father died this morning. Mother insists you continue your concerts and not disappoint the public. Will have funeral postponed until your return."

Mother died August 23, 1908, at eighty-three years of age. She was a wonderful, fearless woman whose simple faith in goodness was eternally strong. During war-times, when Father was off with the Marines and we little ones were preparing our lessons for the next day at school, some soldier, either drunk or capricious, would wander into the house. Mother would promptly take him by the arm and lead him to the door, admonishing him not to return. Then she would gather us about her and pray for our safety. She gave birth to ten children and lived her life for them and for her husband. And I suspect that I was always her favorite, even though she never fully understood my "musicking."

It is to her that I owe my faith in mankind. She always had a good word for everybody and was loath to see the wrong things in this world. She came to hear my band only once; it made her so nervous that she never went again, declaring at the time that she knew what I could do and that telling her about my music always satisfied her. When I was only a small boy I used to write little tunes and play them to her on my violin; she was not musical but she always encouraged me by assuring me that they were very beautiful.

MR. SOUSA'S MOTHER IN HER EIGHTIETH YEAR

Chapter XVI

MADAME CHAMINADE AND I TALK IT OVER — POPULAR MUSIC — TRAP-
SHOOTING AND ITS JOYS — HAM AND EGGS — THE PERIL OF SHOES
IN WINTER — PLAYING FOR PRISONERS — MARCHES I SHOULD HAVE
"ROTE" — PANAMA-PACIFIC EXPOSITION, 1915 — CAMILLE SAINT-SAENS
— HIPPODROME DAYS — FIFTEEN COMPOSERS AT THE PIANO — THE
ORIGIN OF SOUSA

O N NOVEMBER 15, 1908, there had appeared a sympo-
sium on music, by Madame Chaminade and myself. The
Sunday Editor of the *New York Herald* had conceived
the idea of presenting the American and the European points
of view on matters of popular interest. Mr. Frank A. Munsey
and Lord Northcliffe gave their opinions concerning the peri-
odic magazine, Mr. Guggenheim and Mr. Zangwill discussed the
Jewish question and other prominent people participated.

Madame Cecile Chaminade, the French composer, proved
an interesting conversationalist on our topic. Mr. Cleveland
Moffatt, the editor of the *Sunday Herald*, was the questioner
and Mr. Rupert Hughes the recorder. Of course the question of
so-called popular music came up. Notwithstanding the credo of
musical snobs, "popular" does not necessarily mean "vulgar" or
"ephemeral." In London a certain conductor had sneered at my
efforts, saying, "He gets the mob because he plays nothing but
marches." Now marches are only a small part of my programmes.
There is rarely more than one listed. If the audience gets others,
it is because they are demanded as encores. Madame Chaminade
asked me how I met this jealous conductor's onslaught.

"By sending word to him that I would give a concert in
London which would consist only of the compositions of the

so-called classic writers, and that I felt confident it would be the largest in point of receipts given that season," I replied.

"What was the programme?" asked Madame Chaminade.

"Miss Maude Powell played Mendelssohn's violin concerto, the most popular of all violin literature, Miss Estelle Liebling sang Mozart's fascinating *Batti-Batti* from *Don Giovanni*; the band played Handel's *Largo*, Bach's *Loure*, Haydn's *Surprise Symphony*, Beethoven's *Leonore* Overture Number Three, Weber's *Invitation to the Dance*, Schumann's *Träumerei* and Mendelssohn's *Wedding March*. Those, I maintain are among the most popular compositions ever written and every one of them is from the pen of a great composer whom the critics would dub a classic writer. I didn't even have to include an opera composer like Wagner."

Madame Chaminade was asked at the conclusion of my recital,

"Would you agree that these nine names stand for the greatest in music?" The answer was, "Yes, yes!"

Probably there is no term more abused and more often mistaken in its real meaning than "popular music." To the average mind popular music would mean compositions vulgarly conceived and commonplace in their treatment. That is absolutely false. Let us take music that has been performed over and over again. In every instance the most meritorious and inspired works, whether based on complex or simple lines, have survived the longest. There certainly is no composition in the world which has enjoyed greater vogue for twenty-five years among a wide range of listeners, from technical musician to uneducated but sympathetic auditor, than the *Tannhäuser* overture. For spontaneity, brilliancy and melodic charm most people will agree that the *Poet and Peasant* Overture is the master work of Suppe — and that piece of music has been thrummed and hammered, scraped and twanged and blown for, lo, these many years. Many a melody, chancing to catch the fickle fancy of the public, becomes temporarily popular, but unless it bears the stamp of genius it soon palls upon the ear and is no longer heard.

I was asked, "What makes a composition popular?"

"Its measure of inspiration. Anybody can write music of a sort. But touching the public heart is quite another thing. My religion lies in my composition. My success is not due to any personal superiority over other people. But sometimes Somebody helps me and sends me a musical idea and that same Somebody helps the public to lay hold of my meaning. It does not always happen, by any means, and I am quick to realize when a composition lacks inspiration. I can almost always write music; at any hour of the twenty-four, if I put pencil to paper, music comes. But twenty-four hours later I am apt to destroy it as worthless. For years I have been able to wear the same size hat!"

I started on a long horseback trip covering all the cities between New York and Washington, returning to Philadelphia to act as a judge at Wanamaker's Competitive Music Festival. The other judges were George W. Chadwick, Horatio Parker, J. Lewis Brown and Arthur Foote. At our first meeting, Mr. Parker, who had had experience at various similar competitions and who, until his death, occupied the Chair of Music at Yale University, said,

"Gentlemen, there is one suggestion I wish to make to you. As soon as you have arrived at your decision, destroy your markings. If you don't, you will be bothered to death by both the successful and unsuccessful contestants." It was good advice, for after I had voted on each contest I invariably received a number of letters requesting grades. My answer was that I had destroyed them all.

The fascinating Octavia Roberts, of the State Journal of Springfield, Illinois — now Mrs. Barton Corneau of Boston

— asked me while I was in that city shooting in the Grand America Handicap, "Won't you tell the public, you who have known all the good things the world can give — fame and honor and travel and wealth — what are life's best gifts?"

"A horse, a dog, a gun and a girl — with music on the side," I replied.

She laughingly said, "Is that a diminuendo or a crescendo?

"Crescendo, crescendo. The last is the best of all."

I went south presently, according to my custom, to hunt ducks, deer and quail on our preserves in South Carolina. Of all sports there is none that appeals to me, like clay bird shooting. I am opposed to the shooting of live pigeons for I feel that it is a wanton destruction of domestic birds, and can in no way be deemed a sport. I made good scores in the clay pigeon contests. At Augusta, Georgia, I led the field both for professionals and amateurs, breaking 98 out of 100. That is my best score, although one year I shot so consistently that my average for 15,000 clay birds was ninety per cent. I have many friends among the trap-shooters; they are clean sportsmen and always ready to applaud the winner.

Clay pigeon, or trap-shooting is comparatively new in America. Like golf it appeals to all ages and all strata of society. On the golf course at Hot Springs, Virginia, I have seen the multi-millionaire Rockefeller wait for John Jones to tee off, even though John Jones is a ribbon-clerk from Wana-maker's, honeymooning at the Springs, spending three days and six months' savings! Millionaire, savant, ribbon-clerk, — all are members of the Ancient and Honorable Society of Golfers. So with trap-shooting. In the State shoot a few years ago, a squad of five included one famous baseball pitcher, one world-renowned divine, one well-known financier, one hard-working carpenter

ON THE FIRING LINE — TRAP-SHOOTING

and "yours truly." None of us had ever met before but we all worked like Trojans to make our squad the "top-notcher." Like love, trap-shooting levels all ranks.

Before returning to New York I went quail-shooting in Virginia. The young farmer with whom I was lodging had never been twenty-five miles from his home and he said it was the dream of his life to go at least as far north as Washington.

"Why don't you do so?" I asked.

"Can't afford it," was his answer.

"Of course you can. This horse I am riding here on your plantation belongs to you and is a good one. Your other horse seems all right, too. Suppose we start on a trip and go as far as Washington. I'll pay for the use of your horse and $5.00 a day for your time.

He was delighted. We started the next day. At noon we stopped at a farmhouse for luncheon. The farmer's wife said, "What will you have — fried chicken or ham and eggs?" My friend chose ham and eggs. We stopped at still another farmhouse for the night and at supper when he was asked what he would like to eat, my companion repeated, "Ham and eggs." Indeed, on that ten day trip to Washington, his invariable choice for breakfast, dinner and supper was ham and eggs. When we finally reached the Capital we went to the Hotel Willard where I handed him the menu card with at least 150 items on it, saying, "This is a first-class hotel, Jim. You must be hungry as a bear, so just take anything and everything you want."

He looked it all over carefully, his face growing more and more serious, and then moaned as he dropped the menu card, "'Tain't here, 'tain't here."

"What 'ain't here'?" I asked.

"Ham and eggs."

Riding for the fifth time from Hot Springs, Virginia, I had as my companion Jim Hamilton, the genial riding master of that famous resort. We each had two horses and carried a surrey containing clothing and the necessities of travel. We started late in February. The Jackson River and the mountains were still blanketed with snow; the river had cakes of ice in it and winter yet lingered in the air. One day we stopped at a plantation for lunch and I was amazed to behold three or four little children running about the grounds barefoot and thinly clad. I called to the farmer's wife, "It seems dangerous to me to allow those little ones to run about without shoes and stockings. They are likely to contract pneumonia from such exposure."

"Don't you worry," said the mother. "A fool man come along here 'bout two years ago and talked just as you are talking and we got plumb scared and Jim (that's my husband) hitched up his team and druv sixty miles to Staunton to buy the little fellow a pair of shoes and stockings. When he got back it was snowing hard and I put the shoes and stockings on the little boy's feet. He went out to play in the snow, got his feet wet and that night he nigh died of croup. My mother took off the wet shoes and stockings, dosed him with kerosene and made him run around outside in the snow for an hour. That cured him. No more shoes for him, nuther. I ain't a-goin' to risk their health with no such foolishness. Why, man, they slides on the ice in Jackson River in their bare feet. I loves 'em too much to let them take any chances with shoes!"

One November we were in Atlanta giving concerts. The warden and the clergyman attached to the Federal Prison wrote and asked if I could not bring my band to the Penitentiary and give a concert for the inmates. The band unanimously volunteered and we gave our concert in a huge hall with the white prisoners on the left and the colored ones on the right. One of the attendants stood at my side as they marched in and pointed out a young man, barely over thirty, handsome but marred by a devil-may-care expression. The attendant remarked, "Notice that man. He's a bad 'un. He was sent here from one of the territories after his sentence had been commuted from hanging to life imprisonment. In a little over a year he was pardoned; within a few months of his release he nearly killed another man, was tried and sentenced to twenty-years and sent here once more. A year later he was pardoned again. In six months he had killed another man, was tried and sentenced to be hanged but the sentence was commuted to imprisonment for life. Here he is and, we hope, here he will remain."

Of course so desperate and perverted a personality won my interest. When we played the first number the applause was deafening but he sat with folded hands, absolutely impassive and evidently determined to remain so. When Miss Root, the vocalist, stepped forward he never wavered an eyelash. I had thought that a pretty girl singing beautifully would arouse him but he gave no sign. As we reached the close of our program I played *The Stars and Stripes Forever*. At the first measures he began to straighten up and presently was applauding as loudly as the others. Apparently the one redeeming trait in his character was a certain patriotic devotion. Despite his evil life it is quite possible that he would have died for his country.

The Stars and Stripes Forever seems to have a unique appeal. A Frenchwoman once told me very quaintly and expressively that it sounded to her like the American eagle shooting arrows into the Aurora Borealis!

The liking for marches is quite universal and I have no doubt that many are written which never see the light of a musical day. I am still treasuring an earnest, kindly and very human letter — with all its inaccuracies — which I received about this time:

> MR. SOUSA Dont get cross at me For Wrighting to you
> Abought theas marches o Gem i have 16 Butiefule marches i
> have Bin right at thos marches For 16 years abought 10 year i
> rote and now i Wood Like to put them in the hands of a Grate
> Band Master and you are the man that i Wood Like to have a

good Look at theas marches, if you Wood be sow kind and so com idatin to poore mane Like me. pleas Let me send 5 or 6 of thes marches to you to satisfised you that the ar as Fine as enny marches ever rote i Will class them With your Directorate march or invincible egle or El capitan and the Bass parts in theas marches are neardner to the stars and Stripes Base part of youres and enny that Was ever rote. They are like the Band Bace part hevy and Fine every Strane is a 16 or 32 mesher of a plane toone esy to play This Tones Will Last, Will not get Stale in 20 years they Will renue your Name agan as the Grate march rite of the World as you held the glory all this years. Duble it up Like rosevelt For president ... Look at the marches. Let me send 5 or 6 to you then tell me What you think of them i neve showed this marches to enny Body or neve tryed to published them, my idea all ways was to place them in your Name years ago. Becose they are hevy masters marches the kind that have classic Movent in them and the Basse solo ar as good as enny ever put in a march outside of the Stars and Stripes of yours that is the Best Base solo ever rote. mine are nearder to that an enny othr one that you ever rote. i have I Base Solo that is 24 meshers soled runs or comatic i takes a violin to play it With ese. i play the piane and Worked them out year after year. now pleas rite to me and Let me send a Few of the marches to you or if that dont soot you pleas tel me now Were i can meet you i Wood Like to Show them toe you and talk to you abought them or place them in your hans some day i am to poor to publishem them my self and i have no mane as a righter and they are to good to Fool away red this over and think as you never thought Before Beleve me this ar perfect marches From end to end

I let myself in for some very puzzling situations in my anxiety to help young composers and to please my public. I suppose I have made my attitude so clear that some people may have taken advantage of it. At any rate, one of my managers, Frank Christianer, resented very strongly certain abuses of my leniency. He acted as if he hated every other composer in the world, except myself, and when he found me inserting works by John Doe and other local composers on our programmes, he cursed roundly at my crazy impulses.

One evening in Cleveland three composers brought me some short pieces and urged me to use them as encores. I was in a dilemma for I did want to help fellow musicians whenever possible. So I said, "But, you see, my audiences seem to want to hear some of my own compositions as encores. Bad taste, of course, but it can't be helped. Then there are two or three minor composers like Strauss and Wagner whom I feel I must include! I can't tuck in all three of these things of yours, but I'll tell you what I'll do…. I'll let you toss up and I'll play the march of the one who wins." And I stuck to my bargain, although the papers "roasted" me heartily for putting miscellaneous and unexpected music on the programme. I still feel the impulse to give young writers a hearing, and I believe I have played more unpublished compositions than any other band leader in the country.

The band contracted to appear for ten weeks at the Panama-Pacific Exposition, so we left New York early in April, 1915, for the Pacific coast, giving concerts as we crossed the continent. We opened on May 22d. I had the pleasure of hearing *The Messiah of Nations*, written by James Whitcomb Riley and myself for the occasion of the dedication of the Soldiers' Monument in Indianapolis, sung by the choir of St. John's Presbyterian church of Berkeley, during their concert at the Exposition. We gave several concerts with the other bands there — Conway's and Cassassa's, — and the combination attracted much attention. M. Camille Saint-Saens, the French composer, wrote the official musical composition for the Fair, a piece written for orchestra, band and organ which was given its initial performance on June 20.

Strange to say, the official music for expositions and world fairs seems always to die an immediate death. Wagner wrote the official march for the Centennial and although he was helped by no less a conductor than Theodore Thomas, the Wagner march died before the Exposition closed its doors. I have had the honor of playing a number of official marches, including that of M. Saint-Saens, but with the single exception of *King Cotton*, the march of the Cotton States Exposition at Atlanta, all of them fell into innocuous desuetude. *King Cotton*, however, for some reason or other still continues to reign.

Saint-Saens and I became the best of friends. We used to wander about the grounds together and he seemed always to have an eye for lovely womankind. Slim beauty seemed to make little impression on him but when one with territorial expansion hove into sight he would nudge me, calling my attention to "yonder beaming beauty!" The broader the "beam" the greater his delight!

I received a telegram from Charles Dillingham which read, "How would you like to play in New York all winter?"

I replied: "What kind of playing?"

"Am sending Harry Askin out to talk it over with you."

Mr. Askin came with the news that Dillingham had obtained the Hippodrome for the winter season and wanted to open it with my band as one of the attractions. I was to give a short concert each evening and on Sunday the entire entertainment. I made a contract with him and remained two seasons under the Dillingham régime.

While we were still in San Francisco the Music Teachers' Association of California adopted a resolution petitioning Congress to make *The Stars and Stripes Forever* and *Dixie* the

A FRANCO-AMERICAN ENTENTE CORDIALE
Saint-Saens and Sousa, 1915

official airs of the United States. The idea did not appeal to me for, though Congress is a powerful body, it cannot make the people sing what they don't want to sing. If *The Stars and Stripes Forever* ever becomes a national air it will be because the people want it and not because of any congressional decree.

We left San Francisco late in July, toured east to Willow Grove and from there to the Pittsburgh Exposition, then on to fulfill our contract at the Hippodrome, where we opened late in September. I had written *The March of the States* during my Western sojourn and when it was played at the Hippodrome it scored a phenomenal success. I wrote the *New York Hippodrome March* which is now in the repertoire of every band in the country. In our Sunday night concerts the band played in conjunction with many well-known artists. Among them were Grace Hoffman, Florence Hardman, Virginia Root, Emmy Destinn, Nellie Melba, Orville Harrold, Belle Story, Margarite Ober, Alice Nielsen, Ernest Schelling, Susan Tompkins, John McCormack, Herma Menthe, Olive Fremstad, Julia Culp, Maggie Teyte, Tamaki Mura, Kathleen Parlow and Anna Pavlowa.

At one time we put on a combination of fifteen composers at the piano: Jerome Kern, Louis Hirsch, Baldwin Sloane, Rudolph Friml, Oscar Hammerstein, Alfred Robyn, Gus Kern, Hugo Felix, Leslie Stuart, Raymond Hubbell, John Golden, Silvio Hein, Irving Berlin and myself. We sat at fifteen different pianos, each playing his most popular hit, accompanied by the others. That night the attendance-record was certainly shattered.

On the eleventh anniversary of the Hippodrome, Mr. R. H. Burnside, the stage manager, conceived the idea of organizing a parade of the entire Hippodrome force, 1274 paraders, with my band leading. At the rehearsals before the opening of the show, as I sat with Dillingham watching the various acts, I was especially pleased with the graceful skating of the charming Charlotte and later, with the antics of a trick mule. After the rehearsal I turned to Dillingham and said in a burst of enthusiasm, "Why, Mr. Dillingham, Charlotte and the mule would carry this show alone."

"Charlotte and the mule," he mused. "Well, I'll talk to the mule about it and if he doesn't kick, I'll do it!"

Many of the great artists who appeared at our concerts were greeted with stirring ovations. Miss Emmy Destinn was having a triumphant evening and at the end of her second encore she walked briskly onto the stage, suddenly took me by the shoulder, and gave me a resounding kiss! The unexpected never fails to make a hit and the audience shouted for joy. After that, every good-natured prima donna would bestow a chaste salute on the blushing conductor; even the doll-like little Japanese opera star, Tamaki Mura, reached up and just about managed to kiss my collar! Fun-loving Maggie Cline, carried away by her applause one evening, advanced on me with determination in her eye. I foresaw a burlesque kissing bee and quickly dodged behind the harp lest she corner me.

The Hippodrome closed the last of May. About this time I received a letter from Mr. James Francis Cook, Editor of *The Etude*, asking me to set one of his correspondents right in regard to my name — whether it was Sousa, So, or Something else. My reply was as follows:

IF there is one thing I dislike more than another it is to spoil a good story. I vividly remember my infantile contempt for the punk-headed pirate who told me that Jack the Giant Killer never existed, and I clearly recall my undying hatred for the iconoclast who calmly informed me that Robinson Crusoe was a myth and his man Friday a black shadow without life or substance. I also despised the man who said that Nero was never a fiddler; hence you can understand my position when you call on me in all seriousness to verify the story that my name is not Sousa but Philipso. When I received your letter my first impulse was to allow you to hang on the tenterhook of doubt for some moons and then in the interest of truth gradually to set you right.

The story of the supposed origin of my name is a rattling good one and like all ingenious fables, permits of international variation. The German version is that my name is Sigismund Ochs, a great musician, born on the Rhine, emigrated to America, trunk marked S. O., U. S. A., therefore the name. The English version is that I am one Sam Ogden, a great musician, Yorkshire man, emigrated to America, luggage marked S. O., U. S. A., hence the cognomen. The domestic brand of the story is that I am a Greek, named John Philipso, emigrated to America, carried my worldly possessions in a box marked J. P. S. O., U. S. A., therefore the patronymic.

This more or less polite fiction, common to society, has been one of the best bits of advertising I have had in my long career. As a rule items about musical people find their way only into columns of the daily press, a few of the magazines, and papers devoted to music, but this item has appeared in the religious, rural, political, sectarian, trade and labor journals from one end of the world to the other, and it is believed that it makes its pilgrimage around the globe once every three years. It emanated first about ten years ago from the ingenious brain of that publicity promoter, Colonel George Frederick Hinton. At that time Colonel Hinton was exploiting Sousa and His Band, and out of the inner recesses of his gray matter he evolved this perennial fiction. Since it appeared I have been called on to deny it in Afghanistan, Beloochistan, Carniola, Denmark, Ethiopia, France, Germany, Hungary, Ireland, Japan, Kamchatka, Lapland, Madagascar, Nova Scotia, Oporto, Philadelphia, Quebec, Russia, Senegambia, Turkestan, Uruguay, Venezuela, Wallachia, Xenia, Yucatan, and Zanzibar, but even with this alphabetical-geographic denial on my part, the story — like Tennyson's brook — goes on forever.

Were it not for the reproving finger of pride pointed at me by the illustrious line of ancestral Sousa, I would let it go at that; were it not for the sister and brothers ready to prove that my name is Sousa, whom I cannot very well shake, I might let your question go unheeded.

My parents were absolutely opposed to race suicide and had a family of ten children, six of whom are now living, all married and doing well in the family line; so well, indeed, that I should say about 1992 the name of Sousa will supplant that of Smith as our national name. Now for the historical record: I was born on the sixth of November, 1854, on G. Street, S. E., near old Christ Church, Washington, D. C. My parents were Antonio and Elizabeth (Trinkhaus) Sousa. I was christened John Philip at Dr. Finkel's church on Twenty-Second Street, Northwest, Washington, D. C. and would say, had I an opportunity to be born again, I would select the same parents, the same city and the same time.

Chapter XVII

A THOUSAND MILES ON HORSEBACK — THE HIPPODROME AND MY
BIRTHDAY PARTY — I AM IN THE NAVY NOW — ORGANIZING THE
BANDS OF A GOVERNMENT AT WAR — OLD GLORY WEEK — THEODORE
ROOSEVELT — CRUSADING FOR THE LIBERTY LOAN — "MILLIONS FOR
DEFENSE" — "A DAY AT GREAT LAKES" — WE CONQUER THE FLU-MASSED
BANDS OF THE ATLANTIC FLEET — THE FLU CONQUERS ME! — DOCTOR
OF MUSIC — "IN FLANDERS FIELD"

IN THE early summer of that year — 1916 — I started on
a thousand-mile horseback journey, as a change from
conducting. On my trip I had my gun with me and took part
in tournaments. I also offered to join General Wood's command
on the border, which inspired a jocular *New York Herald* corre-
spondent to say, "Sousa should play *La Paloma* in order to fasci-
nate the Mexicans into inaction and *The Stars and Stripes Forever*
to inspire the American troops." The war scare petered out,
however, and I didn't go, but turned to Willow Grove where we
opened on August 20th.

That fall I went to New York to rehearse with the Hippodrome
company and we opened in Philadelphia on October 16th. *The
Boy Scout March* was written that season.

On November sixth, my sixty-second birthday, at the
Metropolitan Opera House, Mr. E. T. Stotesbury presented me
with a beautiful loving cup, the company gave me a silver platter
and the band also gave me a loving cup. I'm glad I wasn't born on
the 29th of February; it would be so long between loving cups!

On May 20, 1917, — six weeks or so after the United States
entered the World War — I received a telegram from Mr. John
Alden Carpenter, a composer-friend of mine: "The Naval Station

has an undeveloped band which needs the inspiration of a master hand to start them on the right track. Could you come here if only for a few days to start the work and bring with you a bandmaster of the right personality to continue the instruction? I realize how much I ask and know your enthusiasm for the cause."

I left as soon as I could arrange my affairs, met Mr. Carpenter in Chicago, and we went on to the Naval Station at Great Lakes. I was introduced to the Commandant, Captain Moffett, since promoted to Admiral. He summoned the band to the parade grounds, a collection of seventy-five young fellows. They played a march or two and then returned to their quarters. After lunch we chatted of his plan and the Navy's necessity for good music.

"You, Sousa, know the game better than any man in the country, with all your years with the Marines, your knowledge of discipline and the best way to handle men. I don't know where to look if you fail me."

"I won't fail you," I replied. "I'll join. I'm past sixty-two, but you'll find me a healthy fellow."

"When will you join?"

"Right away," I answered.

On my return to Chicago I telegraphed to my wife my intention of joining the navy and was sworn in as lieutenant in charge of the music. I had explained to the Commandant that I had contracted for various dates which must be fulfilled before I could remain permanently at the station. Until I came to stay I volunteered to be placed on the one-dollar-a-month basis. I celebrated my new position with a verse which was reprinted in many an American newspaper:

I JOINED the Reserves on the last day of May,
I gave up my band and a thousand a day,
A dollar a month is my government pay,

CONDUCTING IN THE NAVY, 1918

My God, how the money rolls in!

During my service in the Navy, from May, 1917, to March, 1919, I learned to love and admire Admiral Moffett. Every man who had the honor to serve him felt the same. His own hours for work were all hours. He asked no man to do more than he was willing to do himself. Certainly his executive ability was unusual and although he was a great disciplinarian he had nothing of the martinet about him.

In a month we had over six hundred enlistments for the band. It was a cumbersome number to handle. One day as the Commandant and I were returning from a banquet at the Chicago Club, I said,

"Commandant, the musical forces are degenerating into an unruly mob. I have a plan to propose which I hope will meet with your approval. I should like to form a band battalion of three hundred and fifty, with military commander, musical director, surgeon, master-at-arms and petty officers. After that I propose to organize, as enlistments warrant it, bands to consist of double-battleship units of the *Delaware* type, assigning a band to each regiment at the Station. Will you issue an order to that effect?"

"Order be hanged," said the amiable Moffett. "You're the musical director. Go ahead, and if it doesn't work you will be the first to realize it."

Next day I sent for the senior bandmaster and asked him for a list of all the musicians in the station, with their rating, ability and age. From this I formed a battalion which became my special care during the war. We had in all about 350 musicians. My system proved to be advantageous for whenever we received a telegram from the Department asking us to send a band to some ship or another station I was able to send an organized whole — a group of men who knew one another, possessed a common repertoire and understood how to play together.

One request from Admiral Mayo, commander of the Atlantic Squadron, was for a band for his flagship, the *Pennsylvania*. Captain Moffett decreed that we send the finest regimental band we had. I suggested a bright young bandmaster named V. D.

Grabel and we sent him and his men along to the *Pennsylvania*. Later, when I was ordered aboard that ship to dine with Admiral Mayo, he said enthusiastically, "Sousa, you gave me a great surprise when you sent me that band. They reported at six o'clock and gave a concert at seven, an achievement which I have never heard equalled in the Army or the Navy!"

In September my battalion was ordered to Kansas City to take part in "Old Glory Week" where we gave a concert in Electric Park. Thousands surged about the bandstand and very near us I observed Colonel Roosevelt and his family. I asked him if there was anything special he would like to hear. He replied warmly, "It would make me very happy if you would play *Garryowen*.

By the way, in 1917 Roosevelt made a speech to the Naval forces at Great Lakes and he said, with that famous grin of his, "I'd give anything if I could go to war with you, but so far this has seemed to me a very exclusive war and I was blackballed by the committee on admission."

It was in 1917, too, that I went over to Oyster Bay from my home at Port Washington to talk with Colonel Roosevelt about some features of my work with Navy Band Battalions, and in the course of the conversation, he put his arm around the shoulders of a young naval officer, who was with us and said feelingly, "My boy, you should be proud to be wearing that uniform — I wish I were!"

Back at the Great Lakes a telegram awaited me from Mr. Henry P. Davison asking if the band would play for the Red Cross Drive in New York. The Commandant permitted us to go, and we laid out a further itinerary which included the Rosemary Pageant at Huntington, a concert in Carnegie Hall and then engagements in Philadelphia, Baltimore and Washington.

The band battalion included young men between the ages of eighteen and twenty-five, many of whom were members of college bands and small town bands of the west and southwest. They were a bright, pleasing lot and full of enthusiasm. I had exercised great care in selecting the music, making sure that it was all within the comprehension and execution of the band. I had chosen the most effective street marches, such as *The Thunderer*, *The National Emblem*, *Semper Fidelis*, *Washington Post*, and *The High School Cadets*. The drum major, a splendid sailor named Micheaux Tennant, was an excellent drill master and trained the boys to step off briskly. When we reached Philadelphia we were gathered in front of the Union League Club on Broad Street. An old Civil War general came out of the Club and proceeded to inspect each file of the band. We were at rigid attention. He came up to me and said, "Sousa, you have a remarkable lot of men."

"Yes, sir, I think so, too," I replied.

"I have inspected every file of the three hundred or more and there isn't a belly in the whole band!" I thanked him again.

Our next assignment was the First Liberty Loan Drive in Baltimore. Mr. Van Lear Black, chairman of the Committee, in discussing the probable success of the drive, said to me, "I'm very much encouraged since the arrival of your band. Now I believe we will be able to raise eight million dollars."

Before it was over we had raised nearly twenty-one million dollars! Patriotic Baltimore responded nobly. The banks had already named the amount of their subscriptions before we arrived, but when our concerts began in the Fifth Regiment Armory thousands of people came forward to make magnificent gestures. I would have a man with a megaphone call out to the assemblage,

"If somebody will subscribe one hundred thousand dollars the band will play *Dixie*." We would get that sum in a very few minutes. Presently the man would announce, "If someone will subscribe two hundred thousand dollars, the band will play *Maryland, My Maryland*. The subscription was forthcoming.

From Baltimore we went to Washington to assist in the Liberty Loan drive there. My home town was good to me. Here was a gratifying refutation of the old saying that a prophet is without honor in his own country! During the Washington stay I planned a serenade to the President. We marched from Hotel Willard up to Sixteenth Street and came to a halt beside the executive offices. The streets were crowded and the officers and clerks from the War, Navy and State Departments overflowed the steps and balconies of those buildings. I played three pieces and at the third fully expected the appearance of the President for that is the custom in serenades. I played still another and no President. One more and then we closed with *The Star Spangled Banner* and marched off, three hundred and fifty disappointed boys who had had a yearning to behold their Chief Executive.

In New York we gave a concert at the Hippodrome for the Women's Auxiliary Naval Recruiting Station and our receipts were eleven thousand dollars. For that occasion I wrote *The United States Field Artillery* March and *Blue Ridge*. I had put together a medley of airs and called it *A Day at Great Lakes*. It began with reveille and continued through a day's doings to the midnight patrol. In it I introduced not only instrumental but vocal music and arranged to have a song popular at that time, *Throw Me a Rose*, sung by a handsome young sailor lad named Mix. At times the stage was littered with roses thrown by admiring and patriotic ladies!

How we tooted and trumpeted to charm the dollars out of American pockets! We toured Milwaukee, Cleveland, Columbus, Cincinnati, Pittsburgh and other cities. I verily believe we were the strongest drawing card in all the war drives. Millions were

WHO'S WHO IN NAVY BLUE
Band Battalion of Great Lakes Naval Training Station on Fifth
Avenue, New York City, First Liberty Loan Drive, 1917

subscribed to the Liberty Loans and the dollars came pouring
in for Red Cross drives and naval relief campaigns. Nor did we
scorn fifty, a hundred, or two hundred dollars at a time. Some
attractive sailor lad would hold up my twenty-cent baton and ask
what he was offered for it. If he received a bid of only fifty dollars
he would drawl, "Say, this is a money affair. We can't let this
priceless baton go for fifty dollars," whereupon the bids would
rise as high as three or four hundred dollars.

One of the most important musical events during the war
was the performance of Mendelssohn's oratorio, "Elijah" at the
Polo Grounds in New York. I received orders from the Navy
Department to conduct the performance for the War Thrift
festival. I found a chorus of ten thousand voices drilled by men

famous in oratorio work. The principals were Marie Sundelius, Sophie Breslau, Betty McKenna, Charles Harrison and Oscar Seagle. The orchestra was recruited from the symphony orchestras and was entirely wood-wind and brass.

During the terrible epidemic of Spanish influenza I received orders from the Treasury department to visit a number of cities in the interest of the Liberty Loan. Just as we were on the point of departure, the medical director at the station quarantined the entire force. The Treasury representative, of course, became much excited but he was in the position of Canute, for medical directors are as relentless as the waves of the sea. No officer ever presumes to question the mandate of an official medical adviser. So it was that we remained in station until the quarantine was raised. An appalling number of men had been lost during the epidemic. The medical adviser sent for the battalion surgeon, Dr. A. H. Frankel, and said, "Doctor, the band battalion leaves the station to-day for an extended period. If you bring half these boys back alive it will be a miracle."

Before we entrained Dr. Frankel had converted one car into a sick bay and placed the hospital corps in charge. He brought plenty of Dobell's Solution and other medical stores to discourage the "flu" and we started off. Throughout the entire tour Dr. Frankel labored for the health of my men. In my subsequent report to the Commandant, I said: "We left home with three hundred and fifty officers and men. We returned with three hundred and fifty officers and men. Dr. Frankel's fidelity was wonderful; I do not believe the man slept four hours a night. Twice a day the entire command was required to spray with detergents. Every possible means was used to ward off the 'flu.'" Faithful Frankel was a junior lieutenant but the Commandant was so delighted with his diligence that he immediately promoted him to senior.

Wartime feeling led the American Defense Scouts to organize a committee to suppress all things German and they passed a resolution to request me to write an American wedding march. I agreed and the march was first played in Philadelphia August 6, 1918. The *Pittsburgh Gazette* said of it: "The march approaches classical intricacy and brings forth a very sweet melody symbolic of happy affection." I was mighty busy composing, for the Fourth Liberty Loan Committee suggested that I write a Liberty Loan March. We played it in Detroit a number of times when we were dollar-chasing for the Government.

In Detroit in May, 1918, Mr. Charles M. Schwab came to town the day we were scheduled to leave. I knew and admired him and so I marched my men to his hotel and serenaded him. Schwab appeared and, throwing his arms about my neck, said to the band: "Until I heard you I thought I had the best band in the world at my Bethlehem Steel Works. Now I know otherwise. I take off my hat to you. You're a wonderful bunch and you ought to be — under such leadership!" Mayor Marx in addressing the sailor-musicians and myself, said:

"Detroit is more than proud to have you with her, she is more than sorry to have you leave and she will be more than glad to have you return. You have brought an inspiration to Detroit. You and your peerless leader have made vivid the Great War to us and with your departure we are losing something very near and dear." When we started off for Cleveland we were followed by veritable seas of men and women cheering us loudly and unceasingly.

On June 11, 1918, I was ordered to report to the Flagship of the Commander-in-chief of the Atlantic Fleet and so I sought out the *Pennsylvania*. After some days we gave a concert ashore with the massed bands of the fleet and had for our audience half of the crews of the entire squadron. As the squadron stretched out to sea it seemed to me one of the most formidable armadas in the world. I received the following letter from Admiral Mayo:

UNITED STATES ATLANTIC FLEET

U. S. S. PENNSYLVANIA, FLAGSHIP

June 28, 1918

MY DEAR MR. SOUSA:

I wish to thank you for the music for the Flagship band and orchestra which I am sure we will enjoy very much. And please also let me thank you for the piano music which you so kindly sent to Mrs. Mayo. She is delighted with it and asks me to convey her appreciation.

I have heard a great many compliments of the Fleet band under your direction and hope that some day you will give us the pleasure of another visit.

With kind regards,

Sincerely,

H. T. MAYO

Admiral U. S. Navy

In November of that year we were ordered to Toronto, Canada to assist the Canadian Government in their Victory Loan campaign. The Armistice came during our sojourn there. Never was there such a night! Not a soul in the city slept. Certainly I did not, for aside from the excitement, I had at last caught "flu" and my right ear was abscessed. A Toronto surgeon cut me three times — but what were pains and pangs and abscesses to the frantic delight of knowing that war was over? Still suffering horribly with my ear, I telegraphed Admiral Moffett asking for permission to return to New York and see my physician. It was granted and I went on, happy over the Armistice but a mighty sick man. A week later I was, at my own request, transferred to the Third Naval District.

In January, 1919, I received this:

NAVY DEPARTMENT

Bureau of Navigation

WASHINGTON, D. C.

Jan. 20, 1919

To: Lieutenant

JOHN P. SOUSA, USNRF

Port Washington, L. I., N. Y.

Subject: RELIEVED FROM ALL ACTIVE DUTY

1. At such time as you are able to travel, proceed to New York, New York and report to the Commandant of the Third Naval District for temporary duty and physical examination and to have your health and service records closed out.

2. Upon the completion of this temporary duty proceed to your home and regard yourself relieved from all active duty.

3. Advise the Bureau of Navigation immediately upon your arrival home, giving the date thereof, and also your full address.

4. The Bureau takes this opportunity to thank you for the faithful and patriotic services you have rendered to your country in the war with Germany.

VICTOR BLUE

Rear Admiral U. S. Navy

Chief of Bureau

A year later I received this notice:

NAVY DEPARTMENT

Bureau of Navigation

WASHINGTON, D. C.

Feb. 24, 1920.

From: BUREAU OF NAVIGATION
To: Lieutenant Commander JOHN PHILIP SOUSA, USNRF
Port Washington
Long Island, N. Y.

Subject: Provisional assignment of rank and grade of Lieutenant Commander.

Enclosures: (a) Assignment of rank and grade.

(b) Four blank forms of Acceptance of Office and Oath of Allegiance.

1. Having been given the provisional rank and grade of Lieutenant Commander in the Naval Coast Defense Reserve, Class 4, for general service to rank from Feb. 11, 1920, the Bureau encloses herewith your assignment dated February 24, 1920.

2. Please acknowledge receipt.

THOMAS WASHINGTON

Rear Admiral, U. S. N.

Chief of Bureau

This letter awaited me on my return from the exercises of the Pennsylvania Military College on February 27, at which the College conferred upon me the honorary degree of Doctor of Music. It was at that time that Senator Warren G. Harding received the degree of Doctor of Laws from the same college. And three years later, on November 26, 1913, I was honored with the degree of Doctor of Music by Marquette University.

My naval duties officially over in 1920, I called my band together and took up again the practice of giving concerts all over the country. Now that the tumult and the shouting of those World War days has died, there comes to my mind one priceless memory — the message of Colonel John MacCrae to his brothers-in-arms and to us, who, when he wrote it, were almost ready to take up his "challenge to the foe." He sent to me, through Mr. Walker of Montreal, the manuscript of *In Flanders Fields* and asked me to give it a musical setting, as a song. I was deeply touched by the beauty of his verses; and I should be happy if the music which I made for them may serve, however slightly, to keep that message sounding in the hearts of all lovers of human liberty.

DOCTOR OF MUSIC, MARQUETTE UNIVERSITY

Chapter XVIII

AMERICA'S PROGRESS IN CREATIVE MUSIC — THE POPULAR SONGS OF
BIBLE DAYS — DAVID AS BANDMASTER AND MUSICIAN — SYMPHONIC
COMBINATIONS — INSTRUMENTS AND THEIR TEMPERAMENTS,
VAGARIES, AND USES — THE INCONGRUOUS IN MUSIC

NO NATION as young as America can be expected to become immediately a power in the arts. In the early days, commerce and invention were bound to be of greater importance than music, pictures, or the drama. Therefore it is not strange that the best brains were busily employed with those things most important to the material progress of the country.

Up to fifty years ago there had been produced here only one or two serious operas by native composers. But now, far from being a suppliant at the door of the theatrical manager, the American composer who has something worth telling to the public is received with open arms. Of course this happy state of affairs is traceable to commerce, because the business man, having won his residence on Easy Street through his commercial pursuits, looks about for enjoyment and is entirely willing to pay for it. It is pleasant to contemplate the number of first-class orchestras in America and also the number of really prosperous musicians.

Our unusually fine motion picture houses, such as the Paramount, Strand, Rivoli, Rialto, Capitol, and Roxy's, in New York, have contributed materially to the musical education of the country by reaching so many thousands with their well-equipped orchestras. A student of instrumentation is bound to gain much from a close study of the various combinations. Here he can learn the difference between the tone of the trombone and the cornet and distinguish the characteristic voice of oboe and horn. There are certainly two hundred players developed to one composer. America can well expect to develop a goodly amount of composers for she has a goodly number of people.

In my own organization I have had Americans who attained the pinnacle in their own particular branch of the musical art. I have never heard a finer cornetist than Herbert L. Clarke who for over twenty-five years was the solo cornet of my band, and is now director of his own. Nor was there anyone on earth to equal Arthur Pryor, the trombone player, when he was with my organization. John Dolan and many more American instrumentalists honor the bands to which they are attached.

More than two hundred years ago Andrew Fletcher of Saltoun, a philosopher and a keen observer of mankind, said: "I knew a very wise man who believed if a man were permitted to make all the ballads he would not care who might make the laws of a nation."

At the very beginning of the recorded history of man we have a series of laws, now known as the Decalogue, that have remained through all the ages as a very Gibraltar of universal justice. Biblical history says that the people heard these commandments in fear and trembling. They have remained as a monument erected on a foundation of everlasting truth. Tomes upon tomes of statutes have been enacted since the days when the finger of God traced the Decalogue upon the tablets of stone, but very few man-made laws have survived. Macklin says: "The law is a sort of hocus-pocus science that smiles in your face while it picks your pocket and the glorious uncertainty of it is of more use to the lawyers than the justice of it."

Music, on the contrary, reassures and comforts. It tends to soften the hardships of life and add joys to our days. Its appeal is to the tenderest traits in man's nature; therefore it is not difficult

EXCERPTS FROM MANUSCRIPTS OF "THE DWELLERS
IN THE WESTERN WORLD"

to understand why Fletcher's wise man preferred writing the songs of a nation to making its laws.

One of the first popular songs ever written was the one sung by Moses and the children of Israel in exultation over the destruction of Pharaoh's hosts. Nothing but song and dance wereadequate to celebrate that great event. In triumphant unison they sang, "I will sing unto the Lord; the Lord is a man of war," and Miriam and her women played upon timbrels and danced in graceful abandon to the accompaniment of the mighty choir.

That happened at the dawn of history. Let us for a moment come down to our own time. The land — Cuba. The year — 1898. Just as the children of Israel raised their voices in those ancient days, so did we in 1898. The unison, the abandon were the same. Only the music was different. Moses and his people sang, "The horse and his rider hath he thrown into the sea; the Lord is a man of war." Uncle Sam and his people sang, *There'll Be a Hot Time in the Old Town To-night* and *The Stars and Stripes Forever*. After all, human nature is much the same throughout the centuries.

With advent of the sweet singer of Israel came the first great writer of popular songs, for by his genius he swayed the multitude and became the idol of all his land — David, the beloved one who wrote the Book of Psalms. He was a musician, a poet and a first-class fighter!

By common consent he is one of the most fascinating figures in history, a child of genius, ample in faculty, fertile in resource and rich in all those qualities that stir admiration and evoke respect. To quote Hillis, "What the *Iliad* did for Greece, what Dante's *Inferno* did for the Renaissance, what the *Niebelungenlied* did for the German tribes, what *The Legends of King Arthur* did for the age of chivalry, that and more David's songs did for the ancient church and the Jewish people. If Moses' laws laid the foundation, David's songs and psalms built the superstructure."

Singing the forty-sixth Psalm, "God is our refuge and strength, a very present help in trouble," Polycarp went toward his funeral pyre as did Savonarola. Centuries later, strengthened by this Psalm, Martin Luther braved his enemies. Cromwell's soldiers marched forth to their victory at Marston Moor chanting the songs of David.

Time has kept for us a record of David as a poet, as a ruler and as a fighter but not one vestige remains of David as a composer. More's the pity, for he must have written splendid music, or he could not have so influenced his people.

David might well be called the first bandmaster mentioned in history. Of course we know in Genesis Jubal is spoken of as the father of all those who handle the harp and pipe. But David was the first orchestral organizer. His band numbered two hundred four score and eight. He no doubt possessed a knowledge of instrumentation and tone-color effect, for he assigns his subjects to special instruments. The fourth Psalm, "Hear me when I call, Oh, God of my righteousness," he directs to be played by his chief musician who was a player of the harp and the sackbut. The fifth Psalm, "Give ear to my words, oh Lord," he assigns to the chief musician who was the solo flutist of his band. In the sixth Psalm, "Oh, Lord, rebuke me not in thine anger," the chief musician, a soloist on the string instrument who had a virtuoso's regard for expression, is called upon to perform and so on through the Psalms.

David without question had in his band all the component parts of the modern orchestra — strings, wood-winds, brass and percussion. At the dedication of Solomon's temple an orchestra played before the Lord with all manner of instruments. Some were made of fir wood, there were harps and psalteries, timbrels, castanets, cornets and cymbals and the sound of the trumpet was heard in the land even as it is heard to-day. The records of these ancient concerts are the lamps that light the way to our days, where music has taken its place among the inspirational outbursts of man.

Hugo Riemann, Sir Charles Villiers Stanford and Cecil Forsyth, those indefatigable delvers into the mystical mines of musical antiquity, agree that everything in music, up or down to 900 A.D. should be considered ancient. They record the use of voices and instruments giving melody only, or at most, octaves in singing and playing. Of course the rhythmic instruments of percussion were used to mark time and accentuate the melodies. If, as some insist, music is all man-created, its improvements in the innumerable years that preceded the makers of modern harmony were slight indeed.

It is self-evident that man in the ancient days had brain, eyes, voice and hands, even as he has to-day but polyphonic music did not exist until God breathed into music a soul and the cold mathematical beat gave way to creative genius, inventive skill and inspiration.

The Messiahs who brought the glad tidings — Palestrina, Bach, Beethoven, Wagner and a multitude of divinely-endowed musicians, led the world out of the darkness of crudity into the dazzling realm of the present — a present rich in the treasures of the masters of the past, rich in the promise of those to come.

The precursor of the present Symphony Orchestra dates from the eighteenth century. Joseph Haydn has long been known as the "Father of Instrumental Music." Many of his symphonies remain in the repertoire of the famous orchestras of the world and are played each succeeding year with never-ending delight to the auditor, the performer and the conductor.

Although it is a far cry from the combination of strings, wood-wind and brass of "Papa" Haydn's orchestra to the instruments employed by Richard Strauss, it is to the composer of *The Surprise, The Farewell, The Clock* and other immortal works that the honor of having established the classic orchestra should be given. The favorite group of "The Father of Instrumental Music" in 1766 consisted of six violins, two violas, one 'cello, one bass, one flute, two oboes, two bassoons, two clarinets, and two horns. The earliest of the Haydn symphonies was given to the world through these instruments. The *Alpine Symphony* of Richard Strauss (1914) calls for two flutes, two piccolos, two oboes (doubled), one English horn, one hecklephone, one E-flat clarinet (doubled), two B clarinets, one C clarinet (doubled), one bass clarinet, three bassoons, one contra-bassoon, sixteen horns, four tenor-tubas in B and F, six trumpets, six trombones, two bass-tubas, two harps, organ, celesta, tympani, eighteen first violins, sixteen second violins, twelve violas, ten 'cellos, eight double basses, small drum, bass drum and a host of "effect" instruments, which we, in America, call the "traps." Besides the above instruments, Strauss, in a previous composition, employed saxophones.

It will be noticed that between 1766 and 1914 composers have added a multitude of wood-wind, brass and percussion instruments to the primitive symphonic combination. With the single exception of the harp, there has been no effort since to incorporate into the string band any other stringed instrument. While the guitar, the lute, the mandolin, the banjo, the zither and the viola d'amore have been used in orchestral combinations they have only been employed for some effect believed necessary by the composer. In fact, "The symphony orchestra," says W. S.

Rockstro, "has become a large wind-band plus strings, instead of a string-band plus wind." Why?

The most æsthetic of the pure families of instruments is beyond question the violin group. In sentiment, mystery, glamour, register, unanimity of tonal facility and perfection in dexterity it more than equals all other families. But, aside from its delicate nuances and diffident dynamics, it reduces itself to the skeleton of the symphonic structure, because, like bread served with each course, it loses its novelty; and if violins are used alone beyond a certain time limit, they suggest an Adamless Eden.

Of the separate instrumental groups, apart from the violin, the vocal group, although in compass, lightness and mobility it is not the equal of the violin family, possesses a power for pathos and passion not possible to any other group. The wood-wind has a slightly greater scope than the violin. In coquetry, humorous murmurs and the mimicry of animated nature it is in a class by itself. The last orchestral family, the brass, in gamut decidedly less, has the power to thunder forth a barbaric splendor of sound or to intone the chants of the cathedral.

Therefore, composers have found a greater diversity of tone color in a multitude of wind instruments, cylinder or conical, single-reed, double-reed, direct vibration or cup-shaped mouth-piece than in the string family alone. All these wind instruments have added to the palette of the orchestrator and have enabled him to use his creative power in blending the various colors. In this connection it is not amiss to point out that that giant of the music drama, Richard Wagner, in nearly every instance, enunciates the "leit-motifs" of his operas through the agency of wood-wind or brass.

The so-called Thurmer (watchmen) bands of the Middle Ages were probably the progenitors of the present-day concert band. They were made up of fifes, oboes, zinken, trombones and drums. Trumpets were not at first used because they were for royal ears alone; not for the common herd. As time passed, numerous wind instruments were added to this group; some of the originals became obsolete and others were improved upon, until to-day the wind-band consists of four flutes, two piccolos, two oboes, one English horn, two bassoons, one contra-bassoon, or sarrusophone, two alto saxophones, two tenor saxophones, one baritone saxophone, one bass saxophone, twenty B clarinets, one alto clarinet, two bass clarinets, four cornets, two trumpets, two Fluegel horns or added cornet, four horns, four trombones, two euphoniums, eight basses (double B), one harp, one tympani, one small drum and one bass drum.

The tendency of the modern composer to place in the hands of the wood-wind corps and the brass choir of the orchestra the most dramatic effects of the symphonic body has much to do with the development of the wind-band, although there is no question that the inventive genius of Boehm, Klose, Wieprecht and Sax have been important factors. With the improvements in mechanism so far as purity of intonation and facility of execution are concerned, observant musicians and capable conductors saw the coming of a new constellation in the musical firmament — a constellation of star players on wood-wind, brass and percussion instruments.

The pioneers were Wieprecht and Parlow in Germany, Paulus and Sellenik in France, the Godfreys and George Miller in England, Bender in Belgium, Dunkler in Holland and last but not least, Patrick Sarsfield Gilmore in America. Gilmore organized a corps of musicians superior to any wind-band players of his day, many of them coming from the leading orchestras of the world and possessing a virtuoso's ability on their respective instruments. He engaged his musicians regardless of expense and paid them

AT THE NEW YORK HIPPODROME
First presentation of Lieutenant-Commander John Philip Sousa's 101st March,
"The Gallant Seventh," November 5, 1922, by Sousa's Band and the Seventh
Regiment Band

salaries commensurate with their talents. Conductors and players alike tenderly cherish the memory of Patrick Sarsfield Gilmore for his activities in the interests of instrumental performers.

The only question that can be asked in the name of progressive art comparing the modern string-band and the modern wind-band is — which, at the moment, presents the most perfect massing of sounds and tonal colors? An incessant playing of all groups combined, or the serving of solid blocks of string, wood-wind or brass music becomes wearisome. Recitals by a single vocalist or instrumental performer are made attractive through the personality and technique of the performer rather than through the entertainment itself. When personality is missing the ear is bound to tire.

In placing the string-band and the wind-band on the same plane, I see, in my mind's eye, the lover of Haydn, of Mozart, of

Beethoven and the violin family standing aghast at the thought and asking why wind instruments should attempt the immortal symphonies of these beloved masters. And well may they stand aghast and question. These compositions were created for one purpose only — to be played by the instruments the masters intended for them and *never* by any other combination. The efforts on the part of some misguided conductors and orchestrators to "improve" on the original and the equally self-appointed task of some arranger to transcribe Mozart, Beethoven and Haydn to the wind-instrument combination are greatly to be deplored. The earlier symphonies are the musical flowers grown in the shadowy lanes of the past and it is not pleasant to attempt to modernize them. Either play them as they were or let them alone entirely.

There is much modern music that is better adapted to a wind combination than to a string, although for obvious reasons originally scored for an orchestra. If in such cases the interpretation is equal to the composition the balance of a wind combination is more satisfying.

The chief aim of the composer is to produce color, dynamics, nuances and to emphasize the story-telling quality. The combination and composition which gains that result is most to be desired. To presume that the clarinet, the cornet, and the trombone should be used only to blare forth marches and jazz tunes or that the violin family must devote itself to waltzes, two-steps and fox-trots is ludicrous. The string-band and the wind-band are among the brightest constellations in the melodic heavens. The former may be likened to a woman, the latter to a man, for like maid and man, brought together in divine harmony, they can breathe into life the soulful, the sentimental, the heroic and the sublime.

Chapter XIX

AS I have already said, Sousa's Band was born back in the "gay nineties" when David Blakely called upon me in Chicago where the Marine Band was giving a concert. Blakely had taken it for granted that I would eagerly accept his offer to leave Washington. On the contrary I refused it at first, held by familiar ties in the capital. But the idea pleased me and secretly I was always favorable to it. I had often dreamed of a real band of my own, composed of the most talented musicians, who would provide a perfect response to my aspiring baton. Besides, it meant a considerable financial advancement — six thousand dollars salary, twenty percent of the profits and a five-year contract. Mother told me, after I had made my decision, that Father, only two weeks before his death, on reading the April ninth newspaper report of my opportunity to leave the Marines and go on tour had said to her slowly,

"Well, Philip *ought* to have his own organization. The time has come for him to go!"

At the end of July, 1892, I gave a farewell concert at the National Theater and left for New York, carrying with me hundreds of gratifying and encouraging messages. Then came the organization of my band. I had met one of the leading cornetists in London, Arthur Smith, a splendid musician who had been solo cornet with the Coldstream Guards and soloist at the promenade concerts at Covent Garden. I then engaged Staats, of Boston, a graduate of the Paris conservatory; Henry D. Koch, one of the finest French-horn players in the United States; Arthur Pryor, the talented trombonist; Frank Holton, another fine trombone player; Jambon, a bassoonist, also a graduate of the Paris conservatory; John S. Cox, the Scotch flutist who calmly faced myriad-noted cadenzas; Richard Messenger, oboe; and a glorious array of clarinets, tubas, saxophones, as well as a valiant bass drummer from the Garde du Corps of Berlin. I had good reason to be proud of this assemblage.

I strove in every way to improve the quality and variety of the instruments. Way back when I was with the Marines they used a Helicon tuba wound around the body. I disliked it for concert work because the tone would shoot ahead and be too violent. I suggested to a manufacturer that we have an upright bell of large size so that the sound would diffuse over the entire band like the frosting on a cake! He designed a horn after that description and it has been in use ever since, by many bands, under the name of the Sousaphone.

There are now eighty-four men in my band. It has become almost entirely American in personnel. Last year — 1927 — there was only one player who was born abroad and he is a naturalized American citizen. That is quite in contrast to the early days when nearly all of them were foreigners, and the dramatis personæ reminded you of a concert in Berlin or Rome.

We have a familiar and beloved routine. Every man knows his duty and performs it. Perhaps that is why there is so seldom any display of jealousy — less than in any organization I have known. No man is ever called upon to do another's part. Similar tastes promote a great friendship among them, and if a vain man joins the band he very soon is brought down to earth!

About July first we start on our tour. Contracts have been made from six months to a year ahead by my manager, Mr. Harry Askin. We assemble in New York from every corner of the country — each man with his trunk and his suitcase. The instruments are stowed in specially-designed trunks under the care of the band baggage man. Arrived at our destination, the men go to their hotels, and the band luggage is sent to the hall where we are to appear. The band librarian lays out our music, the accumulation of which is, I believe, one of the greatest libraries of band music in the world. We carry our own music stands and my podium. The men arrive about three quarters of an hour before the concert to tune up, soften their lips, and make sure everything is in order. That is the prelude which the public rarely hears — a pleasant, busy crooning and tuning, plucking of strings and blowing of low, disconnected notes. It is not music — yet, but it is the sign of efficiency and activity to the conductor, and always gives me a satisfactory feeling of "things about to happen."

When the concert is about to begin, the librarian calls out, "All on!" and they file on the stage. Each man is provided with a list of encores which, nine times out of ten, are Sousa marches, for we generally have advance letters containing requests for many of them. It is my invariable rule to begin the encore almost immediately after the programme number. This habit has come in for its share of criticism. I chuckled over this extract from the "pearls" of John F. Runciman when he wrote, "Sousa in London" for a British journal:

AT a Sousa concert, I am given to understand, the great things arc the Sousa marches. We were certainly given plenty of them. After a piece by some lesser man, Sousa would lightly descend from his platform, and as lightly step up, and the band would uproariously break out with the *Washington Post*; and this done with, the gymnastics would be repeated and we would hear some other thing of which I don't know the name. It appears to me that encores must be easily earned in Mr. Sousa's country. In this retrograde one of ours, the audience is invariably given an opportunity of proving that it really wants to hear something a second time. If an English conductor, or even an English band-master, did anything of this sort he would promptly be called a humbug, a charlatan. But I suppose customs differ, and I must add that if we must have encores, the English custom seems to me the better one. And though Sousa may scorn us as a people who don't come from Chicago, and have not been fed on the sacred gospel of "hustle," it may be useful to him to know that our custom is our custom.

Press notices telling how Mr. Sousa was enthusiastically encored are worse than worthless to those of us who observed that he never allowed time for an encore to be demanded. As for the marches, I have heard them in music-halls, panto-mimes, cafés and on street-organs, but until last week I had no notion of their ear-splitting blatancy. Now I understand why Mr. James Huneker falls back on Strauss as a calm refuge. After one hour of Sousa I could have fallen asleep with the battle in "Heldenleben" falling sweetly on my ears as a soothing lullaby.... The Americans are, they themselves state, a great people, and apparently they like great noises. In no other

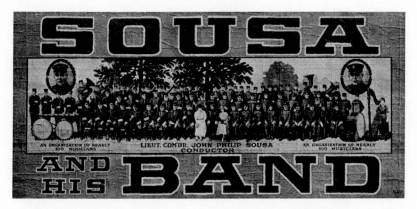

A NOTABLE POSTER — NINE BY TWENTY-ONE FEET

country in the world but America could Sousa and his Band have gained the reputation they have there.

This critic evidently doesn't want an overdose of music. The audiences, however, do not seem to object to my practice. I prefer to respond quickly rather than to await the vigorous smacking-together of tiring hands, hitherto comfortably folded and relaxed.

There has been only one type of uniform for the men and we have not changed it in more than thirty years. Salaries are from seventy-four dollars to two hundred dollars a week, according to proficiency and experience. Everywhere there is manifest good will and impartiality in the entire organization. The human contacts established are, of course, many and interesting. Four years ago one of my original players, Joseph Norrito, a solo clarinetist who had been with me ever since the band was "born," retired and went back to Italy. Sometimes band members marry and settle down, forsaking our nomadic life, but of late many of the men have taken their wives along on tour. Last year half a dozen wives were with us.

We have had basketball and baseball teams of our own and the latter have played the Marine teams at Philadelphia and at various Expositions. In 1900 on our Paris tour, we played the American Guard. We usually make a goodly showing. Recently we have had two teams in the band itself — one of reed players, the other of brass; the average is about equal, even though one might expect the brass to win by virtue of long-windedness!

The Band is unique in the number of concerts given and mileage covered. In the thirty-six years of its existence it has visited every part of the United States and Canada, has made five tours of Europe and one of the world. We have travelled, in all, one million two hundred thousand miles. And this was accomplished quite without subsidy, depending entirely on our own drawing-power. From the ranks of the band have arisen several men who are now conductors of their own bands; among them, Herbert L. Clarke, Arthur Pryor, Walter Rogers, Bohumir Kryl, Fred Gilliland, Frank Simons and others. I am proud to call them graduates of Sousa's Band.

To obtain the best musicians we choose those belonging to the American Federation of Musicians and I have found them unfailingly loyal to me. Every man gives of his best, at all times, uncomplainingly and with spirit and vigor. Their punctuality too, which is the politeness of kings, is admirable. I rejoice at their attitude and at our rehearsals in June, when we go over everything which we are to play for the coming season, I look them over with affection and pride.

I have often been asked the reason for some of my methods of conducting. Is it not the business of the conductor to convey to the public in its dramatic form the central idea of a composition; and how can he convey that idea successfully if he does not enter heart and soul into the life of the music and the tale it unfolds?

The movements which I make I cannot possibly repress because, at the time, I *am* actually the idea I am interpreting, and naturally I picture my players and auditors as in accord with me. I know, of course, that my mannerisms have been widely discussed. They have even said, "He goes through the motions as if he were dancing one of his own twosteps." Now I never move my legs at all. Perhaps my hands dance; they certainly do not make really sweeping motions, for the slightest movement suffices to carry my meaning. In Germany one man said, "Your band is like oil." I knew what he meant. Instead of waving my arms vigorously, I had gone at it smoothly. It struck them as something different. Moreover, they liked the way we did the pianissimo passages.

To my men the raising of a thumb is significant. Whenever we introduce a new man into the band, he invariably stands out too much, particularly if he has been playing under an extremely vigorous conductor. Always I have to jump on him and press him back into the united whole. All organizations work the same way — they must be a unit, and since I strive to paint my melodies usually with a camel's hair brush instead of with the sweeping stroke of a whitewash brush, I must insist upon that delicate oneness of tone.

Very clever players, they are — all of them in the Band — but if their interpretation of a passage does not agree with mine they can and will subordinate their idea to mine. That is why the greatest generals would make the finest privates. These men know that the whole effect will be better if they submit to one dominating spirit — the leader. On the other hand, the leader who doesn't watch for outbursts of genius in his men, in the playing of a phrase, makes a sad mistake. For example: I would be rehearsing a piece and would stop for five minutes to rest. As I went out, I would hear some fellow going over a portion of the piece and playing with it — trying it this way and that, until finally I would hear him play it in a certain way and I would say to myself, "That's the way it *ought* to be done!" Invariably, continuing the rehearsal, I would say to the men, "I heard Jones playing this over a while ago, and his way is better than mine," and after Jones, beaming with delight, had demonstrated, I would lead it in that fashion. If I were not open-minded I could not improve as a director — I am a better director than I was last year, and I hope to be a better one next year!

One of the most amusing and yet perhaps one of the truest things that has been said of me is that I resemble one of those strolling players who carries a drum on his back, cymbals on his head, a cornet in one hand and a concertina in the other — who is, in fact, a little band all in himself. That is what I am constantly trying to do all the time — to make my musicians and myself a one-man band! Only, instead of having actual metallic wires to work the instruments I strike after magnetic ones. I have to work so that I feel that every one of my eighty-four musicians is linked up with me by a cable of magnetism. Every man must be as intent upon and as sensitive to every movement of my baton as I am myself. So, when I stretch out my hand in the direction of some player, I give him the music I feel and, as I beckon to him, the music leaps back at me. But the element which welds us all into one harmonious whole is sympathy — my sympathy for them and theirs for me.

I have always selected my programmes according to my own conception of the dictates of good taste. Of course, this disregard of precedent and tradition gives rise to a good deal of criticism — generally from affronted musicians, not from the public. To a critic who was shocked at my using *Kelly* as an encore on a programme which included Wagner's *Siegfried* I replied, "But

I'd just as soon play *Kelly* for an encore to *Siegfried* as to play *Siegfried* as an encore to *Kelly!*"

Artistic snobbery is so ridiculous! Many an immortal tune has been born in the stable or the cotton-field. *Turkey in the Straw* is a magic melody; anyone should be proud of having written it, but, for musical high-brows, I suppose the thing is declassee. It came not from a European composer but from an unknown Negro minstrel. I am, however, equally enthusiastic about the truly great compositions of the masters. My admiration for Wagner and Beethoven is profound. I played *Parsifal* — or excerpts from it — ten years before it was produced at the Metropolitan. Most audiences had to learn to understand and appreciate it.

Once upon a time, however, the *Parsifal* music was wildly applauded. We were giving a concert in a Texas town during a howling blizzard. The hall was frigidly cold. The audience retained overcoats and even added blankets to their equipment. There was about $124.00 in the house — and I can safely say that it was the smallest, politest, coldest audience I had ever encountered. There was absolutely no applause. During the intermission, the mayor of the town, the editor of the local newspaper and the manager of the hall came backstage to request two encores, *Dixie* and *The Stars and Stripes Forever*. They added an apology for the small attendance. "I don't mind the attendance," I exclaimed, "I don't blame anybody for dodging a blizzard. But if they appreciate our presence here as you say they do, why don't they at least give us a little applause?" They hastened to assure me that the audience, out of consideration for us, had purposely refrained from applauding; they knew that we, on the stage, were equally chilly and they didn't want us to feel obliged to give encores. Said I, "Never you mind about encores! There is one thing that freezes

EXCERPTS FROM MANUSCRIPTS OF "IN FLANDERS FIELDS"
(By kind permission of G. Schirmer, Publisher) and "THE LAST CRUSADE" (By kind
permission of The John Church Company, Publishers)

a musician more than the deadliest physical cold, and that is the spiritual chill of an unresponsive audience! Just give us a little applause — have some man let his leg fall off the chair, and you shall have both *Dixie* and *The Stars and Stripes Forever!*"

The next selection was from *Parsifal*, a long and very dignified number. But the audience well-nigh lifted the roof off. Applause was vociferous and prolonged. The men woke up — we played encore after encore — we gave what was practically another concert. Overcoats came off and the audience went wild. *Parsifal* had loosened the tension. Everybody was more than happy and the blizzard raged unnoticed.

Nowadays I allow myself a bit more of vacationing than formerly. Up to the time of the World War I toured with the Band practically the entire year, often following the road for fifty weeks, including both summer engagements and winter tours; but since the War I travel from July to December and then gather together my guns and equipment and go south for the shooting season. Then to Pinehurst for golf, and back to Long Island to write and to enjoy my home and my family. When June comes, I turn to programme-arranging for the next tour, to determining the personnel of the Band and to rehearsals. Once the tour is mapped out by my business manager it is submitted to me. On long engagements, and on foreign tours, I have always had my family with me.

I have been singularly blessed with a home life which has given me peace, harmony and understanding between the tours that demand so much of my energy, a home life far different from that of many a composer and musician. Surely nothing is so invaluable to a professional musician as the sincere and considerate affection of a loyal family. I have had it — and all because of Mrs. Sousa's sympathy and foresight.

THE HOME AT SAND'S POINT, PORT WASHINGTON,
LONG ISLAND

When we were first married and lived in Washington (on A
Street, S. E., then on 6th Street and finally at the corner of 4th
and B Streets, Capitol Hill) Mrs. Sousa realized that my life work
was to be music, that music was an exacting mistress and that
domestic affairs would have to be subordinated to the musical
demands of the moment. She was therefore careful never to
interrupt my train of thought or disturb me at my work. She has
always had the kindliest words for my achievements, proving
herself a constant inspiration because of her incurable belief that
I can "do it better than anybody else!"

When I left Washington and my directorship of the Marine
Band in 1892 I established my family in an apartment in New
York City and the children began school there. We kept an apartment in New York until 1915 when we moved to the present
family residence at Sand's Point, Port Washington, Long Island.

Our children have brought us only happiness. Mrs. Sousa has been the most devoted of mothers — and grandmothers. My son John Philip, Jr. married Eileen Adams, who has presented us with five fine grandchildren, Eileen, John Philip, 3rd, Jane Priscilla, Thomas Adams and Nancy. My daughter Jane Priscilla is with us at Port Washington, and my other daughter, Helen, the wife of Hamilton Abert, has brought us still another lovely little Jane Priscilla.

At home, this family of mine has given me cooperation, appreciation and constructive criticism. As I write, I can recall the many conferences — frank in the extreme — about my work, and I have always profited by them. My wife and my children have been companions, editors, critics and audience, sharing my hopes and my hobbies, one harmonious company — like my Band.

"Recollection is the only Paradise from which we cannot be turned out," says Richter. Every day has been and still is rich in its contacts with beautiful and talented women and gifted men. Their public often sees them as lovable but remote. I have found them lovable and human — in their play hours the most delightful of grownup children — Chaplin "in the wings" or De Koven at a dinner table.

I met De Koven when the American composers formed a Baton Society and we immediately became warm friends. He was a stickler for proprieties — his fastidious appearance being equalled only by the perfection of his manners, but at one banquet he said to me with the engaging candor of a child, "I wish you'd let me call you 'Philip.' "

"All right," was my reply, "but I should like to call you 'Reggie.' " So thereafter it was "Philip" and "Reggie" although I doubt if many people addressed the dignified De Koven with so little ceremony. He had been educated in Vienna and England — at Oxford, in fact, and his excellent accent showed it. Of all De Koven's operas, and there are twenty-five or more, *Robin Hood* retains best its pristine youth and vigor. It was first presented in England under the title of Maid Marian and was played here with great success by "The Bostonians." I believe that it is the most popular opera ever written by an American composer.

To talk of light opera is, inevitably, to talk of Victor Herbert. It is always a pleasure to me to include many of his compositions on my programmes. I was handicapped in my own opera-writing by the difficulty of getting first class librettos and by the arduous demands of my long band tours, but I followed with interest the creative work of Herbert. He was the best-equipped man of his time for this work; curiously enough he always did his best when he was composing for some particular star; evidently it was necessary to him to have a definite human picture in his mind. Herbert was an excellent example of fine musicianship and it was a distinct aid to his success that he could give so much of his time to operatic writing. Perhaps no two men in the profession have been paired more often in the minds of the people than Herbert and myself. When I planned to go to Europe with my band for its first overseas tour (which the approach of the Spanish War prevented) Herbert, then conductor of the Twenty-Second Regiment Band, formerly Gilmore's famous group, took my place at Manhattan Beach. Since Herbert was a 'cellist, orchestra work was naturally his first love and so it was that he formed an orchestra and became conductor of the Pittsburgh Symphony; before he left his New York band he presented me with a number of military pieces he had arranged and I still have them all. In those good old days, the three names most familiar to patrons of light opera were certainly Herbert, De Koven, and Sousa. Herbert, I am sure, wrote more light operas of high quality than any other composer in Europe or America.

The younger composers of to-day are immensely pleasant fellows to meet. It was at my first attendance of a "gambol" of the Lambs that I met Irving Berlin. William Courtleigh, Shepherd of the Lambs, had asked me to become an honorary member; I accepted gratefully, since I had many warm friends in the club. I went along on that famous "gambol" as general musical conductor. I wrote what is perhaps the only medley overture ever designed to be "acted out," in which I had introduced solos, duets, choruses and dances in a new style of an old-time minstrel overture. It was a novelty and Frank McIntyre (of *Travelling Salesman* fame) afterwards told me that there had been some doubt as to whether it would "get over." Well, no one ever knows which way "the cat will jump" just as no one ever knows just what will receive the stamp of public approval. In that respect, it resembled every other new creation! Berlin had a special song for that night — about Mexico — and he did it most cleverly. I found him a charming fellow, modest, entertaining and a mighty satisfactory companion. Our friendship is still very much alive.

Rudolph Friml, Berlin's contemporary, has appeared with me several times in the Hippodrome stunt which combined a group of composers, each playing his most popular number. I considered him one of the very finest composer-pianists in the lot, and I might add that I was probably the very worst! I am perfectly sure that Friml knows it.

It was at the Hippodrome Sunday feature concerts in 1915 that I first met that public idol, Charles Chaplin. We had been revelling in the vocal gifts of Melba, Culp, Garden and Fremstad. Charlie was therefore quite a departure.

"I want to lead your band!" said Charlie.

"In what number?" I asked.

"The *Poet and Peasant* overture," he confidently replied.

THREE MASTERS OF MELODY
Victor Herbert, Irving Berlin, and Mr. Sousa

At the rehearsal he mounted the podium, took my baton and as the band started the stately measures of the opening, he proceeded to beat time fully four times too fast! That well-known blank expression came over his face but this time it was involuntary. "That isn't it!" he exclaimed. I smiled. "But I've played it many years," I reminded him. Suddenly I realized that he remembered only the *allegro* and had forgotten all about the *moderato,* so I told the band to begin again, this time with the *allegro,* and we were off! On the night of the performance, the audience, reading his name on the program and never having seen him in the flesh, suspected a trick — some clever impersonation of Chaplin — but, as he came from the wings, he did his inimitably funny little step and slowly proceeded to the band-platform. The house, convinced, rang with applause.

Among many pleasant musical associations has been my friendship with that gifted director and interpreter of music, Walter Damrosch. I have the following cordial letter from him:

November 9, 1915

DEAR MR. SOUSA:

I regret more than I can say that I cannot be present at the presentation of the testimonial on your sixty-first birthday. In fact, having just seen and heard you at the Hippodrome in the full zenith of your activities I refuse to believe that it is your sixty-first!

Your enthusiasm has kept you young and you are a wonderful example of the power of music over such a purely arbitrary thing as the marking of time, for you have "marked time" so ably and successfully that the "March King" has become a household word in every quarter of the globe.

Your stirring rhythms have quickened the pulses of millions and we are all proud of you as a fellow American and fellow musician.

Please accept my heartiest congratulations on this happy anniversary and believe me

Yours most cordially,

WALTER DAMROSCH

I have a host of friends among America's actors. And I have worked with them at the pleasantest of tasks — that of amusing a group of sympathetic people. James T. Powers brought back to New York from Washington a song of mine, written for the Gridiron Club, whose guest he had been and he sang it many times for the Lambs. We had enjoyed the planning of that song and I still quote it at intervals. The refrain was "Do We, We Do!" a confirmation of the poet's predilection for wine, woman and song, and Powers put a lot of energy into his eloquent rendition of "Do We, We Do!"

Then there are Fred Stone, Frank Daniels and Francis Wilson. I came into constant contact with Wilson in my younger days. He was a contemporary of mine — born in 1854. I never wrote an opera for him, but I did do much of his orchestrating — *The Merry Monarch*, *The Lion Tamer*, etc. One of my prized possessions is a gold watch which he gave me in recognition of a "rush order" which I filled for him in the early nineties. He telegraphed me, "Will you orchestrate *The Lion Tamer*?" and I went on to New York immediately. Much of the music and some of the libretto had been taken from the French, but a few American numbers were included. I did the orchestration in one week, working from twenty to twenty-two hours a day. The play was a great success. Then came the gold watch — and Wilson offered me the position of musical director of his company, at a very high salary, which I declined.

Frank Daniels, since our first meeting, has always been extremely kind to me. One night, while he was playing in *The Wizard of the Nile* and I was in a box, thoroughly enjoying his performance, at the end of the first act, when the applause was at its height, someone in the gallery spied me and sent up the shout of, "Sousa!" The whole house turned to me and applauded. Frank rang up the curtain once more, took my hand and led me on to the stage. Of course the next cry was "Speech!"

Fred Stone — excellent shooter, fine horseman, all-round athlete and, incidentally, something of a comedian — has especially endeared himself to me because of his devotion to his daughter, Dorothy. Although we are both busy men, whenever we meet he says, "I'm sure Dorothy would be delighted to see you. Let's go!" And we go.

It may seem a sort of inverted politeness to leave the ladies to the last but it is only following the rule of the most vivid impressions. Certainly it is not likely that I shall ever forget beautiful Maxine Elliott, vivacious Henrietta Crosman or the lovely Violet Heming. When I last saw Maxine we were in London where an English gentleman gave a supper to Nat Goodwin, Maxine, Edna May, Mrs. Sousa, and myself. About midnight, Nat said lugubriously, "Here we are; — all but the host — Americans, and according to my way of seeing it, you're a success in London and so are Edna and Maxine, and *I'm* the only failure!" Nat never spoke to failure!

I am always looking for beauty everywhere, and I am among the first to pay it homage. I found it raised to the nth degree when I first met glorious Violet Heming. If all women were as beautiful as she the managers of marriage license bureaus would be working overtime!

In 1927 I met delightful Henrietta Crosman while she was appearing as one of the three stars in *Merry Wives of Windsor*. The others were Mrs. Fiske and Otis Skinner. I also renewed my acquaintance with Mrs. Fiske and was set right about the conductor in New Orleans who told me about that many-times-dedicated polka. To my friendly, "I knew your father well!" she contradicted me, "Why, no, that was my uncle!"

Marie Tempest sang with us at Manhattan Beach and the members of my Band won her heart completely. In one of her songs — *Vogelhander* — they hummed the chorus, as she sang. The combination, a new one at the time, "brought down the house."

Lillian Nordica — there was a glorious voice! I was invited by the Rubenstein Society of New York to be toastmaster at a banquet at which Nordica was a guest. When I introduced her, I said, "We have the very great pleasure of having with us to-night the first 'brass band girl'!" (For Gilmore, planning his trip to Europe in 1878, wanted a girl of talent with an American name and found both qualifications in this Maine girl — Lillian Norton. Once having heard her sing, of course he took her. The gifted girl found it a short step from brass band soloist to queen of the operatic stage.) That night she sang song after song, with the greatest generosity and with magnificent artistry. I shall never forget it, though the voice is stilled.

THERE comes to me out of the Past
A voice, whose tones are sweet and wild
Singing a song almost divine
And with a tear in every line.

THE LONG AND SHORT OF THE BAND
Miss Winfred Bambrick — Harp — 5 feet
Mr. Jack Richardson — Sousaphone — 6 feet, 6 inches

Chapter XX

MUSIC VITAL TO AMERICA — COMPOSER-FRIENDS — EUROPEAN
INFLUENCES BECOMING NEGLIGIBLE — NO NATIONALITY IN MUSIC —
MY FAITH IN AMERICAN MUSIC-MAKING — OUR NATIONAL LOVE OF
HYMNS — THE RADIO — THE JAZZ CULT — WHY THE MARCH? — THE
WRITING OF MARCHES — INSPIRATION — THE UNITED STATES AS THE
PATRON OF MUSIC — ADVICE TO YOUNG COMPOSERS — MY DBBT TO
THE AMERICAN PUBLIC AND THE AMERICAN PRESS — A WEALTH OF
HAPPY MEMORIES — IN CONCLUSION

MUSIC, whatever may be the opinion prevailing at home and abroad, is a vital and integral part of American life. What I have said earlier in this book concerning the capacity of Americans to write good music is not intended to apply to the future alone — I am proud to have known many and admired all of a host of American composers, Charles Wakefield Cadman, George W. Chadwick (Director of the New England Conservatory of Music), Arthur Foote (dean of American composers), Frederick S. Converse, Horatio Parker (a singularly brilliant and talented man), Stillman Kelly, John Alden Carpenter (my dear Western friend), Ethelbert Nevin, Henry Hadley, Homer N. Bartlett, Mrs. H. H. A. Beach, Howard Brockway, George F. Bristow, Dudley Buck, Arthur B. Whiting, Edward MacDowell, Ernest Richard Kroeger, Adolph Martin Foerster, Reuben Goldmark and John Knowles Paine. Every one of these stands out in musical annals as an originator, not an imitator, and as a typical American.

When the question arises as to influences, I feel sure that the only influence which American composers can be said to have had on others is that shown in imitations of Stephen Foster's darky ballads, or of my marches. The European has had a style of his own to pursue and accordingly has not often attempted ours. On the other hand the younger country has of necessity been influenced by Continental methods. America has given us many harmonists, and men who have produced excellent examples of the purest music; ninety-nine percent of these men were educated in Europe and are dominated by foreign methods. However, just as opera programmes now display with pride such typically American names as Tibbets, Johnson, Hackett, Talley, Homer and Farrar, and foreign names are no longer particularly helpful to success in grand opera, so the influence of the German, French and Italian composers upon American composers is becoming almost negligible. I have always believed that ninety-eight percent of a student's progress is due to his own efforts, and two percent to his teacher. We are rapidly developing teachers of rare ability, and students of talent and purpose; with such a combination, the whole hundred percent ought to emerge triumphant. Moreover, American teachers have one indisputable advantage over foreign ones; they understand the American temperament and can judge its unevenness, its lights and its shadows. They bring a native understanding to their pupil.

Such discussion leads inevitably to the question of nationalism in music. Mark Twain tells a story of a celebrated actor who was absolutely confident of the power of the human face to express the passions hidden in the breast. He claimed that the countenance could disclose more surely than the tongue what was in the heart.

"Observe my face," said he. "What does it express?"

"Despair."

"Bah! It expresses peaceful resignation. Now, what is this?"

"Rage!"

"Nonsensetit means terror. This?"

"Imbecility."

"Are you mad? It is smothered ferocity. Can you tell this?"

"Joy!"

"The devil take you! Any ass can see it means insanity."

An attempt to place a melody within geographical limits is bound to fail. Rhythmic qualities are imitated in all popular forms, but music, although it has many dialects, is, after all, a universal language. The waltz may have been German in the beginning but it certainly belongs to the world to-day. It is true that a phase of nationality *can* be depicted by national instruments but not always infallibly. A bagpipe can play a German melody quite as well as *Comin' Thro' the Rye*. The only true nationalism I have observed is that of imitation — where a man writes something fresh and original and is slavishly imitated by lesser lights who repeat the rhythmic flow in other compositions. If nationalism were a factor in music, would it be Wagner or Brahms in Germany who would represent the German in music, Debussy or Gounod in France, Sullivan or Elgar in England, Puccini or Respighi in Italy? We speak of music which is typically Irish; I have in my library nearly five hundred compositions by Irishmen and not one of these works shows the slightest trace of what we have been pleased to call the Irish note in music. And in Scotch, French and Spanish music we find any number of compositions that bear not the slightest tinge of localism.

Nor can one nationalize a melody by the placing of its harmonic structure. Because you meet a blonde in Spain, is she a Swede; or a brunette in Sweden, is she a Spaniard? From a melody itself one cannot deduce its birthplace. *Yankee Doodle* is old English and not American at all. It is the individuality and the genius of the composer that matters, not the individuality

SOUSA AND EDISON

JUDGE LANDIS AND SOUSA
EXCHANGE WEAPONS OF
WARFARE

CHAPLIN TAKES THE BATON

WITH CLARENCE D. CHAMBERLIN
AT IOWA STATE FAIR

of his race. Americans like the martial rhythm of the march but that does not make it more distinctly American than it is Serbian or Norwegian!

If there were absolutely national schools of music, then there would be no Wagnerian style, no Weberian style, nor would there be much difference between Schumann and Schubert. Mozart's style is a combination of his own individual genius and the imitation of certain early Italians — is he then to be classed as typically German, when, instead, he is typically Mozart? We often hear that Chopin wrote essentially Polish music; he did not. He interpreted his own soul. His music is the faithful poetic revelation of the enigma of his heart. If that resembles the revelation of other Polish hearts it is because Poles feel things much as the rest of the great human family. No, I do not believe there is any such thing as nationalism in music.

I have every sort of faith in America's meed of musical artists and music-lovers. I firmly believe that we have more latent musical talent in America than there is in any other country. But to dig it out there must be good music throughout the land, a lot of it. Everyone must hear it, and such a process takes time. Most schools to-day have bands and orchestras for boys and girls; I have often met high school bands (one-third girls) who were not confined to ordinary routine instruments but joyfully executed pieces on tubas, trombones, clarinets, etc. This enlivening of interest means an increase in the number of American concert-goers and, accordingly, in the number of concerts. I think that the quality of all bands is steadily improving and it is a pleasant thought to me that perhaps the efforts of Sousa's Band have quickened that interest and improved that quality.

It is fascinating to watch the barometer of public favor and to observe what gains interest and how. We have a secret love for the old hymn tunes and the American response to these melodies is a keen one. There is a deep-lying foundation of religious sentiment in our temperament which quickens to those songs, and the simple fervor of hymn tunes (the older the better) makes a profound impression upon American audiences. True, we do not wear our religion on our coat-sleeves, but we are nevertheless strongly affected by religious impulses.

At the moment, radio is undoubtedly wielding a tremendous influence over the public. By this medium the masses are becoming acquainted as never before with the best of the world's music. It is pleasanter, moreover, at times to give oneself up to the charms of music with pipe and foot-stool at hand than in the crowded concert hall. I cannot tell whether this influence extends to the student of music in his practice, for I am sure that the progress of any student depends largely upon the urge he feels *within* him. But even at its highest and finest degree, radio will never take the place of the personal performance by the artist. It fulfills its purpose, just as the movies do, but its scope is limited. The rapport between performer and audience is invaluable and can be fully attained only through actual vision. I have refrained from broadcasting for this very reason; I am reluctant to lose the warm personal touch with my audience.

Still, the radio is excellent for our busy people. Americans have such a diversity of interests! The United States has, I think, a greater variety of sport attractions than any other country. We have clubs where much time is given to encouraging and perfecting tennis, golf, baseball, trap-shooting, hockey, prize-fighting — even dominoes! Therefore the American man, rising from his dinner and seeking diversion, may often be torn between two loves — the lure of a concert and the stronger lure of a hockey match or a track meet. It is just another case of "t'other dear charmer!" Variety is the spice of life to an American and so he doesn't always choose the opera or the concert. Your German or your Frenchman has fewer attractions from which to select his programme for the evening — and the opera or the concert has become a habit with him.

Certainly "jazz" takes up a goodly share of the American's time, — too much, to my way of thinking. "Jazz," like the well-known little girl with the curl, when it is good is very, very good, and when it is bad it is *horrid*. The greater part of it is very bad. Its popularity is the result of the avowed tastes of those people who care only for music which is strongly rhythmical. Its harmonic structure is not new and its melodic design is very, very old. I have seen advertisements offering to teach the "art" of jazz in *twenty lessons*! And this wonderful art will, I am positive, some day-disappear — when the dancer tires of it — unwept, unhonored and unsung. It is raging now, to be sure, and has a considerable following, but it does not truly represent America to the world; it does reflect a certain phase of the world's life (not America's alone) since it employs primitive rhythms which excite the basic human impulses. It will endure just as long as people hear it through their feet instead of their brains!

Almost every good tune in the world has been unmercifully jazzed — exquisite melodies whether grave or gay — themes from Aida and the lovely creations of Saint-Saens and Tchaikowsky. Some of the writers of jazz are not composers at all. "Jazz" permits people of no talent whatever to write stuff and call it music. There is no short cut to skill in composition.

Marches, of course, are well known to have a peculiar appeal for me. Although during a busy life I have written ten operas and a hundred other things — cantatas, symphonic poems, suites, waltzes, songs, dances and the like — marches are, in a sense, my musical children. I think Americans (and many other nationals for that matter) brighten at the tempo of a stirring march because it appeals to their fighting instincts. Like the beat of an African war drum, the march speaks to a fundamental rhythm in the human organization and is answered. A march stimulates every center of vitality, wakens the imagination and spurs patriotic impulses which may have been dormant for years. I can speak with confidence because I have seen men profoundly moved by a few measures of a really inspired march.

But a march must be good. It must be as free from padding as a marble statue. Every line must be carved with unerring skill. Once padded, it ceases to be a march. There is no form of musical composition where the harmonic structure must be more clean-cut. The whole process is an exacting one. There must be a melody which appeals to the musical and unmusical alike. There must be no confusion in counterpoints. The composer must, to be sure, follow accepted harmonization; but that is not enough. He must be gifted with the ability to pick and choose here and there, to throw off the domination of any one tendency. If he is a so-called purist in music, that tendency will rule his marches and will limit their appeal.

How are marches written? I suppose every composer has a somewhat similar experience in his writing. With me the thought comes, sometimes slowly, sometimes with ease and rapidity. The idea gathers force in my brain and takes form not only melodically but harmonically at the same time. It must be complete before I commit it to paper. Then I instrument it according to the effects it requires. Often I fix my mind upon some objective — such as the broad spaces of the West, the langorous beauty of the South, the universal qualities of America as a whole. And then comes its musical expression — be it thunder or sunshine!

I do not, of course, manufacture my themes deliberately; the process isn't direct or arbitrary enough for that. It is not a nonchalant morning's work. I often dig for my themes. I practice a sort of self-hypnotism, by penetrating the inner chambers of my brain and *receiving* the themes. Any composer who is gloriously conscious that he is a composer must believe that he receives his inspiration from a source higher than himself. That is part of my life *credo*. Sincere composers believe in God.

Curiosity has often been expressed as to the building up of a musical background, of the whole complex orchestration. The process is difficult of description. In the fashioning of the orchestration the theme occupies somewhat the relation to the whole structure that a leader does to his orchestra — forever weaving in and out, emerging vividly here and subordinating itself there. Of course it is necessary to understand the science of music-making. I might say the theme sounds through the brain — it wakens vibrations from the memory chords of the brain and produces creative activity; the mind quickens, hovers intently about the suggested theme, and gradually the theme, the technique and artistry of the composer all work together to build up the orchestration.

Composers are an odd lot, but I sometimes think visiting ones are oddest of all. I remember one composer-musician who made a tour of the United States and later abused the country in general but added that one part of it was charming — California. The explanation was that, at the time, — years ago — the Californians were not as relentless in their criticisms as were the Easterners. So it is that wounded egotism often permits itself ridiculous untruths.

Despite such occurrences nearly every European artist looks forward with eagerness to the day when he can vend his musical wares in the U. S. A. He never gives a thought to presenting them

to the Patagonians. Why not? Because there would be no mone-
tary *quid pro quo* and because he could not find an intelligent
public. These artists — at least the honest ones — must feel that
in the United States they are well paid for their efforts and that
those efforts if worthy, are invariably appreciated. Moreover, the
symphonic orchestras of America are as well equipped as those of
Europe (often better equipped) to provide an adequate medium
for composer or soloist, and the range of musical literature is
greater here. I know that we have greater variety in that field, for
when I toured Germany they knew little and cared less about
French music; the same attitude prevailed in France concerning
German music. Our population is more cosmopolitan in character, our tastes are less limited and we are more open to the
delights of eclecticism in music. Europeans claim to be international in their tastes, but to my interested eye they were patheti-
cally provincial, perhaps deliberately so, for they always magni-
fied their own music.

Once in Germany I met a sour-faced man who informed
me that my outfit played well enough but that their music was
too *sugary*! Well, Wagner, Tchaikowsky and Saint-Saens were
included on that programme and although I was guilty of
choosing the pieces and my audience was guilty of liking them,
primarily the composer was guilty of having written them!

It is much easier to ridicule the taste of a nation than to
improve or correct it. Foreigners laugh at our naïve taste in the
arts, and we, with equal thoughtlessness, journey abroad and
find food for mirth in their obsolete customs. There are plenty of
explanations for both. *Our* limitations are due to the fact that we
have been developing an enormous territory in an astonishingly
short time and have been trying simultaneously to absorb the
literature, art and music of Europe.

We can afford the best in this country, and once convinced that we desire it, we shall achieve it; the desire is rapidly being implanted, therefore we are going to achieve the best in music. Of course our cousins across seas, like all affectionate relatives, persist in prolonging our infancy. Witness Williams of the English Grenadier Guards Band, who said, indulgently, upon his return to London after an American tour: "We did not try to force upon the American people too 'hifalutin' music — and that is no doubt the secret of our success."

If I could meet the rising army of young American composers face to face, I should say to them, speaking with a veteran's privilege of frankness, "*Be yourself and never an imitator. Do not be obscure, and do not be a materialist* — it will ruin your work. Remember always that the composer's pen is still mightier than the bow of the violinist; in you lie all the possibilities of the *creation* of beauty. You need turn to the orchestra, the piano and the band only for the faithful interpretation of what you have envisioned."

The rest of the world has had a long start, but the American composer with his heritage of creative genius from a race which has produced thirteen out of twenty of the great inventions of the past three centuries, is well qualified to catch up! We require time but (to employ the American vernacular) "we'll get there!"

To-day, if I were a young composer, I would rather submit my chances of success or failure to an American public than to any other public in the world. It is essentially music-loving. I have "laid my ear to it, to see if it be in tune" for these many years, and it has never discouraged or disappointed me. I can think of a thousand glorious and satisfying responses. Moreover, there is concrete evidence of musical interest all over the country. Looking over the field of the finest, I find some twenty-five orchestral societies giving series of concerts; some forty-five festival associations appearing before the public every year; some hundred choral groups and musical ensembles; some eight grand opera companies; at least a hundred and fifty pianists and an equal number of violinists and 'cellists; more than two hundred agencies, and a myriad of singers going up and down the highways and byways of this great land. All this confirms my assertion that ours is a musical nation.

As for myself, I began my apprenticeship as an orchestral player — a violinist, and I paid little attention to wind organizations until I led the Marine Band. Like most people who are, so to speak, brought up on the fiddle, I didn't have a proper respect for wind combinations. To me, band instrumentation in those early days left a void that cried out to be filled — I was never satisfied. Wholly lacking were the qualities I felt a band should and could possess — a tone as sustained as that of an organ and a brilliancy of execution similar to that of the piano. I began my career with the Marines determined to develop a musical body as important in its own field, as any orchestra. This determination was bound, of course, to deflect my sympathies and affection from orchestra to wind-band.

Since the day when I strove to lift the Marine Corps Band out of its narrow rut of polkas, grand opera cavatinas and national airs, the public has accepted my offerings graciously. The press too, has always treated me with the utmost consideration, and has ever shown a kindly spirit toward the work I produced. Whenever I look over my unwieldy tomes of clippings, I feel like saying, "Gentlemen of the press, I salute you!" Success is, after all, only the friendly fusion of the feelings of giver and receiver and I appreciate every cordial handclap and every printed word which has paved the way to the long continuation of my band appearances. Had I not received so overwhelming a reception thirty years ago I could not have proceeded with enthusiasm and confidence; in those days when the air resounded to the strains of Sullivan, Strauss and Sousa, I was warmed and delighted by this appreciation of my work.

But inevitably there will come a time when I shall be too feeble to serve my public longer. When that time comes I shall lay down my baton and say, "God bless all of you — every member of a faithful following. The love shown me is returned a hundredfold, I assure you, and I am proud to say it. I thank you, every one, for what you have done to make my life so rich in happy memories. I hope that, long after my marches have been forgotten, the clarion call of America which I tried to make the keynote of my compositions will continue to inspire her children with undying loyalty."

Well, every concert must reach its last number, the echo of the last fine fanfare must fade away and the conductor's baton be laid aside. At the behest of the Baton of Memory I have called back the melodies of a thousand happy concerts, re-awakened the echoes of many a stirring march and tuneful opera. If, out of the cadences of Time, I have evoked one note that, clear and true, vibrates gratefully on the heartstrings of my public — I am well content.

THE CLEVELAND, OHIO, BIRTHDAY CAKE, 1924

THE ORIGINAL MANUSCRIPT OF "THE STARS AND
STRIPES FOREVER"

The Works of John Philip Sousa

CANTATA: *The Last Crusade*, for mixed voices, chorus and orchestra

SYMPHONIC POEM: *The Chariot Race* from "Ben Hur"

SCENE HISTORICAL: *Sheridan's Ride*

TE DEUM in B flat

OVERTURES
Katherine
Vautour

OPERAS
The American Maid
The Bride Elect
The Charlatan
Chris and the Wonderful
    Lamp
Désirée
The Dragoons
El Capitan
The Free Lance
The Queen of Hearts
The Smugglers

SUITES
At the King's Court
Camera Studies
Cuba-Land
Dwellers in the Western
    World
Impressions at the
    Movies
Last Days of Pompeii
Leaves from My
    Note-Book

Looking Upward
Maidens Three
People Who Live in
    Glass Houses (Ballet)
Tales of a Traveller
Three Quotations

SONGS
Ah, Me
The Belle of Bayou Teche
Blue Ridge
Boots
The Card Song
The Carrier Pigeon
Crossing the Bar
'Deed I Has To Laugh
    Do We? We Do
The Faithless Knight and
    the Philosophic Maid
Fanny
The Free Lunch Cadets
The Golden Cars
The Goose Girl
Have You Got That Tired
    Feeling?
Hoping
In Flanders Fields

I Never Was Right in My
    Life
In the Dimness of
    Twilight
I've Made My Plans for
    the Summer
I Wonder
Kelly and Burke and
    Shea
Lily Bells
Little Brown Thrush
Maid of the Meadow
Mallie
Messiah of Nations
The Milkmaid
My Own, My Geraldine
Non-Committal
    Declarations
Oh, Sunlit Sea Beyond
    the West
Oh, Warrior Grim
Oh, Why Should the
    Spirit of Mortal Be
    Proud?
Oh, Ye Lilies White
Only a Dream
Only Thee
O'Riley's Kettle Drum

Pushing On
The Red Cross Nurse
Right Up On the Firing
 Line
Serenade in Seville
The Snow Baby
Song of the Sea
Sweet Miss Industry
Tally-Ho
We March to Victory
When Navy Ships are
 Coaling
When the Boys Come
 Sailing Home
When You Change Your
 Name to Mine
Where is Love?
Will you Love When
 Lilies are Dead?
The Window Blind
You Cannot Tell How
 Old They Are

WALTZES
Co-Eds of Michigan
Colonial Dames
La Reine de la Mer
Moonlight on the
 Potomac
Paroles d'Amour
Sandalphon

MARCHES
Across the Danube
America First
The American Wedding
 March

Anchor and Star
Ancient and Honorable
 Artillery
The Atlantic City
 Pageant
Beau Ideal
Belle of Chicago
Ben Bolt
Black Horse Troop
Bonnie Annie
Boy Scouts
The Bride Elect
Bullets and Bayonets
Chantymans
The Charlatan
Comrades of the Legion
Corcoran Cadets
The Crusaders
The Dauntless Battalion
Désirée
The Diplomat
Directorate
The Dragoons
El Capitan
Fairest of the Fair
The Federal
Free Lance
From Maine to Oregon
The Gallant Seventh
The Gladiator
Glory of the Yankee
 Navy
The Golden Star
Grand Promenade at the
 White House
The Gridiron Club
Guide Right

Hail to the Spirit of
 Liberty
Hands Across the Sea
High School Cadets
The Hippodrome
Homeward Bound
The Honored Dead
 (dirge)
Imperial Edward
In Memoriam of
 President Garfield
 (dirge)
Invincible Eagle
Jack Tar
Kalorama
Keeping Step with the
 Union
The Lambs
Liberty Bell
Liberty Loan
Loyal Legion
Magna Charta
The Man Behind the
 Gun
Manhattan Beach
March of the Mitten
 Men
Marquette University
The Mikado (*medley*)
Minnesota
Mother Goose
Mother Hubbard
National Fencibles
The National Game
Naval Reserve
The New Century

Nobles of the Mystic
Shrine
Occidental
On the Campus
On the Tramp
Our Flirtation
Pathfinder of Panama
The Pet of the Petticoats
The Picador
Power and Glory
Powhatan's Daughter
Pride of Pittsburgh
Pride of the Wolverines
Resumption
The Review
Revival
Riders for the Flag
Rifle Regiment
Right Forward
Right Left
Sabre and Spurs
Saint Louis Exposition
Salutation
Semper Fidelis
Sesquicentennial
The Smugglers
Solid Men to the Front
Sound Off
Stars and Stripes Forever
The Thunderer
The Transit of Venus
United States Field
Artillery
University of Nebraska
Volunteers
Washington Post
We Are Coming

When the Boys Come
Sailing Home
White Plume
The White Rose
Wisconsin Forward
Yorktown

FANTASIES
A Bouquet of Beloved
Inspirations
A Study in Rhythms
Fancy of the Town
In Pulpit and Pew
In the Realm of the
Dance
International Congress
(*Fantasia on National
Airs*)
Jazz America
Music of the Minute
On With the Dance
Over the Footlights of
New York
Showing Off Before
Company

**MISCELLANEOUS
COMPOSITIONS**
Caprian Tarantelle
The Coquette
Cuckoo Galop
Dance Hilarious
The Gliding Girl
Myrrha Gavotte
Nymphalin
On Wings of Lightning
Peaches and Cream

Presidential Polonaise
Queen of the Harvest
Russian Peasant Dance
Silver Spray Schottische
The Summer Girl
Willow Blossoms

BOOKS, VERSES, ETC.
A Book of Airs for the
Violin
A Book of Instruction
for the Trumpet and
Drum
The Fifth String (*a novel*)
Libretto of "The Bride
Elect"
Lyrics for "The
Charlatan" and "El
Captain"
The National, Patriotic
and Typical Airs of all
Lands
Pipetown Sandy (a
novel)
Through the Year With
Sousa
Transit of Venus (*a
novel*)

Index

d by J. P. S.: